SLASHER

CHARLES FORSMAN

FLOATING
WORLD COMICS

SLASHER

ISBN 978-1942801849

© 2017 Charles Forsman. All rights reserved.

Floating World Comics.
400 NW Couch Street
Portland OR

EDITOR AND PUBLISHER: Jason Leivian
BOOK DESIGN & PRODUCTION: Charles Forsman
COPY EDITOR: Colin Murchison

First Printing. December 2017.

Printed in Canada

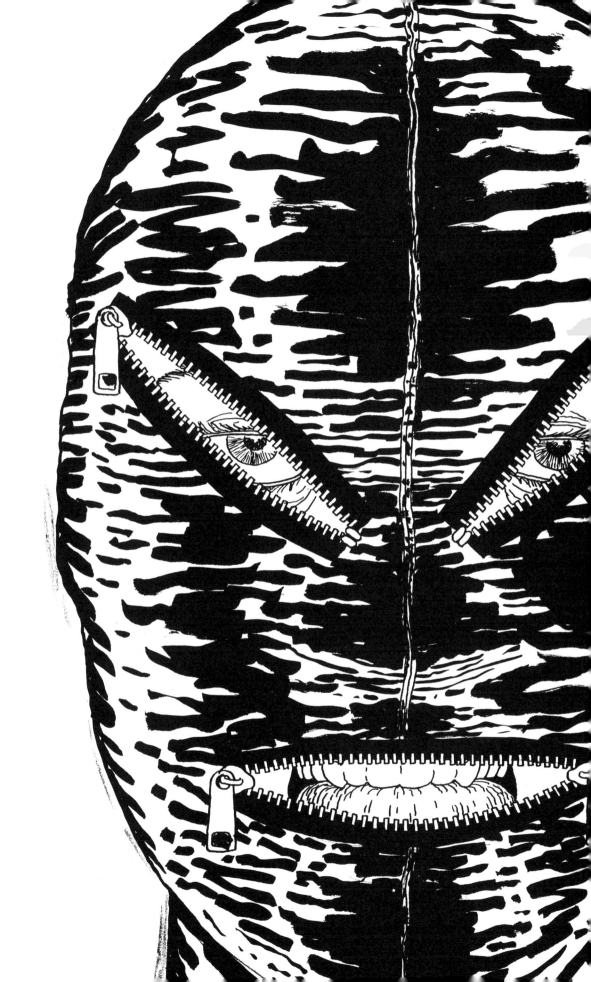

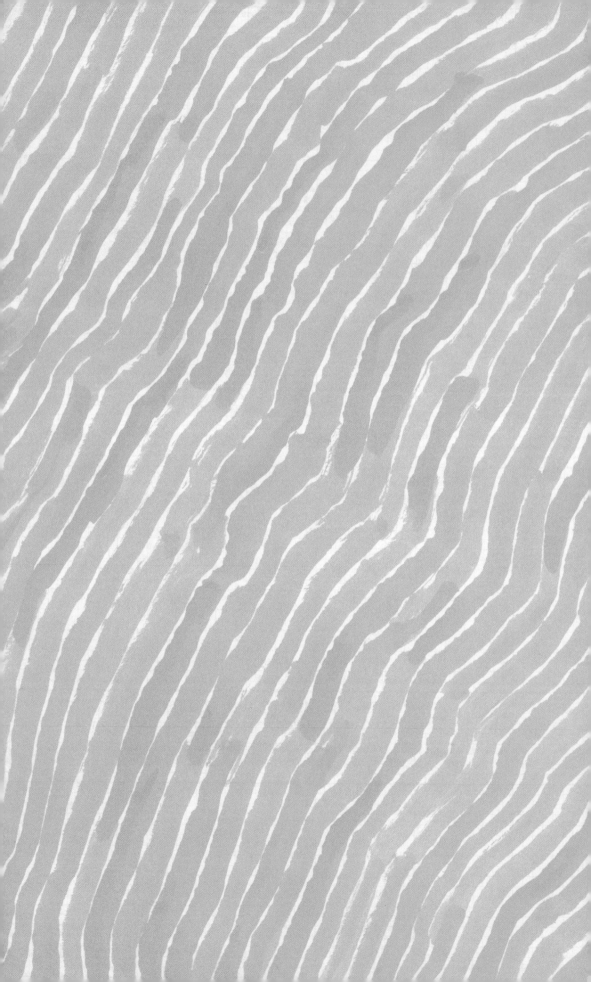

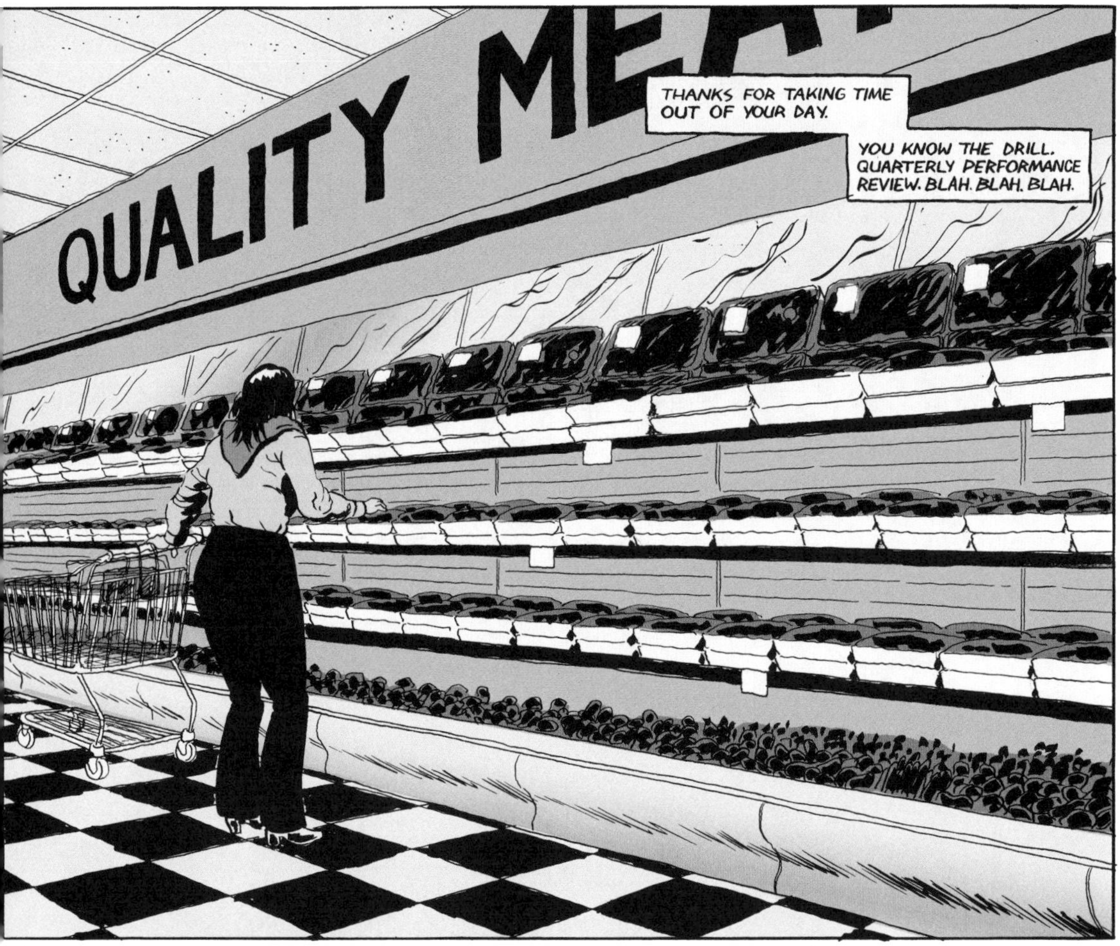
QUALITY MEA
THANKS FOR TAKING TIME OUT OF YOUR DAY.
YOU KNOW THE DRILL. QUARTERLY PERFORMANCE REVIEW. BLAH. BLAH. BLAH.

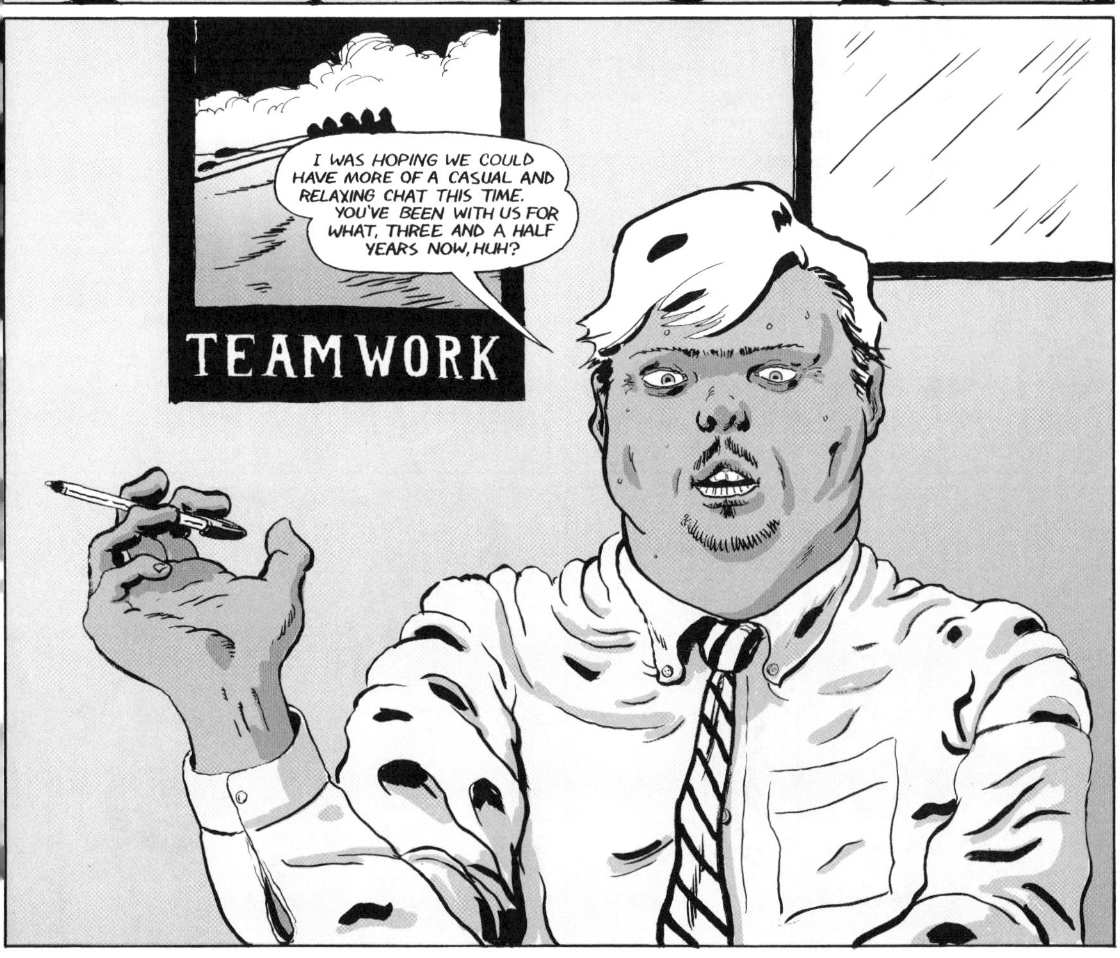
I WAS HOPING WE COULD HAVE MORE OF A CASUAL AND RELAXING CHAT THIS TIME. YOU'VE BEEN WITH US FOR WHAT, THREE AND A HALF YEARS NOW, HUH?
TEAMWORK

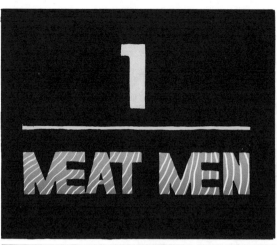

1
MEAT MEN

YES.

IT GOES WITHOUT SAYING YOU ARE ONE OF OUR BETTER PERFORMERS HERE. YOUR WPM SCORES ARE ROCK SOLID AND SHOW STEADY IMPROVEMENT.

YOU SEEM TO GET ALONG WELL WITH YOUR CO-WORKERS, IF NOT A BIT SHY.

I USED TO BE LIKE YOU BEFORE I BECAME THE HEAD-CHEESE.

I WAS A MEEK LITTLE WORKER BEE, BELIEVE IT OR NOT.

I'M SERIOUS.

ME?!

UH, WOW.

HA! HA!

RIGHT? CRAZY, HUH?

I'M NOT THAT SHY...

ANYWAYS, CHRISTINE, YOU'RE A FINE EMPLOYEE AND IF I MAY SAY SO, A REAL PRETTY LADY.

I HOPE I'M NOT MAKING YOU UNCOMFORTABLE. I JUST WANT YOU TO KNOW YOU ARE APPRECIATED.

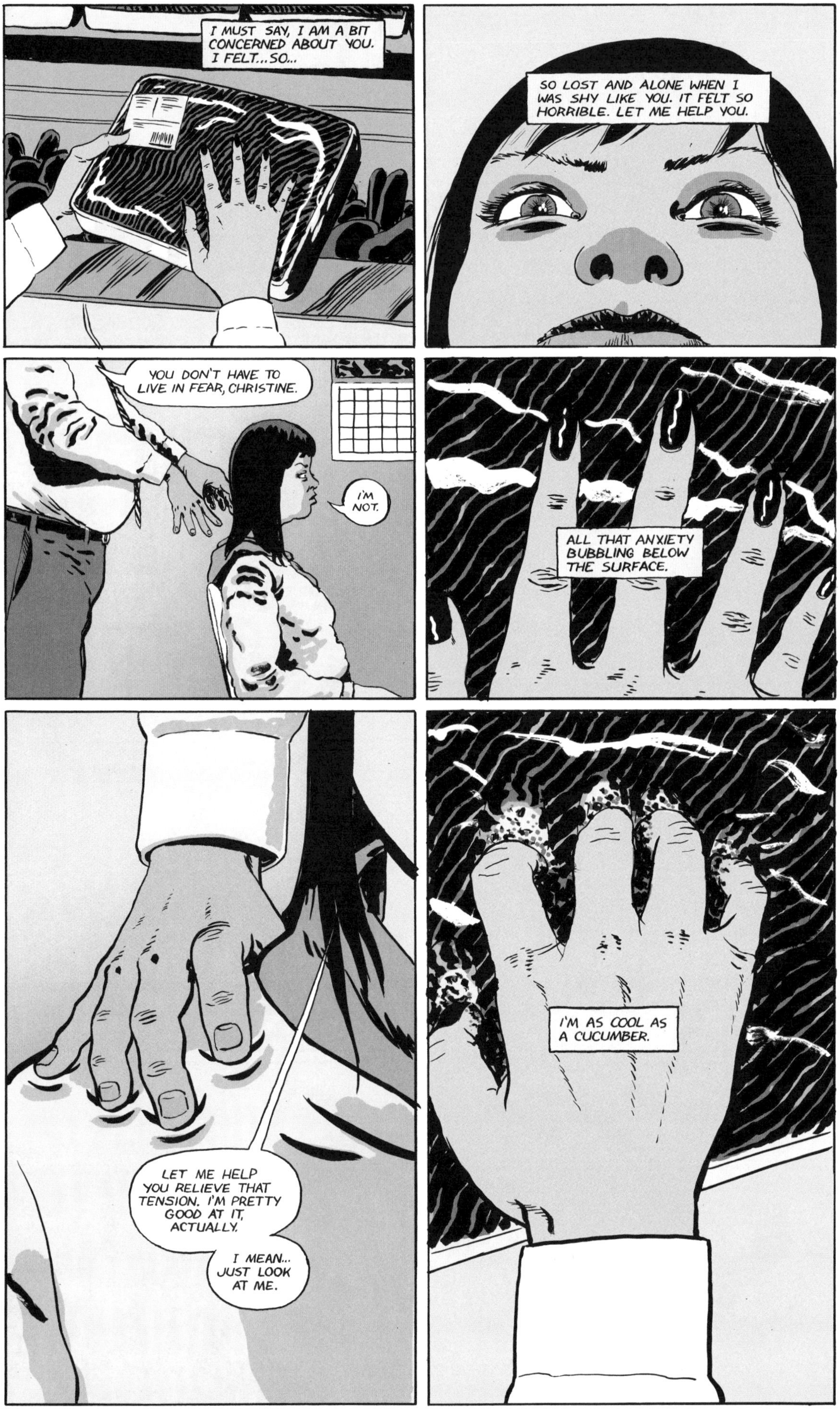
I MUST SAY, I AM A BIT CONCERNED ABOUT YOU. I FELT...SO...
SO LOST AND ALONE WHEN I WAS SHY LIKE YOU. IT FELT SO HORRIBLE. LET ME HELP YOU.
YOU DON'T HAVE TO LIVE IN FEAR, CHRISTINE.
I'M NOT.
ALL THAT ANXIETY BUBBLING BELOW THE SURFACE.
LET ME HELP YOU RELIEVE THAT TENSION. I'M PRETTY GOOD AT IT, ACTUALLY.
I MEAN... JUST LOOK AT ME.
I'M AS COOL AS A CUCUMBER.

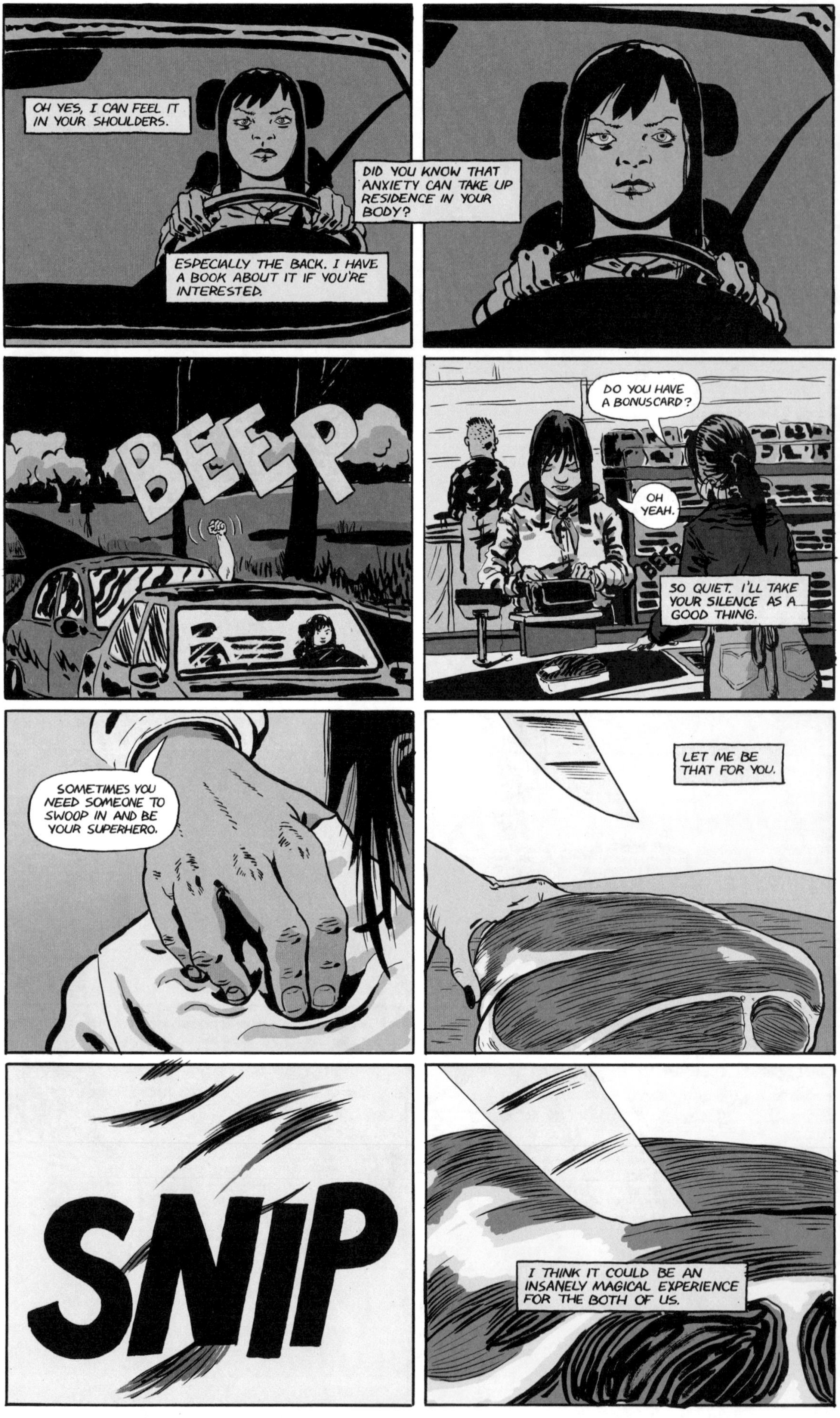
OH YES, I CAN FEEL IT IN YOUR SHOULDERS.
DID YOU KNOW THAT ANXIETY CAN TAKE UP RESIDENCE IN YOUR BODY?
ESPECIALLY THE BACK. I HAVE A BOOK ABOUT IT IF YOU'RE INTERESTED.
BEEP
DO YOU HAVE A BONUSCARD?
OH YEAH.
BEEP
SO QUIET. I'LL TAKE YOUR SILENCE AS A GOOD THING.
SOMETIMES YOU NEED SOMEONE TO SWOOP IN AND BE YOUR SUPERHERO.
LET ME BE THAT FOR YOU.
SNIP
I THINK IT COULD BE AN INSANELY MAGICAL EXPERIENCE FOR THE BOTH OF US.

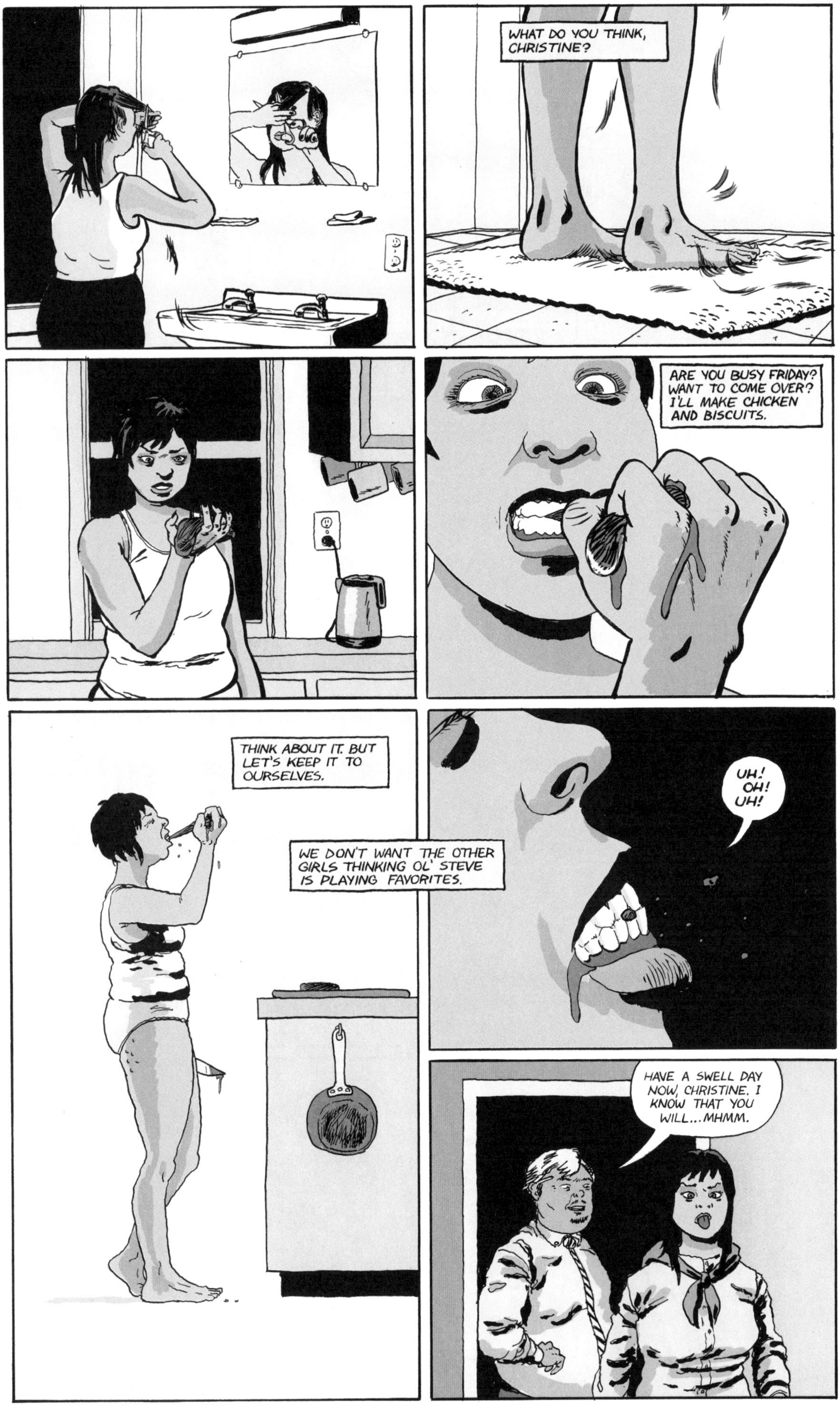
WHAT DO YOU THINK, CHRISTINE?
ARE YOU BUSY FRIDAY? WANT TO COME OVER? I'LL MAKE CHICKEN AND BISCUITS.
THINK ABOUT IT. BUT LET'S KEEP IT TO OURSELVES.
WE DON'T WANT THE OTHER GIRLS THINKING OL' STEVE IS PLAYING FAVORITES.
UH! OH! UH!
HAVE A SWELL DAY NOW, CHRISTINE. I KNOW THAT YOU WILL... MHMM.

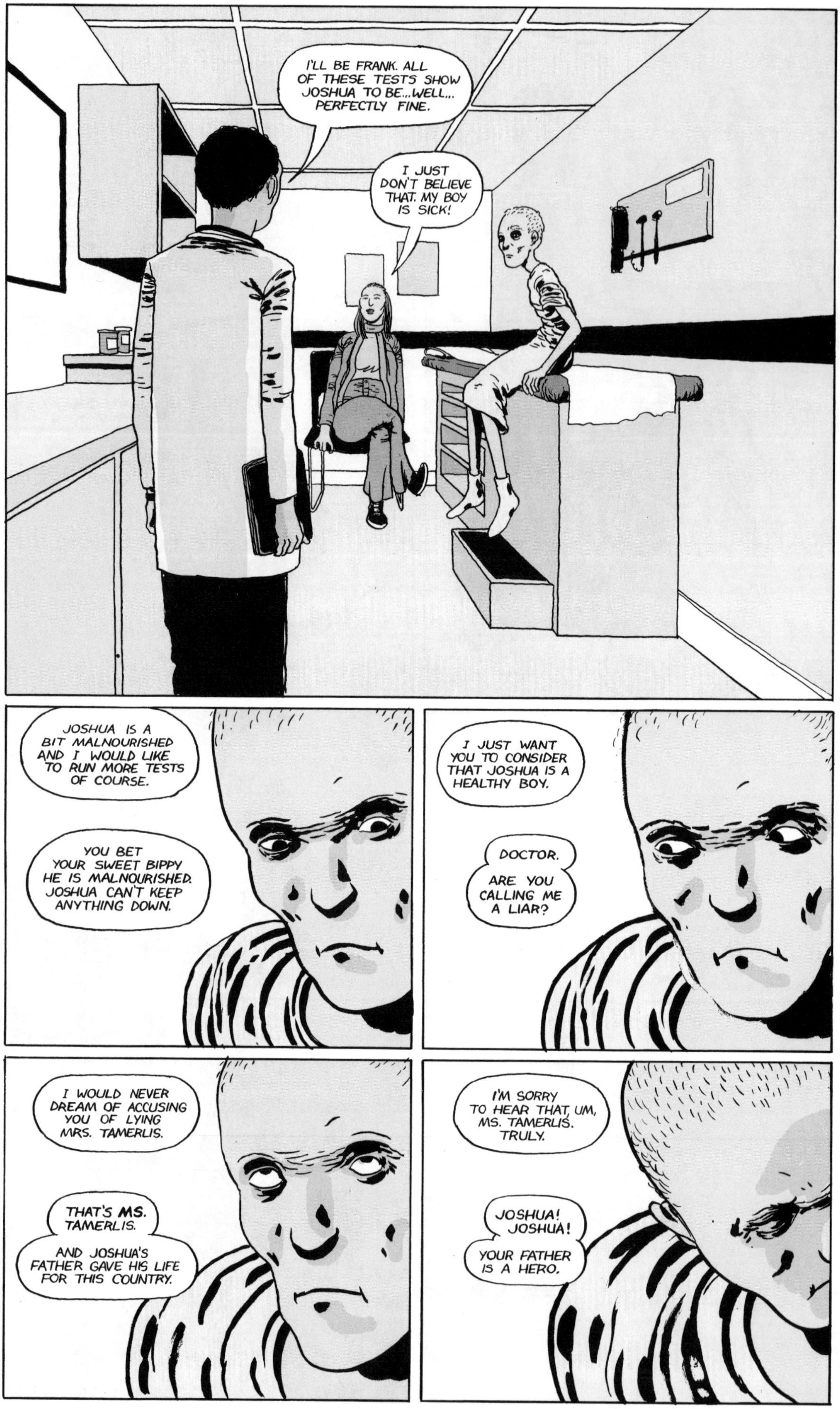
I'LL BE FRANK. ALL OF THESE TESTS SHOW JOSHUA TO BE...WELL... PERFECTLY FINE.
I JUST DON'T BELIEVE THAT. MY BOY IS SICK!
JOSHUA IS A BIT MALNOURISHED AND I WOULD LIKE TO RUN MORE TESTS OF COURSE.
YOU BET YOUR SWEET BIPPY HE IS MALNOURISHED. JOSHUA CAN'T KEEP ANYTHING DOWN.
I JUST WANT YOU TO CONSIDER THAT JOSHUA IS A HEALTHY BOY.
DOCTOR.
ARE YOU CALLING ME A LIAR?
I WOULD NEVER DREAM OF ACCUSING YOU OF LYING MRS. TAMERLIS.
THAT'S **MS.** TAMERLIS.
AND JOSHUA'S FATHER GAVE HIS LIFE FOR THIS COUNTRY.
I'M SORRY TO HEAR THAT, UM, MS. TAMERLIS. TRULY.
JOSHUA! JOSHUA!
YOUR FATHER IS A HERO.

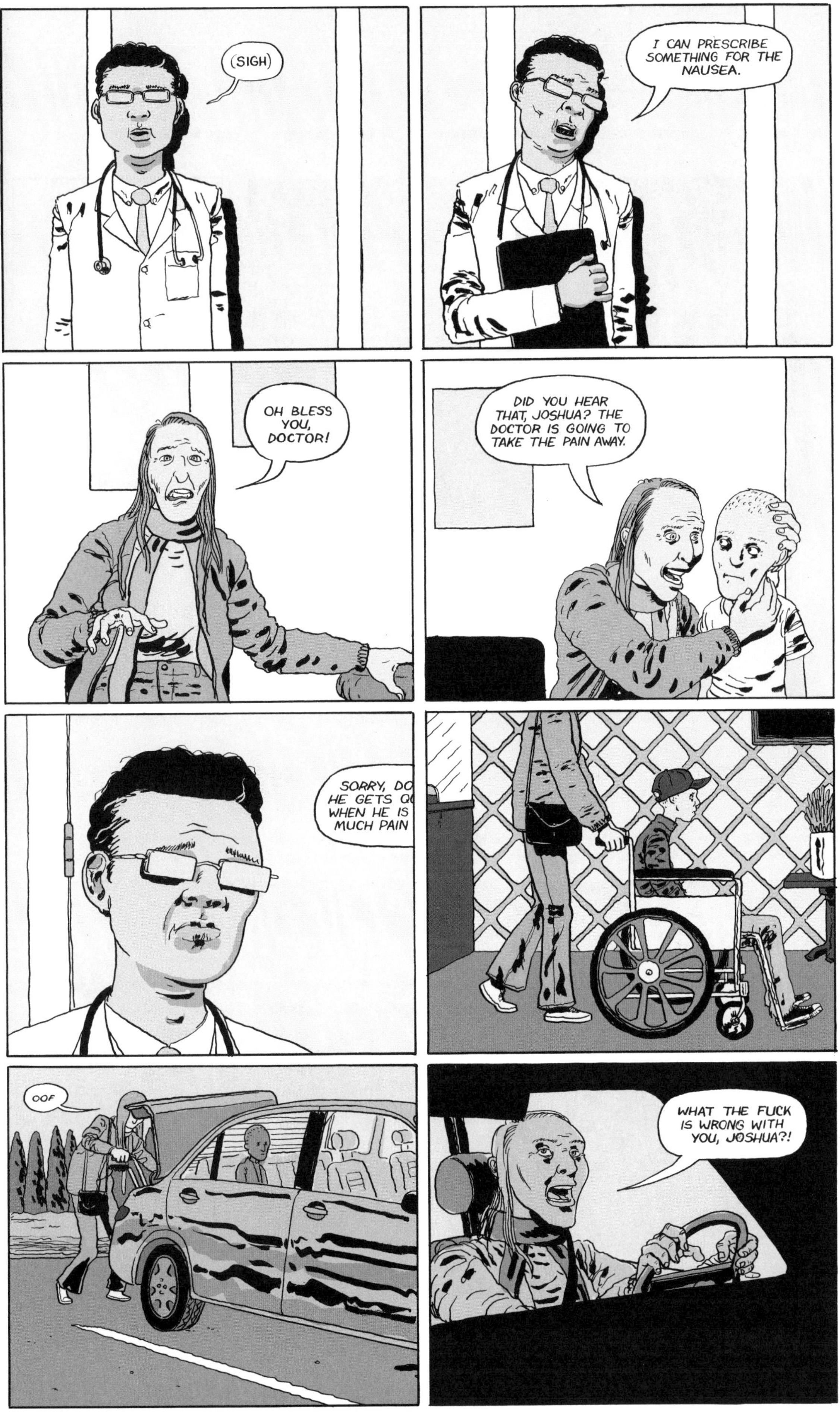
(SIGH)
I CAN PRESCRIBE SOMETHING FOR THE NAUSEA.
OH BLESS YOU, DOCTOR!
DID YOU HEAR THAT, JOSHUA? THE DOCTOR IS GOING TO TAKE THE PAIN AWAY.
SORRY, DO
HE GETS QU
WHEN HE IS
MUCH PAIN
OOF
WHAT THE FUCK IS WRONG WITH YOU, JOSHUA?!

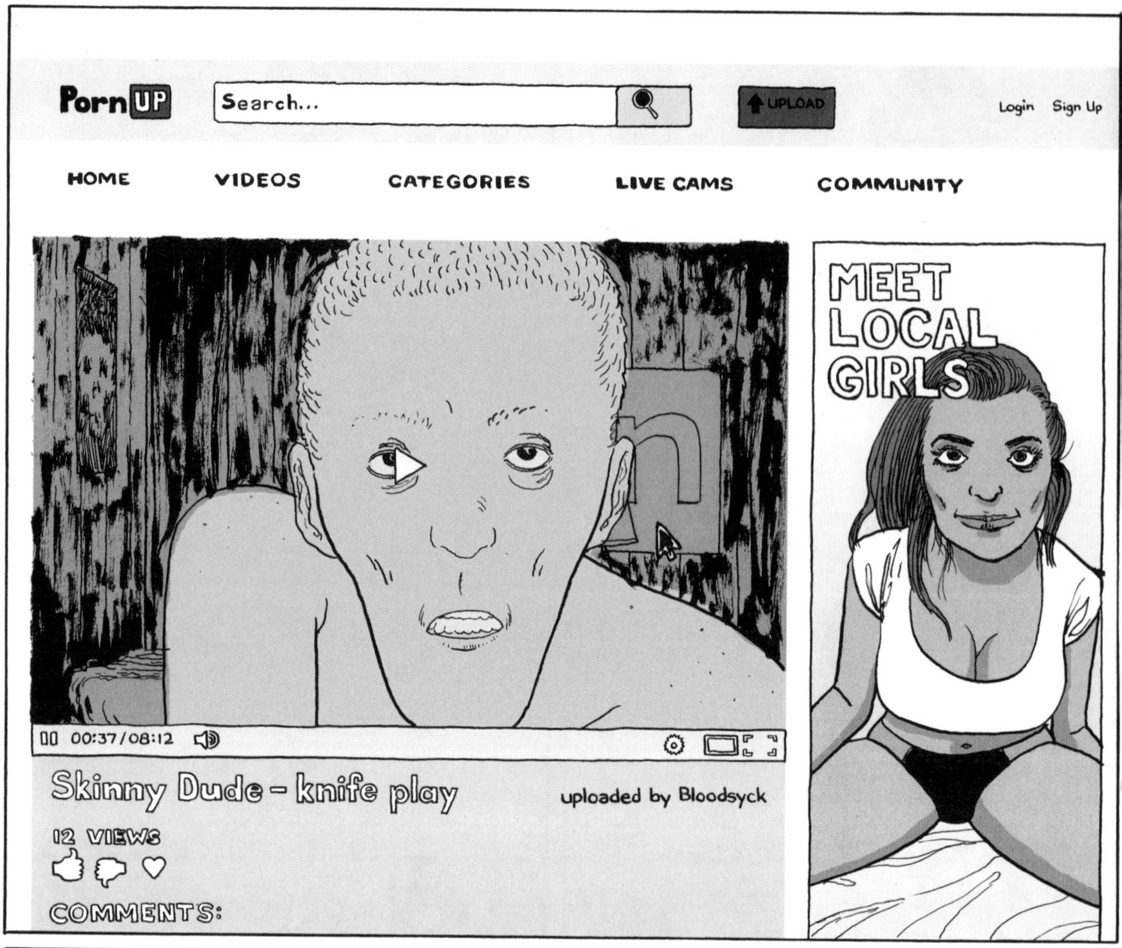

Porn UP
Search...
UPLOAD
Login Sign Up
HOME
VIDEOS
CATEGORIES
LIVE CAMS
COMMUNITY
MEET LOCAL GIRLS
00:37/08:12
Skinny Dude - knife play
uploaded by Bloodsyck
12 VIEWS
COMMENTS:

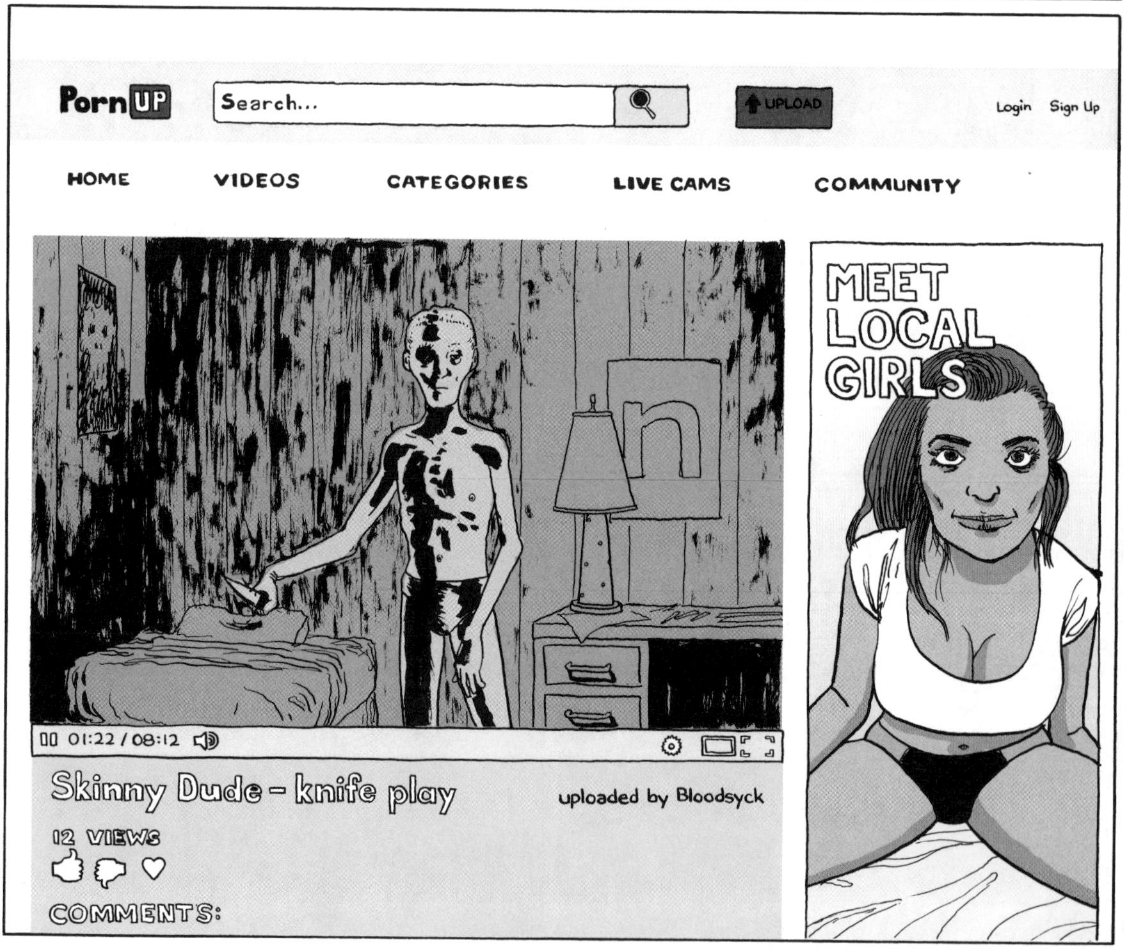

Porn UP
Search...
UPLOAD
Login Sign Up
HOME
VIDEOS
CATEGORIES
LIVE CAMS
COMMUNITY
MEET LOCAL GIRLS
01:22/08:12
Skinny Dude - knife play
uploaded by Bloodsyck
12 VIEWS
COMMENTS:

Porn UP

Search...

 UPLOAD

Login   Sign Up

HOME   **VIDEOS**   **CATEGORIES**   **LIVE CAMS**   **COMMUNITY**

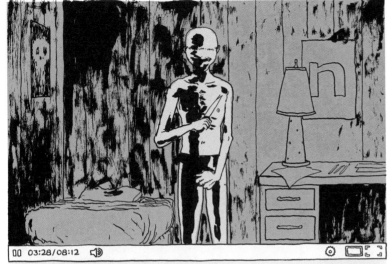

00 03:28/08:12

Skinny Dude - knife play   uploaded by Bloodsyck

12 VIEWS

COMMENTS:

 MEET LOCAL GIRLS

Porn UP

Search...

UPLOAD

Login   Sign Up

HOME   **VIDEOS**   **CATEGORIES**   **LIVE CAMS**   **COMMUNITY**

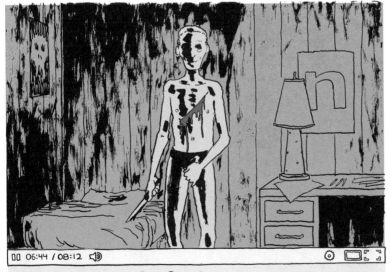

00 06:44/08:12

Skinny Dude - knife play   uploaded by Bloodsyck

12 VIEWS

COMMENTS:

 MEET LOCAL GIRLS

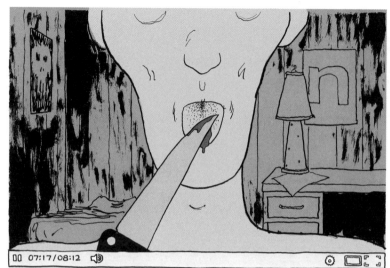

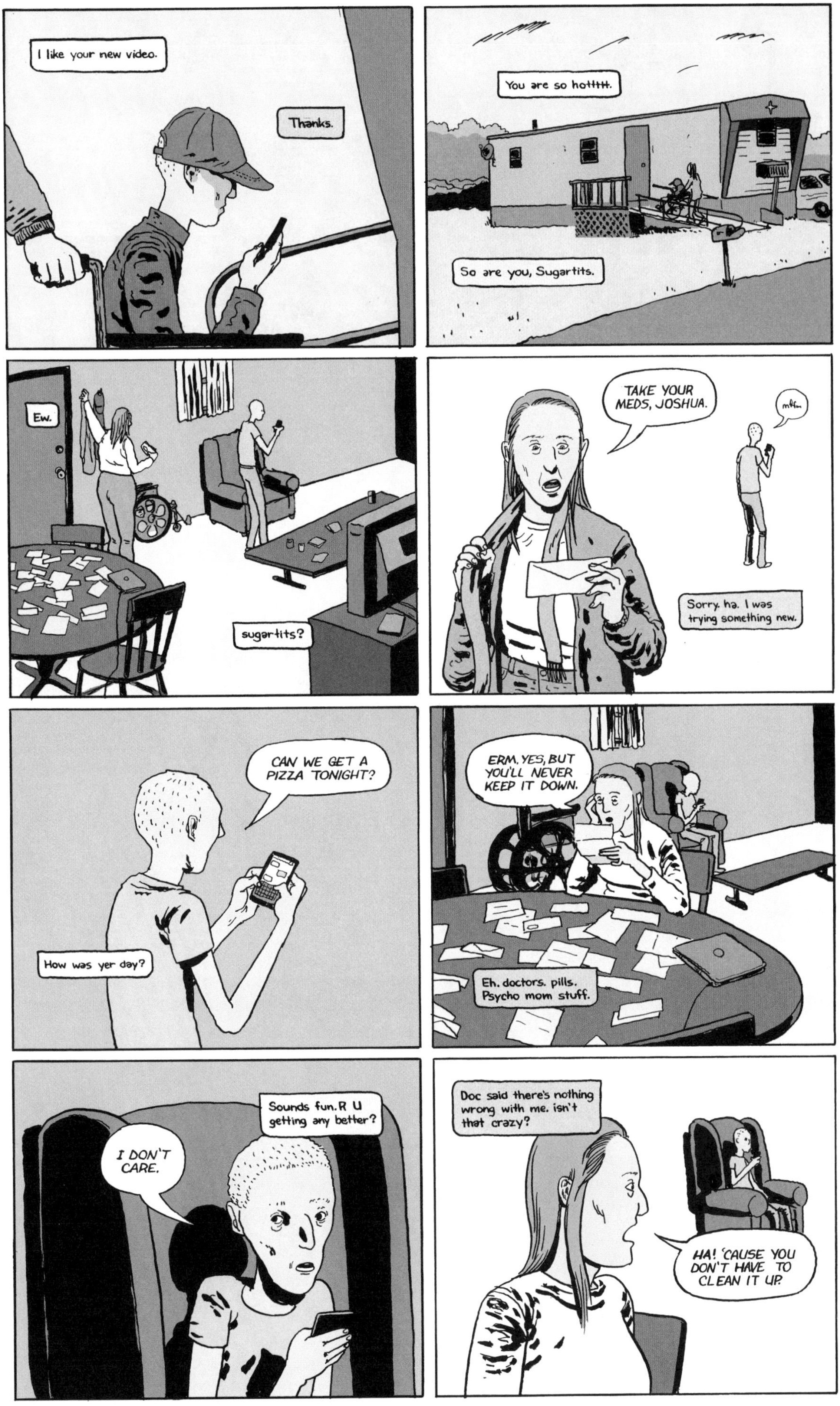

I like your new video.
Thanks.
You are so hottttt.
So are you, Sugartits.
Ew.
sugartits?
TAKE YOUR MEDS, JOSHUA.
Sorry. ha. I was trying something new.
CAN WE GET A PIZZA TONIGHT?
How was yer day?
ERM. YES, BUT YOU'LL NEVER KEEP IT DOWN.
Eh. doctors. pills. Psycho mom stuff.
Sounds fun. R U getting any better?
I DON'T CARE.
Doc said there's nothing wrong with me. isn't that crazy?
HA! 'CAUSE YOU DON'T HAVE TO CLEAN IT UP.

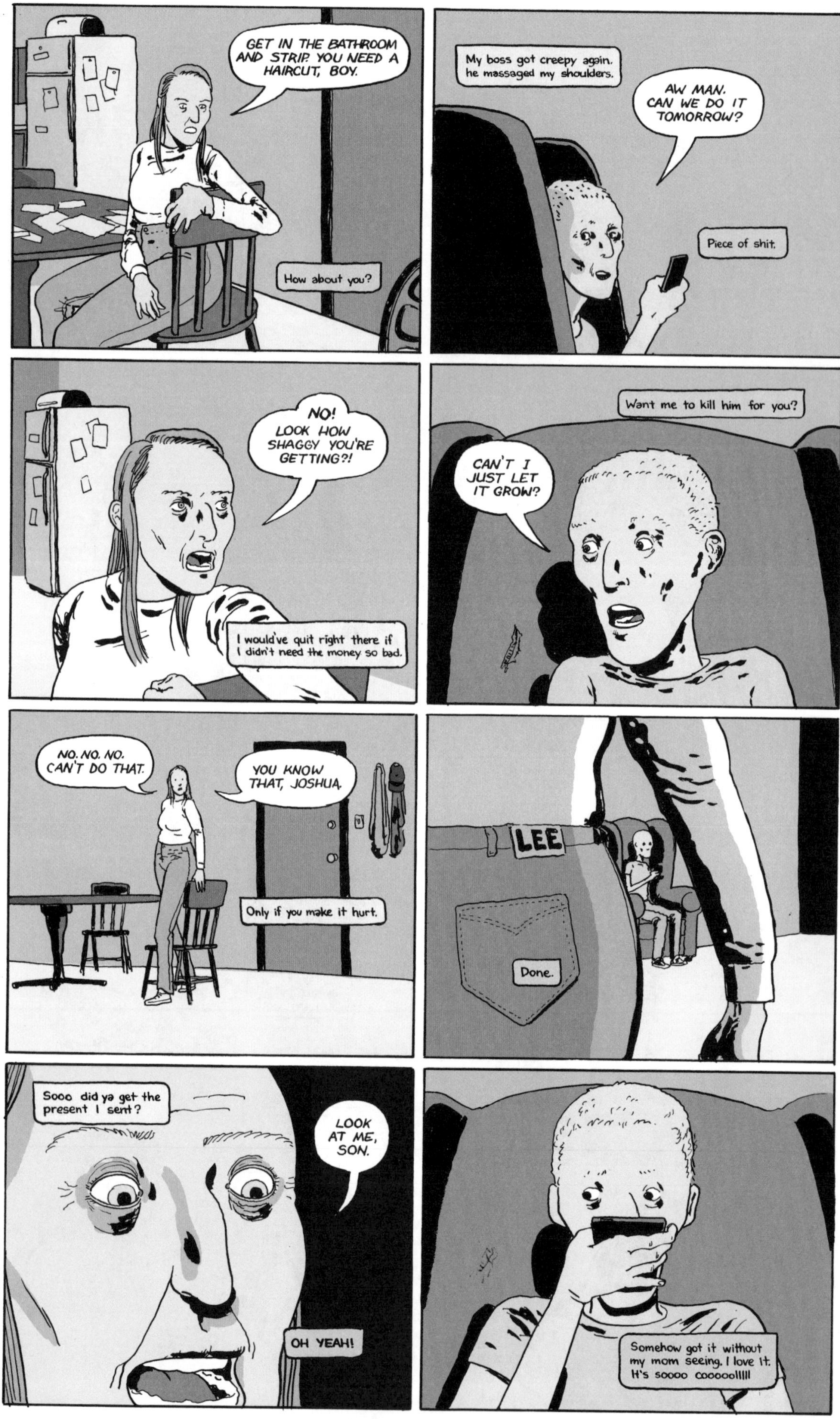
GET IN THE BATHROOM AND STRIP. YOU NEED A HAIRCUT, BOY.
How about you?
My boss got creepy again. he massaged my shoulders.
AW MAN. CAN WE DO IT TOMORROW?
Piece of shit.
NO! LOOK HOW SHAGGY YOU'RE GETTING?!
I would've quit right there if I didn't need the money so bad.
Want me to kill him for you?
CAN'T I JUST LET IT GROW?
NO. NO. NO. CAN'T DO THAT.
YOU KNOW THAT, JOSHUA.
Only if you make it hurt.
LEE
Done.
Sooo did ya get the present I sent?
LOOK AT ME, SON.
OH YEAH!
Somehow got it without my mom seeing. I love it. It's soooo cooooollllll

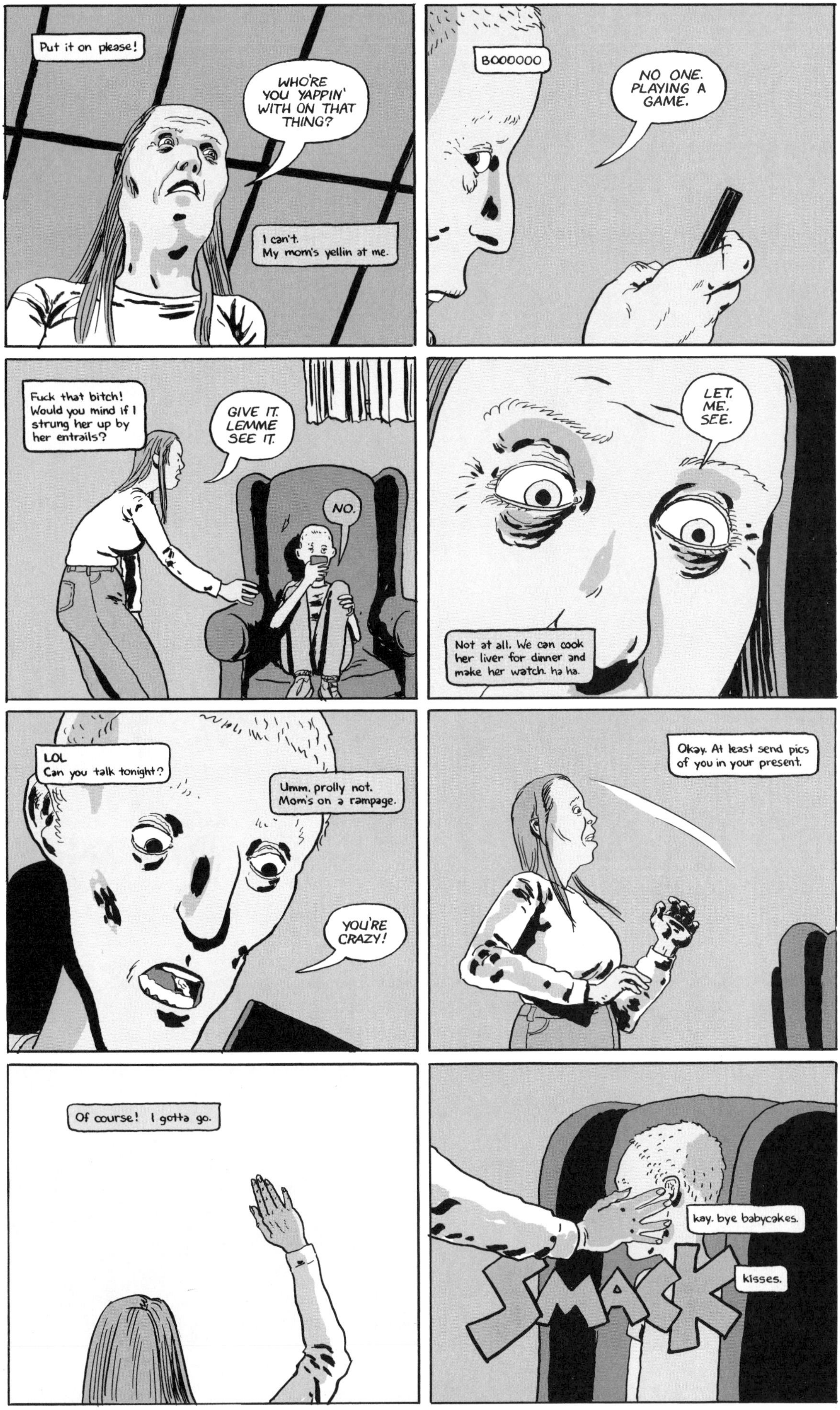
Put it on please!
WHO'RE YOU YAPPIN' WITH ON THAT THING?
I can't.
My mom's yellin at me.
BOOOOOO
NO ONE. PLAYING A GAME.
Fuck that bitch! Would you mind if I strung her up by her entrails?
GIVE IT. LEMME SEE IT.
NO.
LET. ME. SEE.
Not at all. We can cook her liver for dinner and make her watch. ha ha.
LOL
Can you talk tonight?
Umm. prolly not. Mom's on a rampage.
YOU'RE CRAZY!
Okay. At least send pics of you in your present.
Of course! I gotta go.
kay. bye babycakes.
SMACK
kisses.

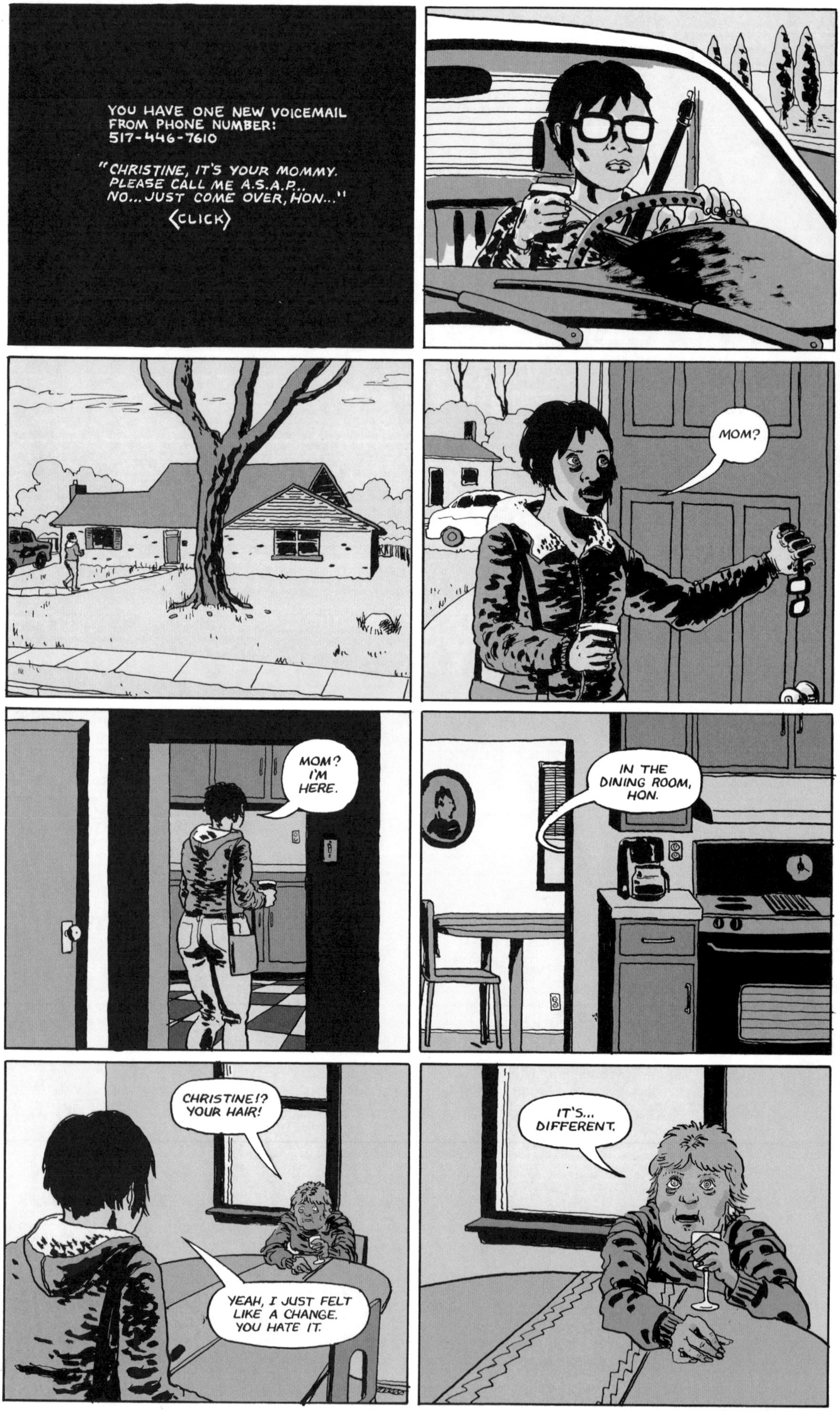
YOU HAVE ONE NEW VOICEMAIL
FROM PHONE NUMBER:
517-446-7610
"CHRISTINE, IT'S YOUR MOMMY. PLEASE CALL ME A.S.A.P... NO... JUST COME OVER, HON..."
<CLICK>
MOM?
MOM? I'M HERE.
IN THE DINING ROOM, HON.
CHRISTINE!? YOUR HAIR!
YEAH, I JUST FELT LIKE A CHANGE. YOU HATE IT.
IT'S... DIFFERENT.

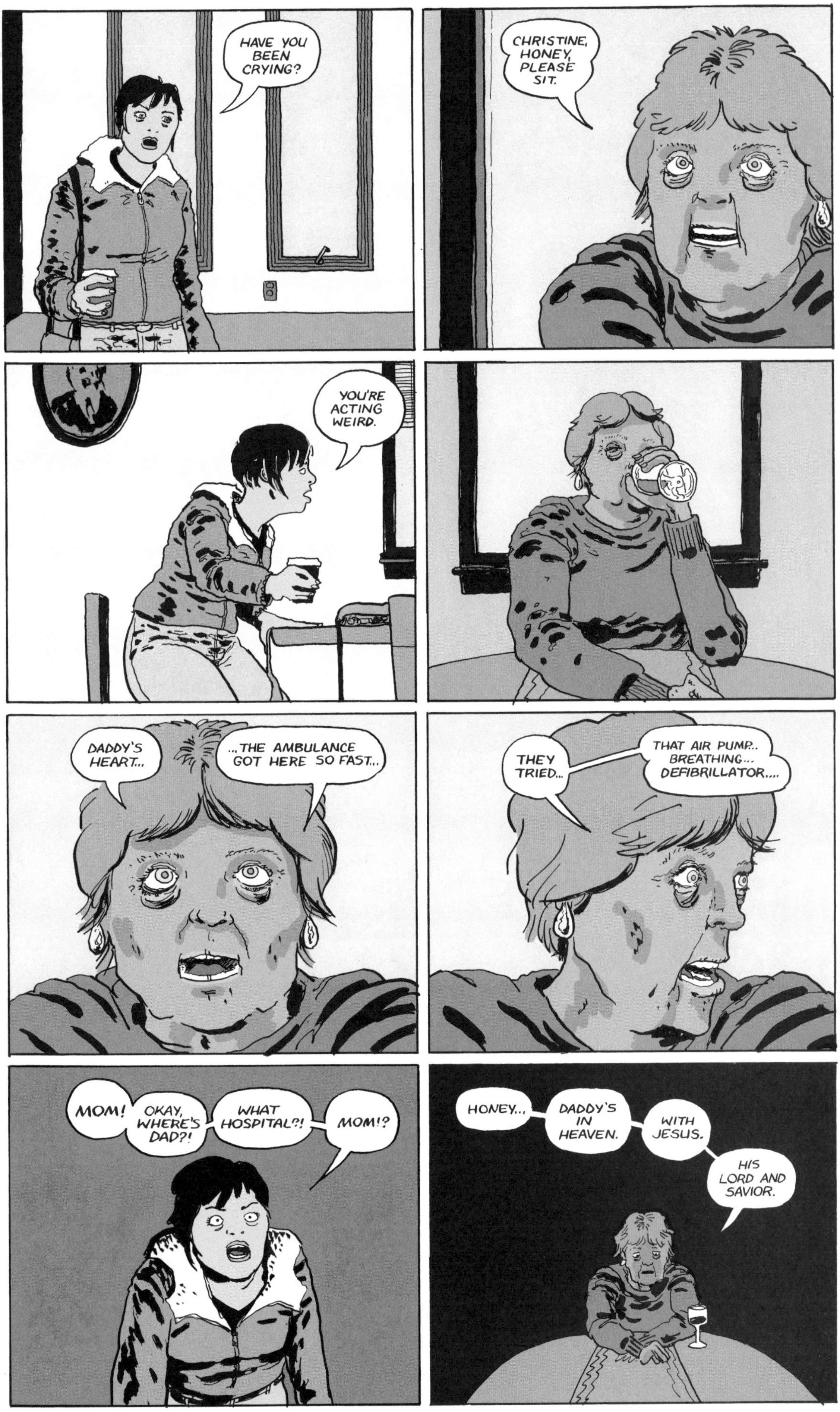
HAVE YOU BEEN CRYING?
CHRISTINE, HONEY, PLEASE SIT.
YOU'RE ACTING WEIRD.
DADDY'S HEART...
...THE AMBULANCE GOT HERE SO FAST...
THEY TRIED...
THAT AIR PUMP... BREATHING... DEFIBRILLATOR....
MOM!
OKAY, WHERE'S DAD?!
WHAT HOSPITAL?!
MOM!?
HONEY...
DADDY'S IN HEAVEN.
WITH JESUS.
HIS LORD AND SAVIOR.

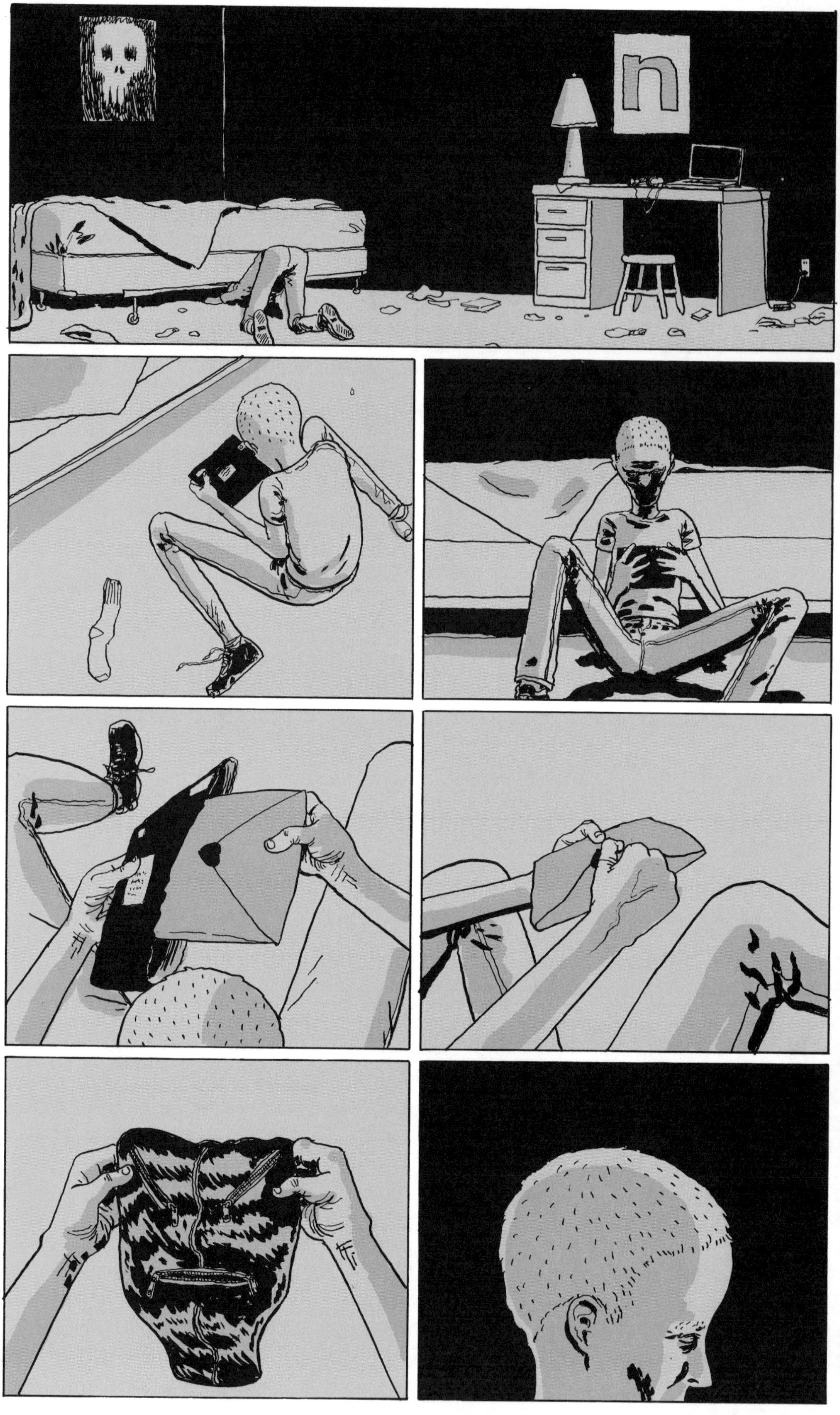
n

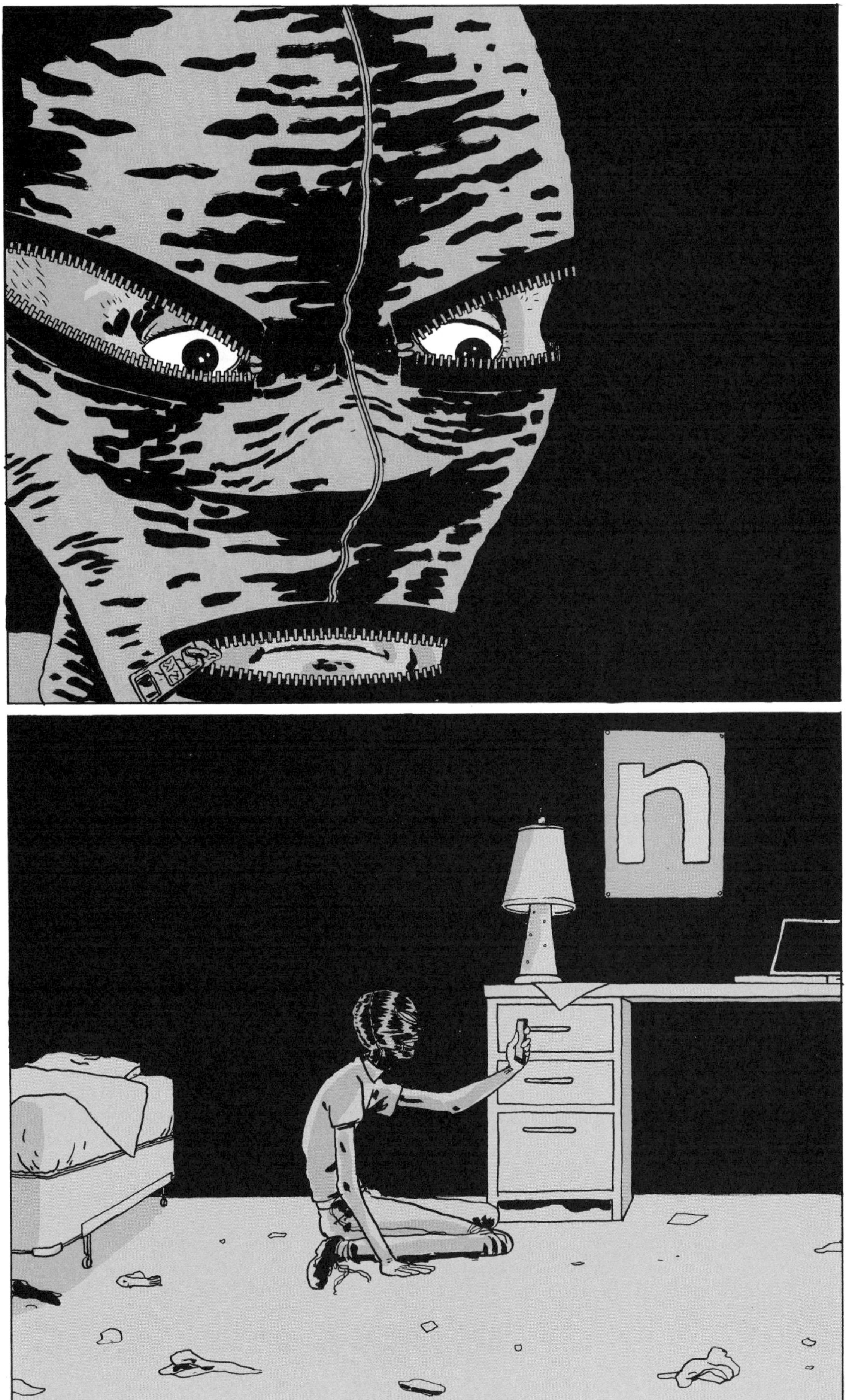
n

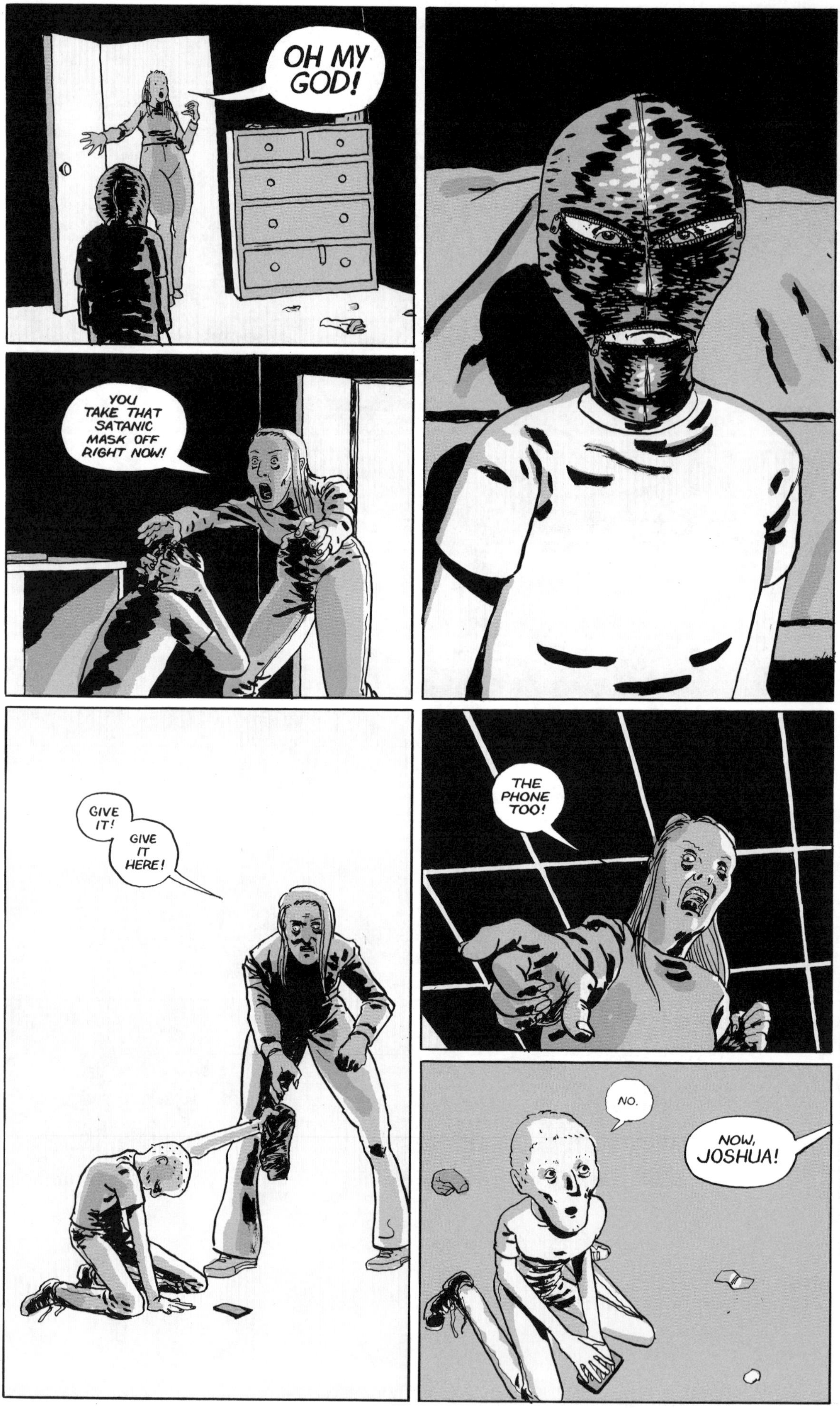
OH MY GOD!
YOU TAKE THAT SATANIC MASK OFF RIGHT NOW!
GIVE IT!
GIVE IT HERE!
THE PHONE TOO!
NO.
NOW, JOSHUA!

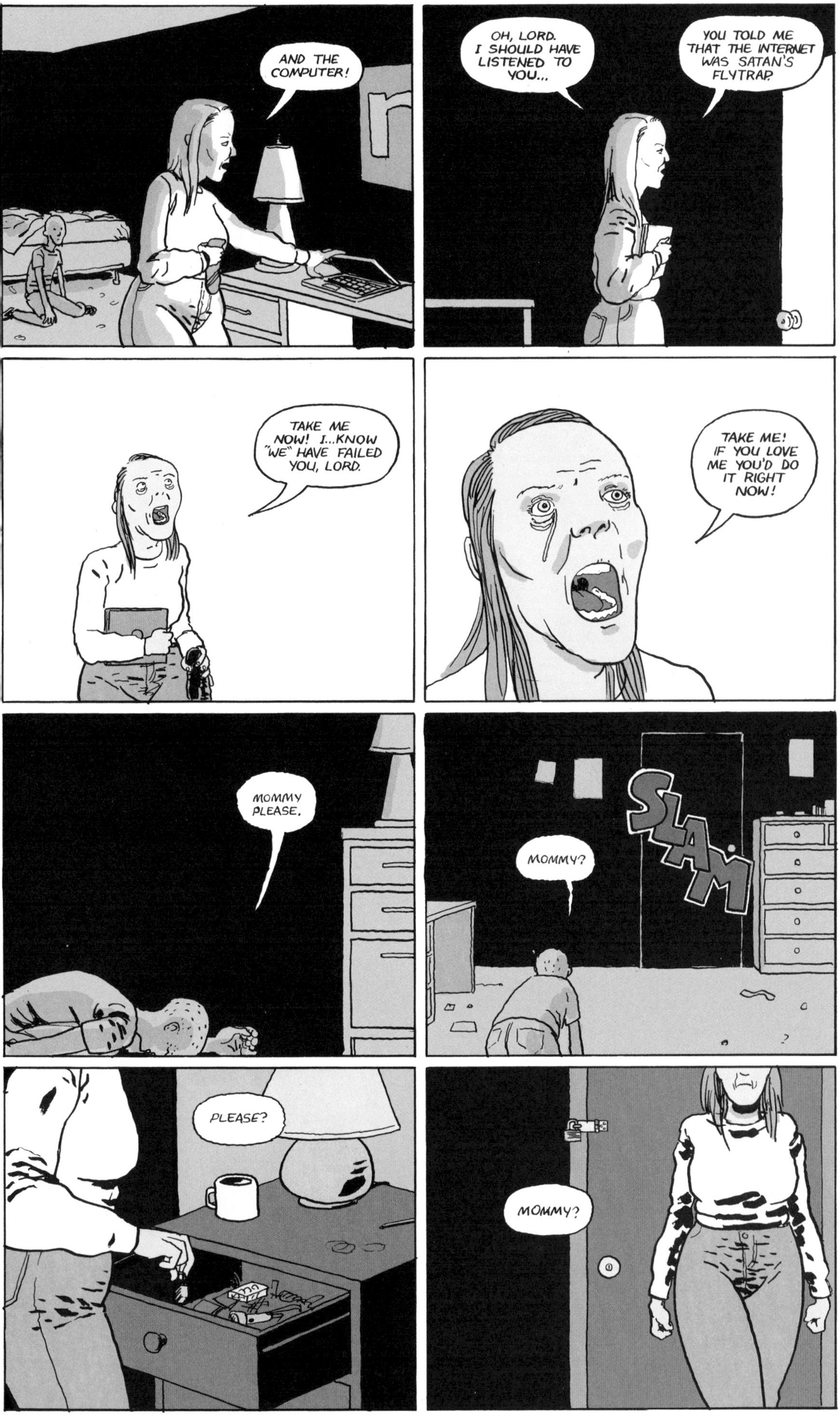
AND THE COMPUTER!
OH, LORD. I SHOULD HAVE LISTENED TO YOU...
YOU TOLD ME THAT THE INTERNET WAS SATAN'S FLYTRAP.
TAKE ME NOW! I...KNOW "WE" HAVE FAILED YOU, LORD.
TAKE ME! IF YOU LOVE ME YOU'D DO IT RIGHT NOW!
MOMMY PLEASE.
SLAM
MOMMY?
PLEASE?
MOMMY?

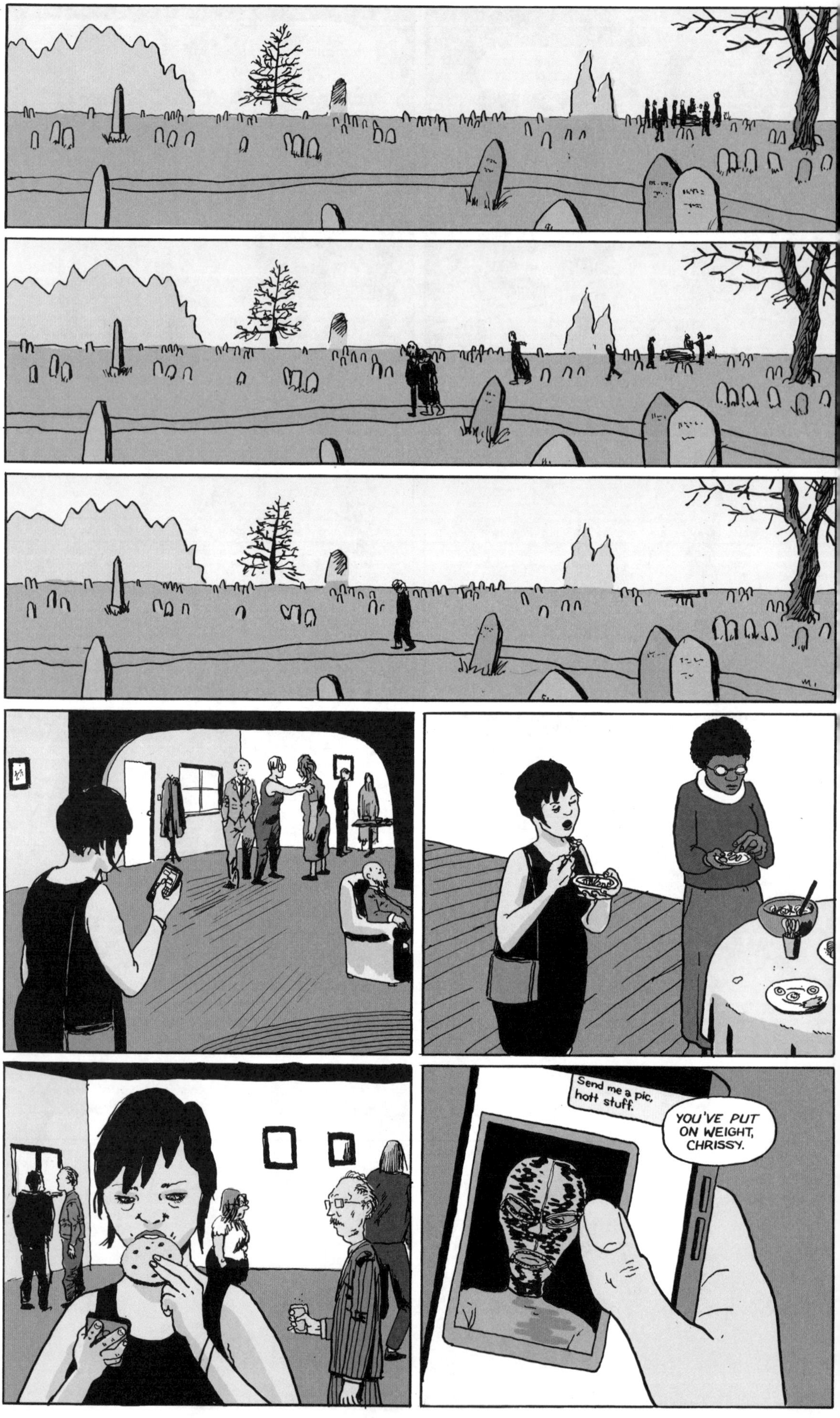
Send me a pic, hott stuff.
YOU'VE PUT ON WEIGHT, CHRISSY.

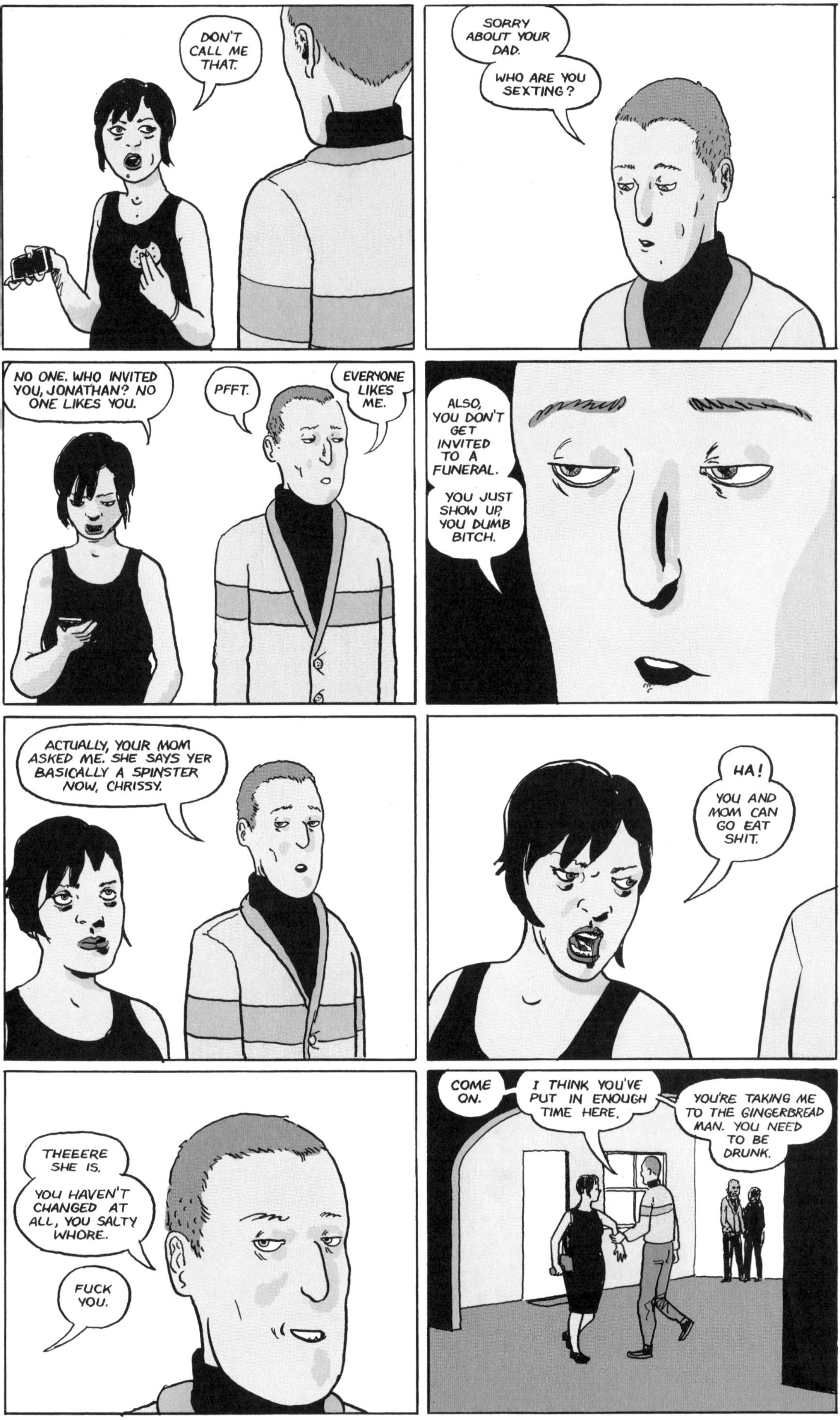
DON'T CALL ME THAT.
SORRY ABOUT YOUR DAD.
WHO ARE YOU SEXTING?
NO ONE. WHO INVITED YOU, JONATHAN? NO ONE LIKES YOU.
PFFT.
EVERYONE LIKES ME.
ALSO, YOU DON'T GET INVITED TO A FUNERAL.
YOU JUST SHOW UP, YOU DUMB BITCH.
ACTUALLY, YOUR MOM ASKED ME. SHE SAYS YER BASICALLY A SPINSTER NOW, CHRISSY.
HA!
YOU AND MOM CAN GO EAT SHIT.
THEEERE SHE IS.
YOU HAVEN'T CHANGED AT ALL, YOU SALTY WHORE.
FUCK YOU.
COME ON.
I THINK YOU'VE PUT IN ENOUGH TIME HERE.
YOU'RE TAKING ME TO THE GINGERBREAD MAN. YOU NEED TO BE DRUNK.

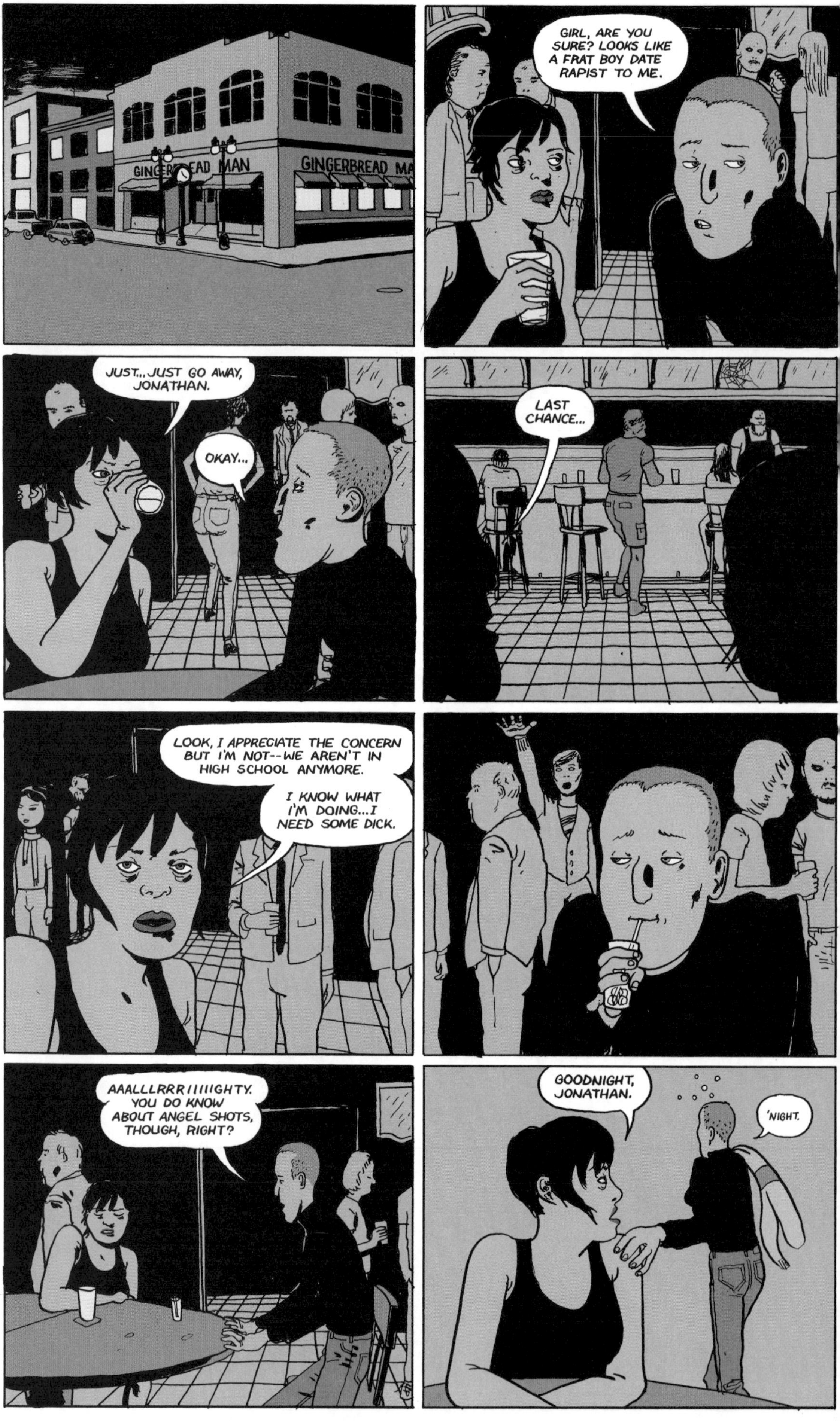
GINGERBREAD MA
GIRL, ARE YOU SURE? LOOKS LIKE A FRAT BOY DATE RAPIST TO ME.
JUST...JUST GO AWAY, JONATHAN.
OKAY...
LAST CHANCE...
LOOK, I APPRECIATE THE CONCERN BUT I'M NOT--WE AREN'T IN HIGH SCHOOL ANYMORE.
I KNOW WHAT I'M DOING...I NEED SOME DICK.
AAALLLRRRIIIIIGHTY. YOU DO KNOW ABOUT ANGEL SHOTS, THOUGH, RIGHT?
GOODNIGHT, JONATHAN.
'NIGHT.

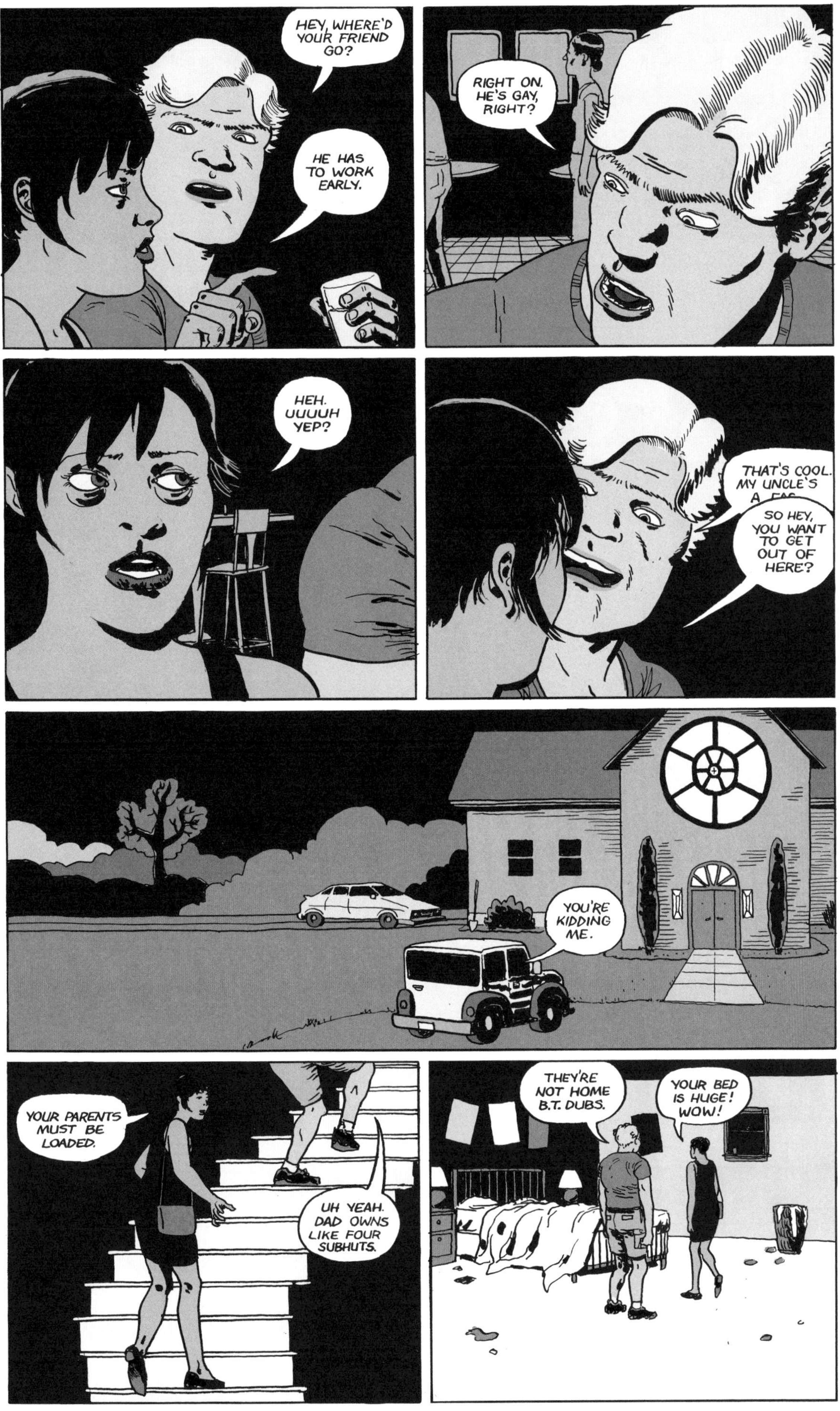
HEY, WHERE'D YOUR FRIEND GO?
HE HAS TO WORK EARLY.
RIGHT ON. HE'S GAY, RIGHT?
HEH. UUUUH YEP?
THAT'S COOL. MY UNCLE'S A FAG
SO HEY, YOU WANT TO GET OUT OF HERE?
YOU'RE KIDDING ME.
YOUR PARENTS MUST BE LOADED.
UH YEAH. DAD OWNS LIKE FOUR SUBHUTS.
THEY'RE NOT HOME B.T. DUBS.
YOUR BED IS HUGE! WOW!

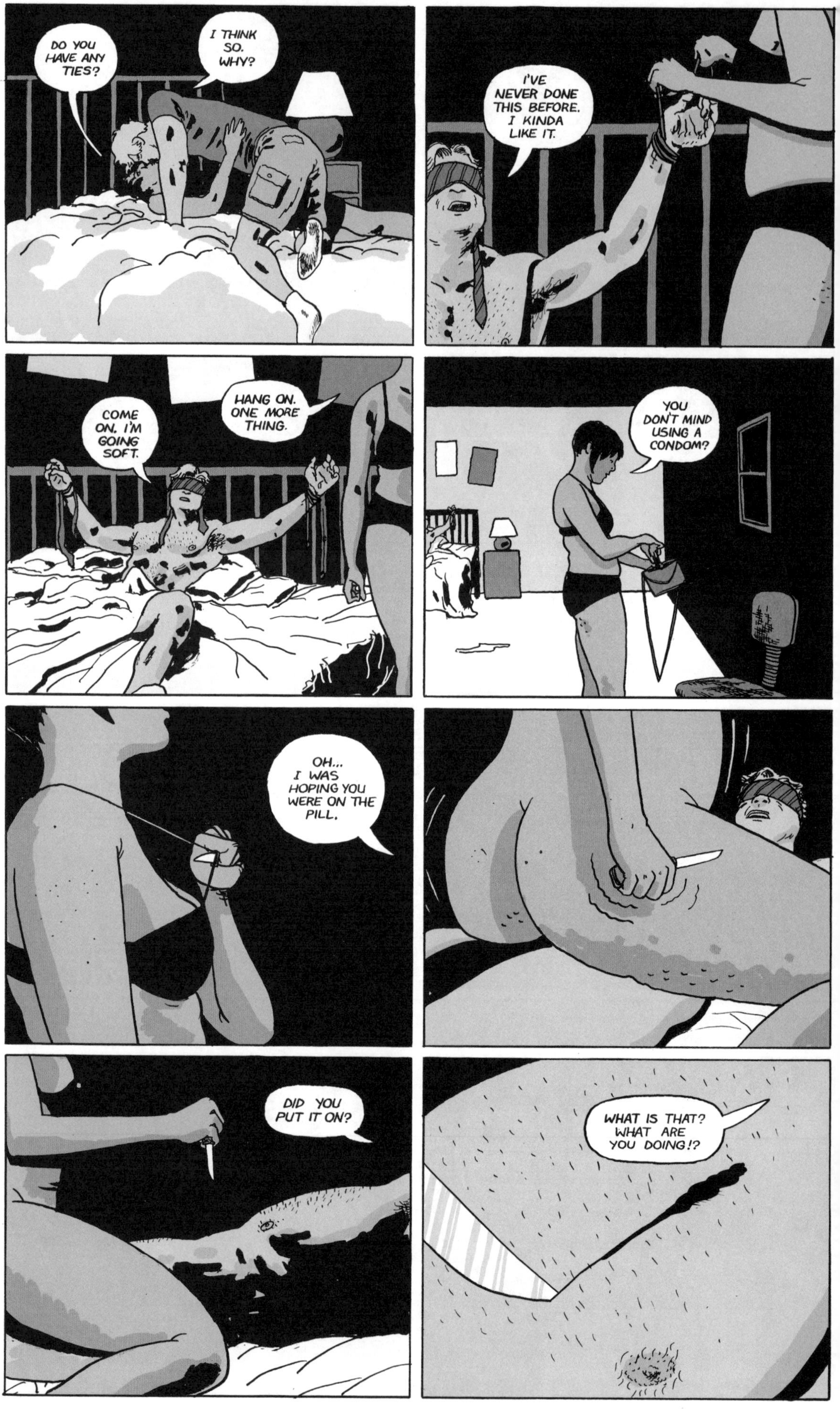
DO YOU HAVE ANY TIES?
I THINK SO. WHY?
I'VE NEVER DONE THIS BEFORE. I KINDA LIKE IT.
COME ON. I'M GOING SOFT.
HANG ON. ONE MORE THING.
YOU DON'T MIND USING A CONDOM?
OH... I WAS HOPING YOU WERE ON THE PILL.
DID YOU PUT IT ON?
WHAT IS THAT? WHAT ARE YOU DOING!?

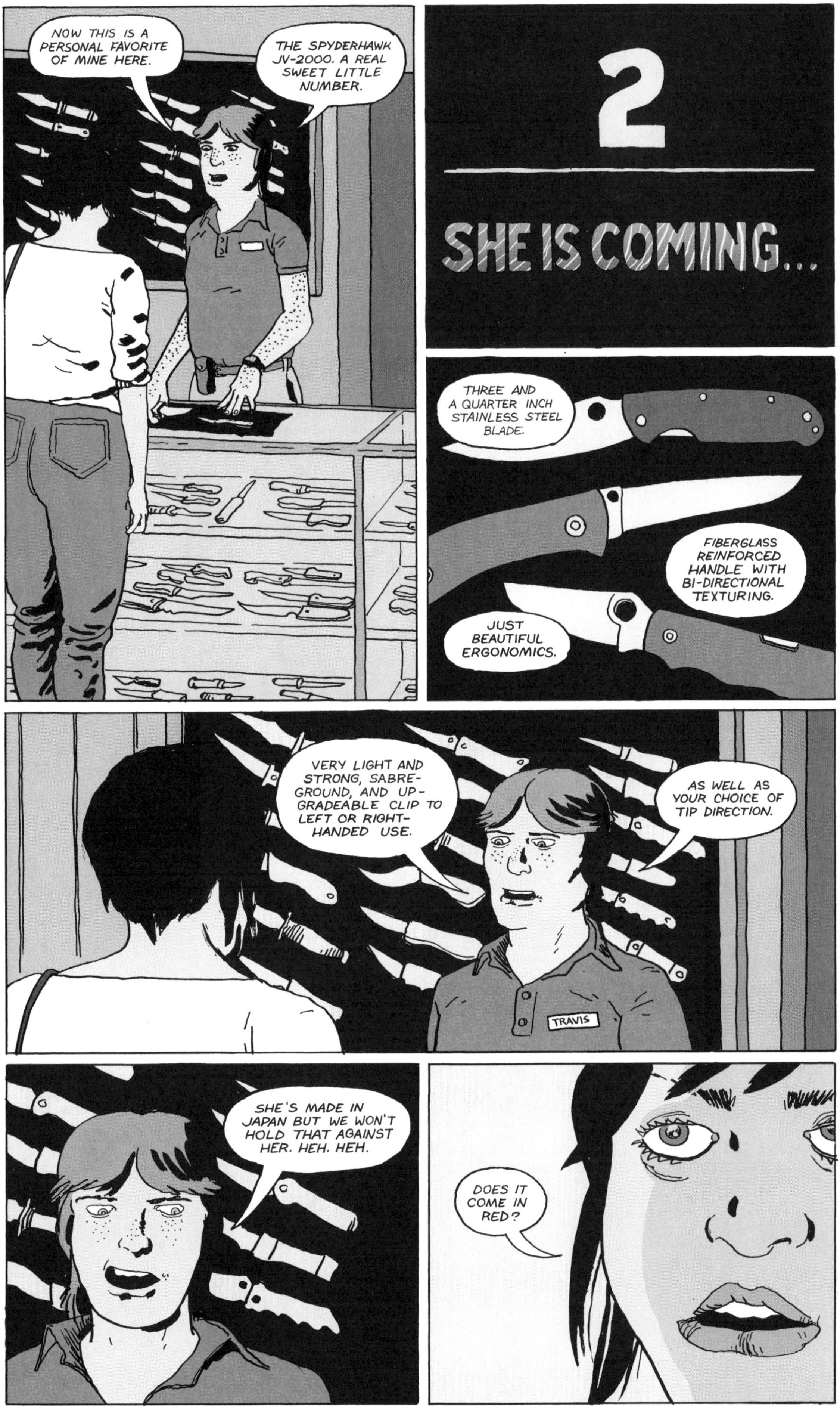
NOW THIS IS A PERSONAL FAVORITE OF MINE HERE.
THE SPYDERHAWK JV-2000. A REAL SWEET LITTLE NUMBER.
2
SHE IS COMING...
THREE AND A QUARTER INCH STAINLESS STEEL BLADE.
FIBERGLASS REINFORCED HANDLE WITH BI-DIRECTIONAL TEXTURING.
JUST BEAUTIFUL ERGONOMICS.
VERY LIGHT AND STRONG, SABRE-GROUND, AND UP-GRADEABLE CLIP TO LEFT OR RIGHT-HANDED USE.
AS WELL AS YOUR CHOICE OF TIP DIRECTION.
TRAVIS
SHE'S MADE IN JAPAN BUT WE WON'T HOLD THAT AGAINST HER. HEH. HEH.
DOES IT COME IN RED?

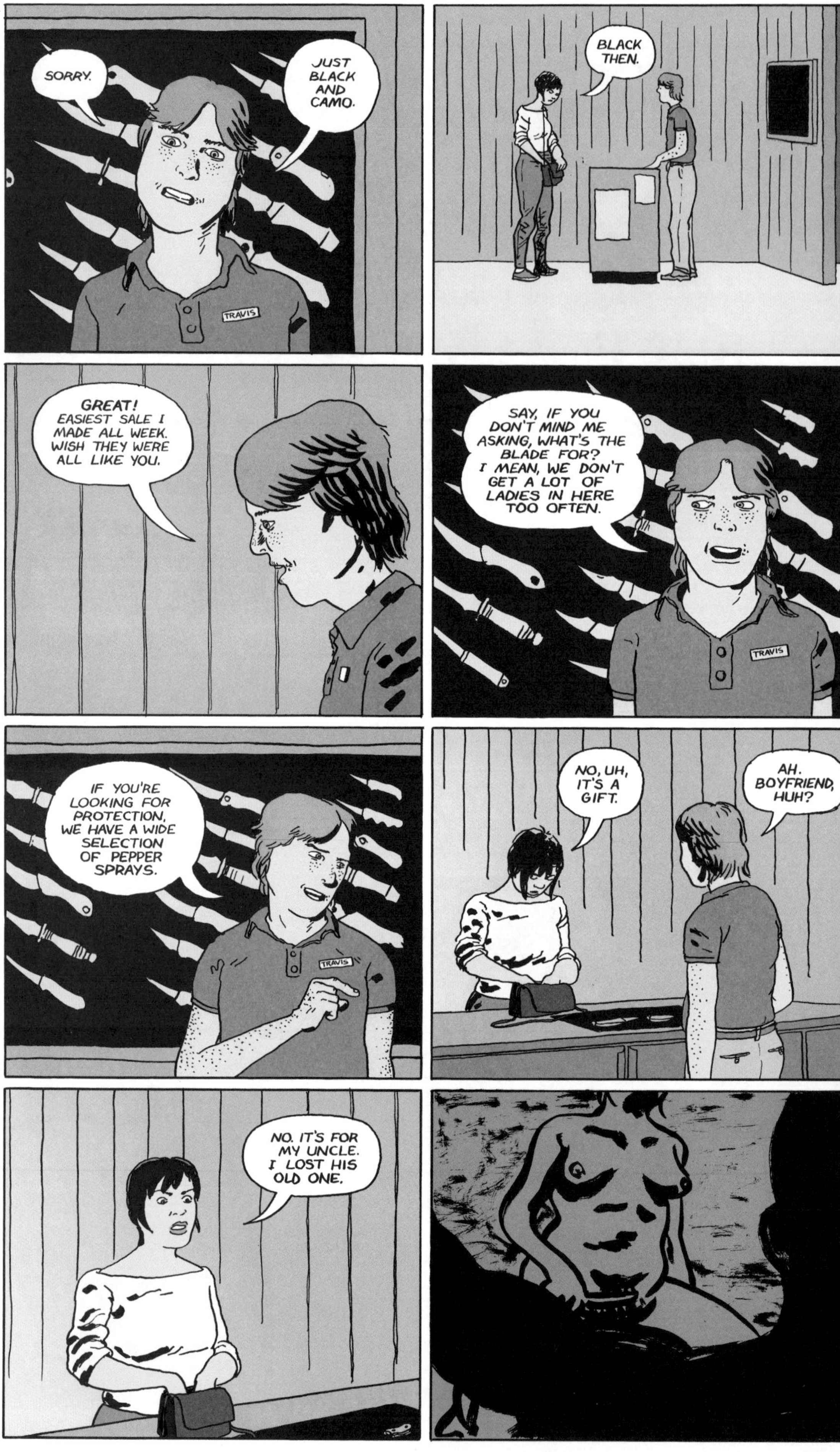
SORRY.
JUST BLACK AND CAMO.
TRAVIS
BLACK THEN.
GREAT! EASIEST SALE I MADE ALL WEEK. WISH THEY WERE ALL LIKE YOU.
SAY, IF YOU DON'T MIND ME ASKING, WHAT'S THE BLADE FOR? I MEAN, WE DON'T GET A LOT OF LADIES IN HERE TOO OFTEN.
TRAVIS
IF YOU'RE LOOKING FOR PROTECTION, WE HAVE A WIDE SELECTION OF PEPPER SPRAYS.
TRAVIS
NO, UH, IT'S A GIFT.
AH. BOYFRIEND, HUH?
NO. IT'S FOR MY UNCLE. I LOST HIS OLD ONE.

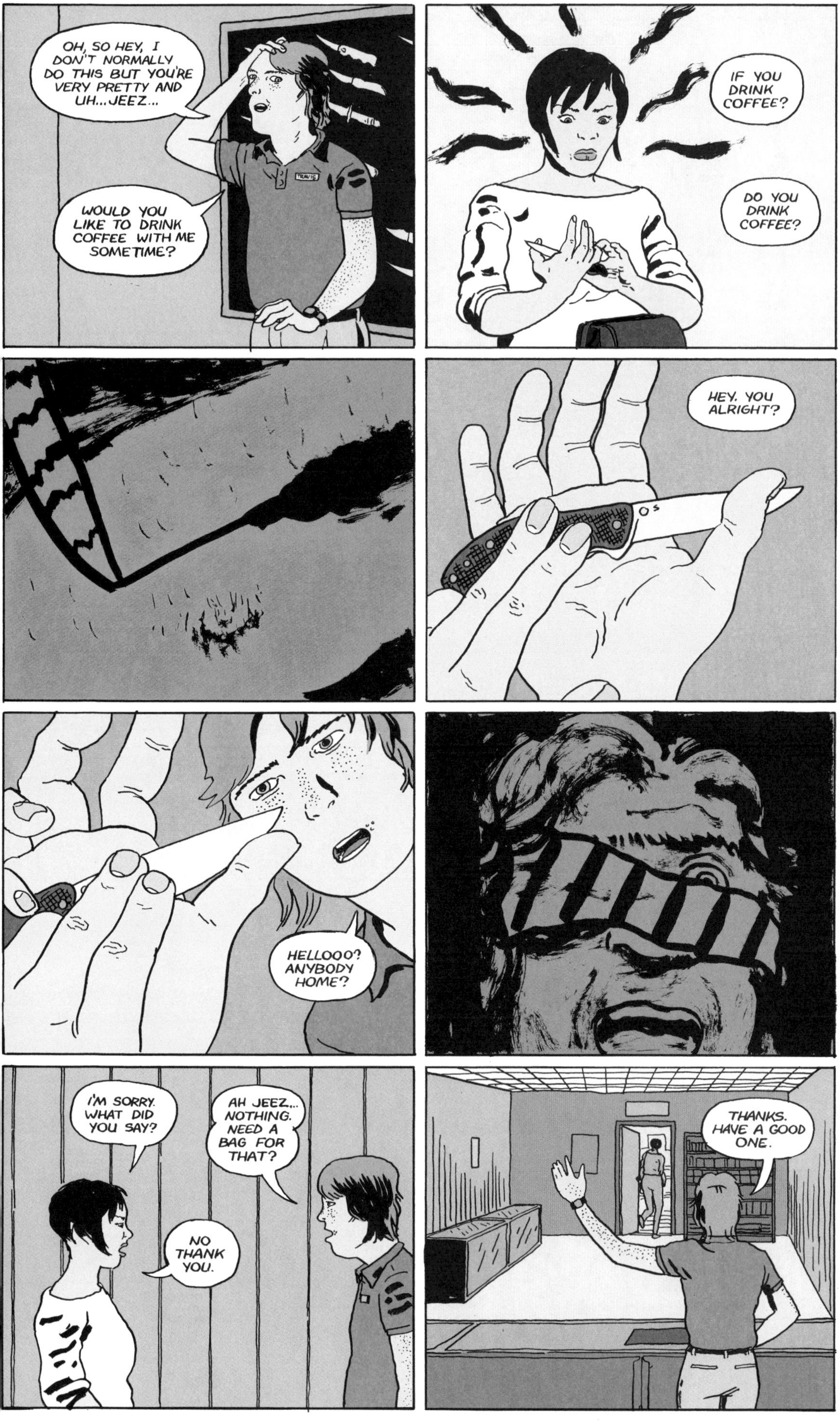
OH, SO HEY, I DON'T NORMALLY DO THIS BUT YOU'RE VERY PRETTY AND UH...JEEZ...
TRAVIS
WOULD YOU LIKE TO DRINK COFFEE WITH ME SOMETIME?
IF YOU DRINK COFFEE?
DO YOU DRINK COFFEE?
HEY. YOU ALRIGHT?
HELLOOO? ANYBODY HOME?
I'M SORRY. WHAT DID YOU SAY?
AH JEEZ... NOTHING. NEED A BAG FOR THAT?
NO THANK YOU.
THANKS. HAVE A GOOD ONE.

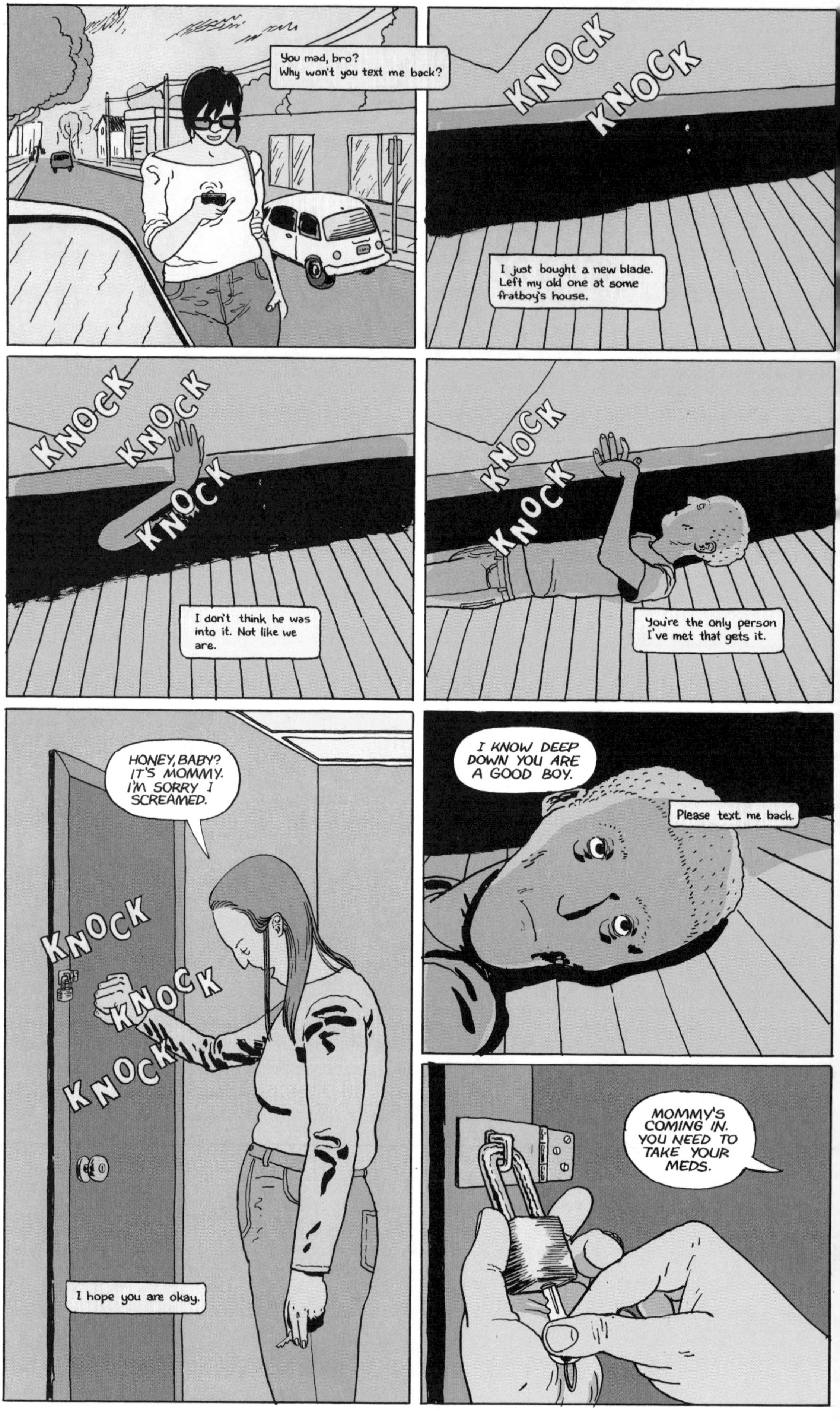
You mad, bro?
Why won't you text me back?
KNOCK
KNOCK
I just bought a new blade. Left my old one at some fratboy's house.
KNOCK
KNOCK
KNOCK
I don't think he was into it. Not like we are.
KNOCK
KNOCK
You're the only person I've met that gets it.
HONEY, BABY? IT'S MOMMY. I'M SORRY I SCREAMED.
KNOCK
KNOCK
KNOCK
I hope you are okay.
I KNOW DEEP DOWN YOU ARE A GOOD BOY.
Please text me back.
MOMMY'S COMING IN. YOU NEED TO TAKE YOUR MEDS.

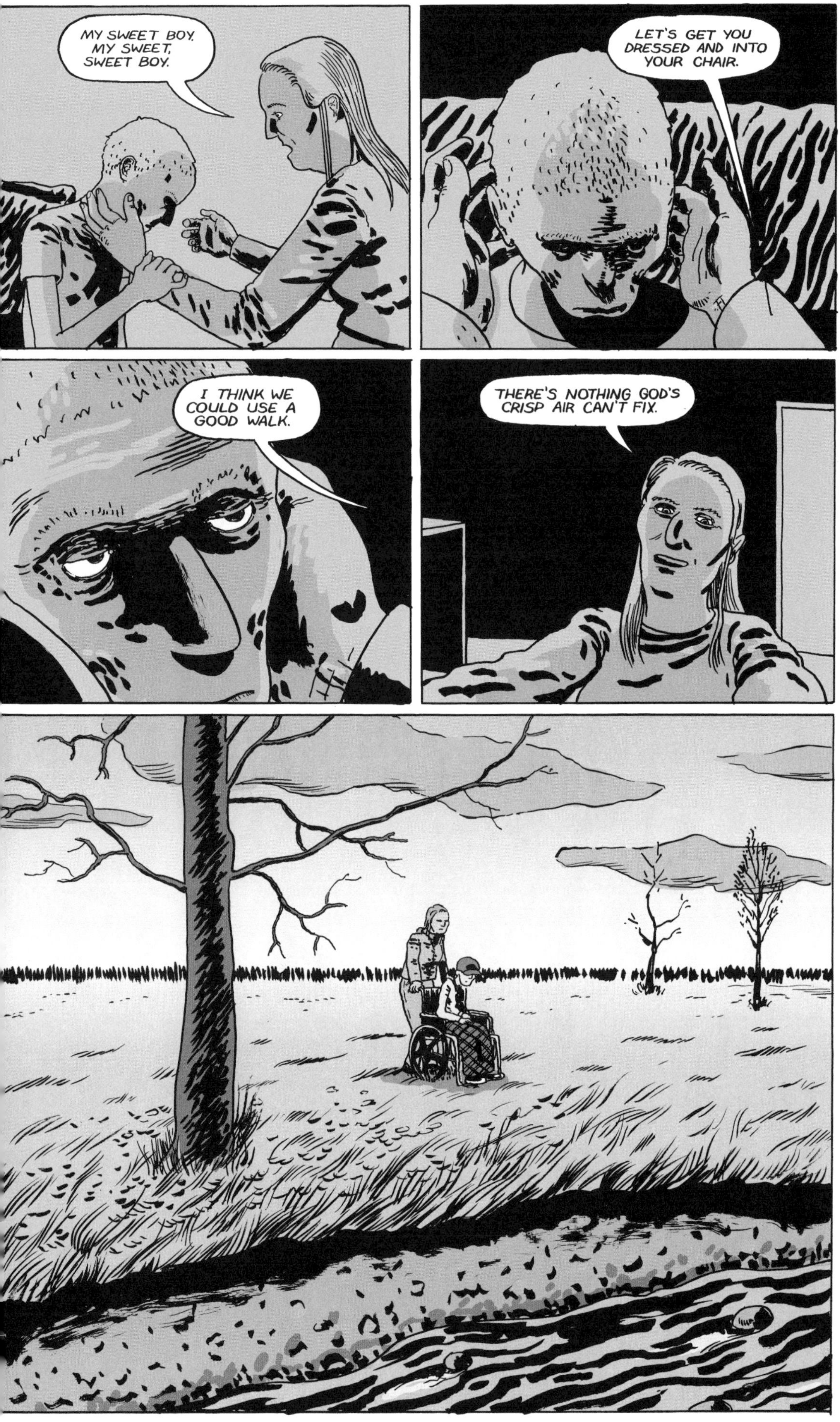
MY SWEET BOY. MY SWEET, SWEET BOY.
LET'S GET YOU DRESSED AND INTO YOUR CHAIR.
I THINK WE COULD USE A GOOD WALK.
THERE'S NOTHING GOD'S CRISP AIR CAN'T FIX.

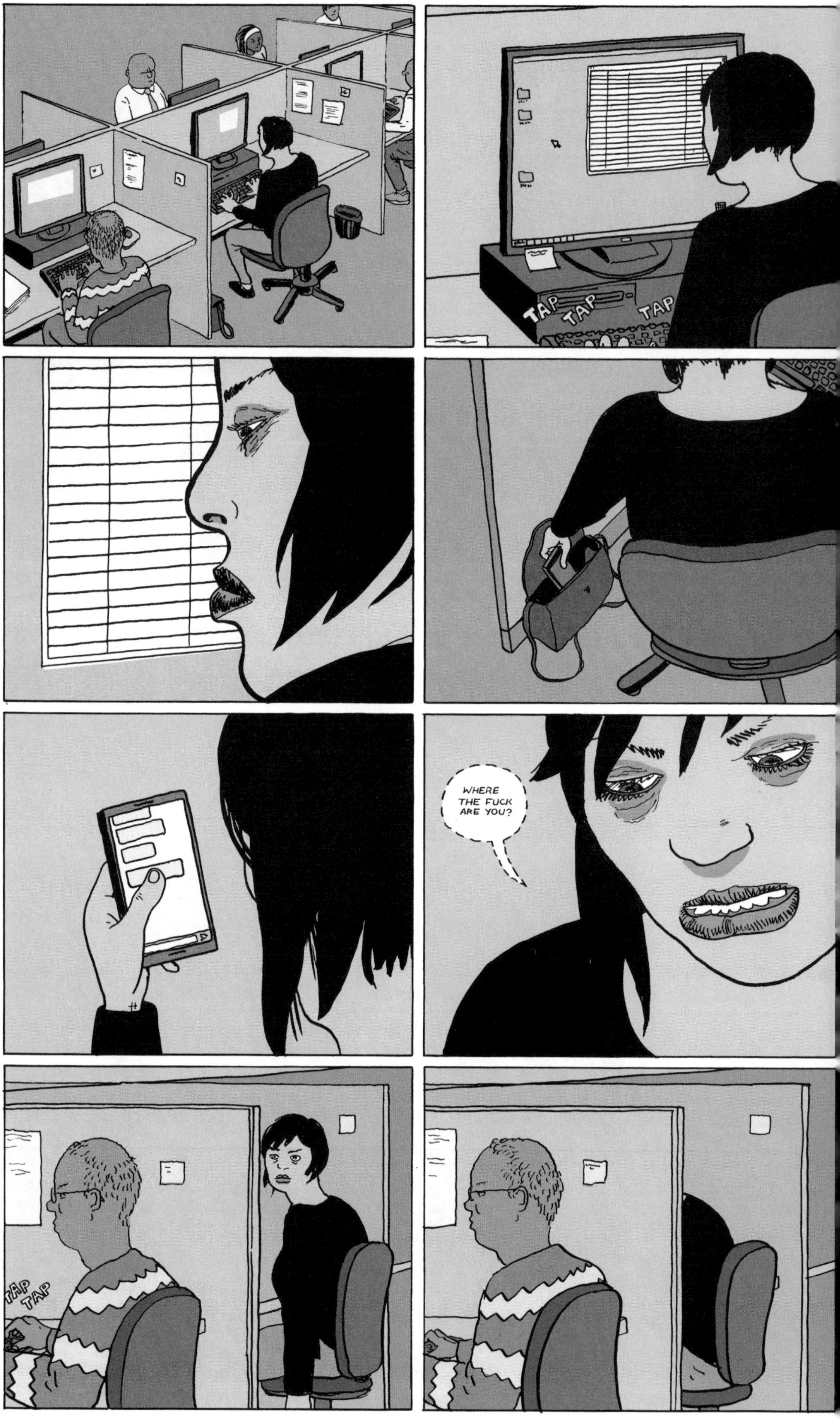
TAP TAP TAP
WHERE THE FUCK ARE YOU?
TAP TAP

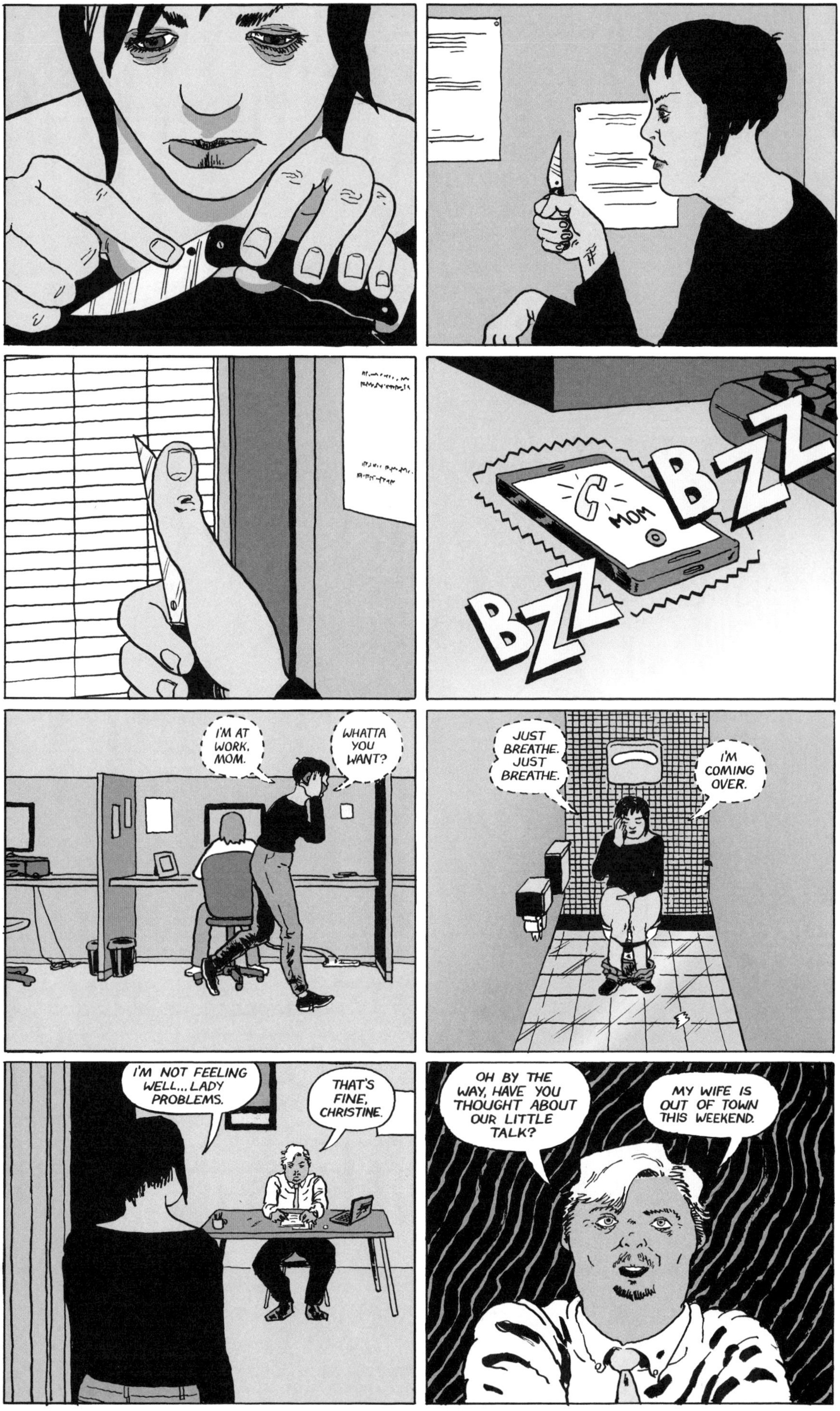
MOM
BZZ
BZZ
I'M AT WORK, MOM.
WHATTA YOU WANT?
JUST BREATHE. JUST BREATHE.
I'M COMING OVER.
I'M NOT FEELING WELL... LADY PROBLEMS.
THAT'S FINE, CHRISTINE.
OH BY THE WAY, HAVE YOU THOUGHT ABOUT OUR LITTLE TALK?
MY WIFE IS OUT OF TOWN THIS WEEKEND.

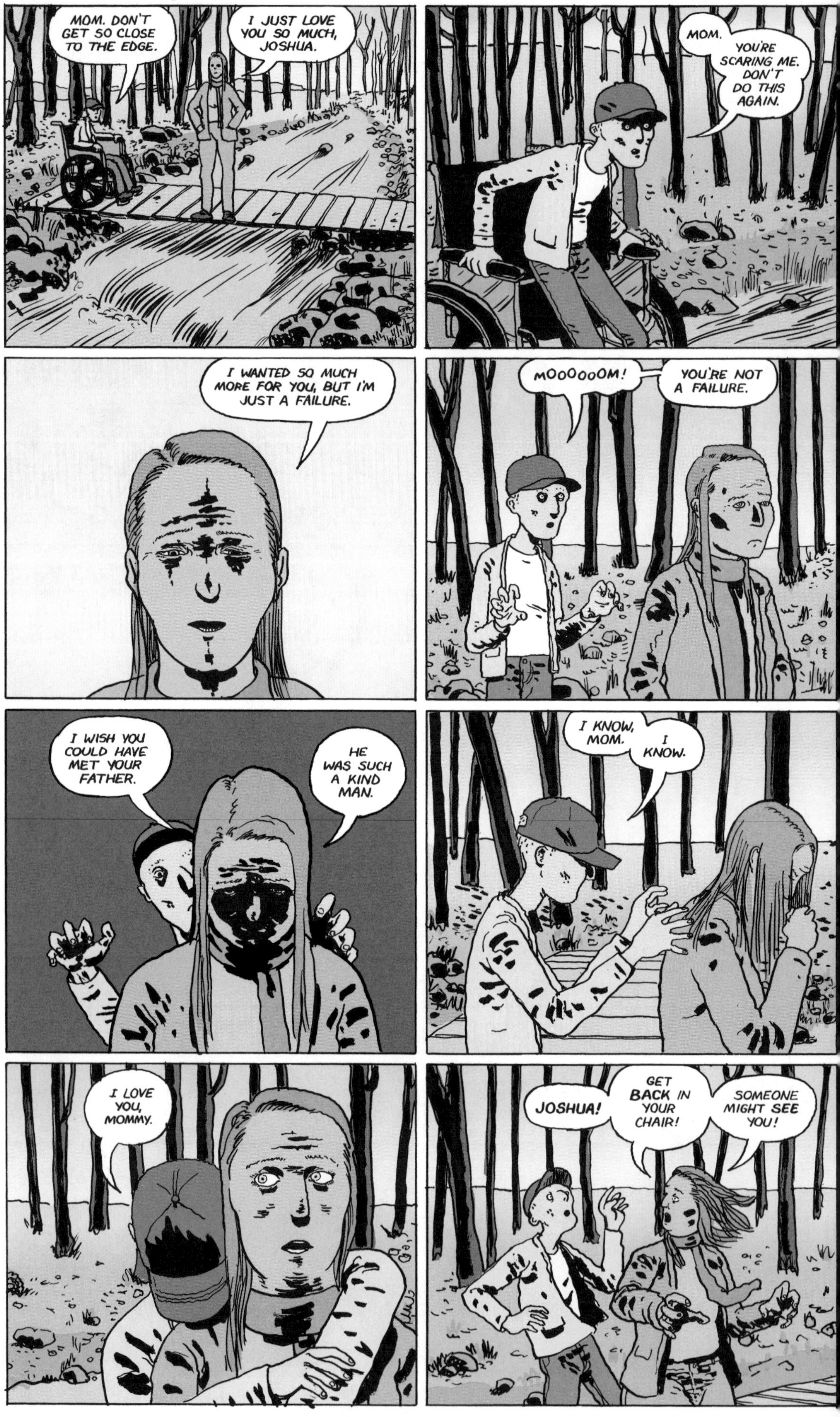
MOM. DON'T GET SO CLOSE TO THE EDGE.
I JUST LOVE YOU SO MUCH, JOSHUA.
MOM.
YOU'RE SCARING ME. DON'T DO THIS AGAIN.
I WANTED SO MUCH MORE FOR YOU, BUT I'M JUST A FAILURE.
MOOOOOOM!
YOU'RE NOT A FAILURE.
I WISH YOU COULD HAVE MET YOUR FATHER.
HE WAS SUCH A KIND MAN.
I KNOW, MOM.
I KNOW.
I LOVE YOU, MOMMY.
JOSHUA!
GET BACK IN YOUR CHAIR!
SOMEONE MIGHT SEE YOU!

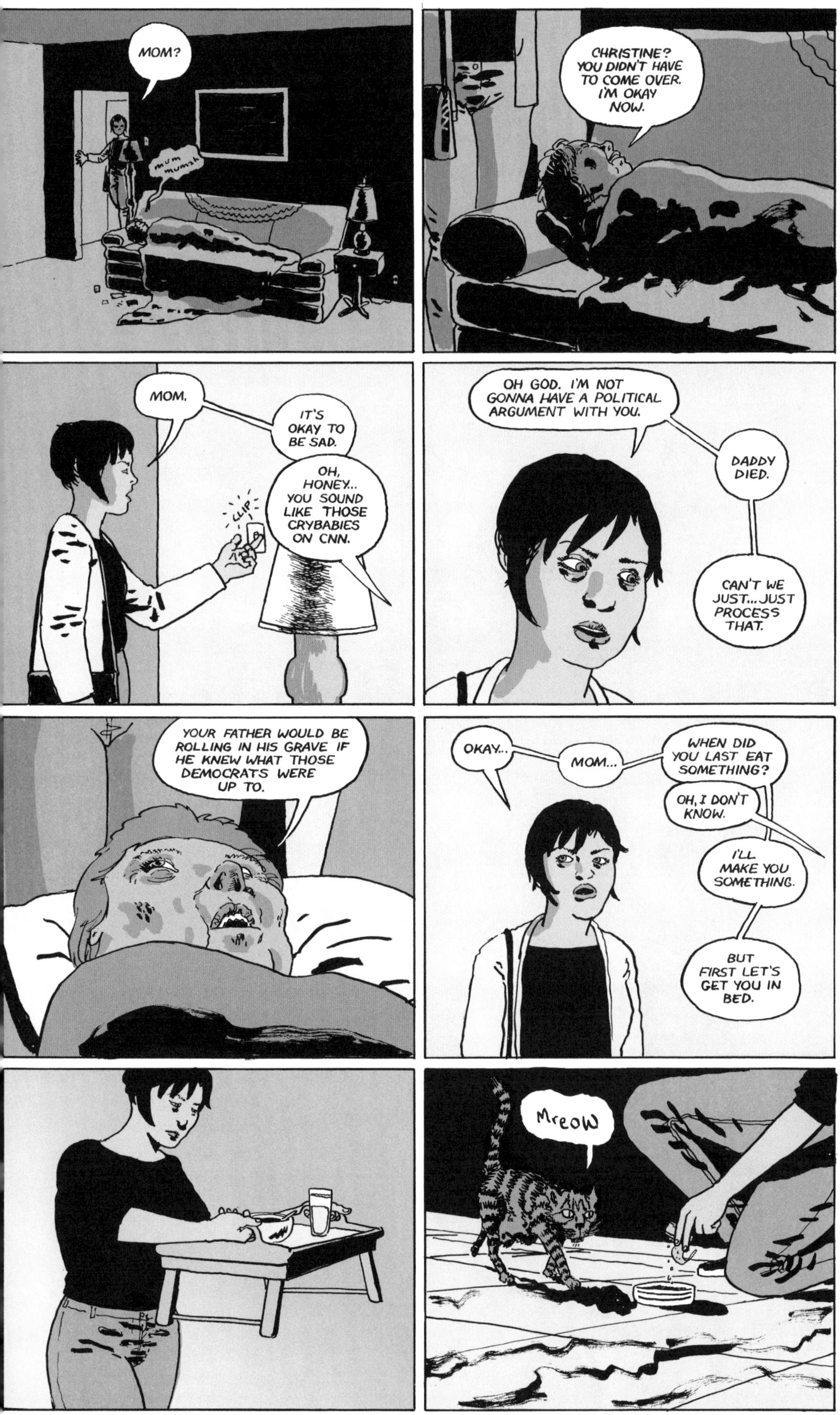
MOM?
mum mumzh
CHRISTINE? YOU DIDN'T HAVE TO COME OVER. I'M OKAY NOW.
MOM.
IT'S OKAY TO BE SAD.
CLIP
OH, HONEY... YOU SOUND LIKE THOSE CRYBABIES ON CNN.
OH GOD. I'M NOT GONNA HAVE A POLITICAL ARGUMENT WITH YOU.
DADDY DIED.
CAN'T WE JUST...JUST PROCESS THAT.
YOUR FATHER WOULD BE ROLLING IN HIS GRAVE IF HE KNEW WHAT THOSE DEMOCRATS WERE UP TO.
OKAY...
MOM...
WHEN DID YOU LAST EAT SOMETHING?
OH, I DON'T KNOW.
I'LL MAKE YOU SOMETHING.
BUT FIRST LET'S GET YOU IN BED.
MreoW

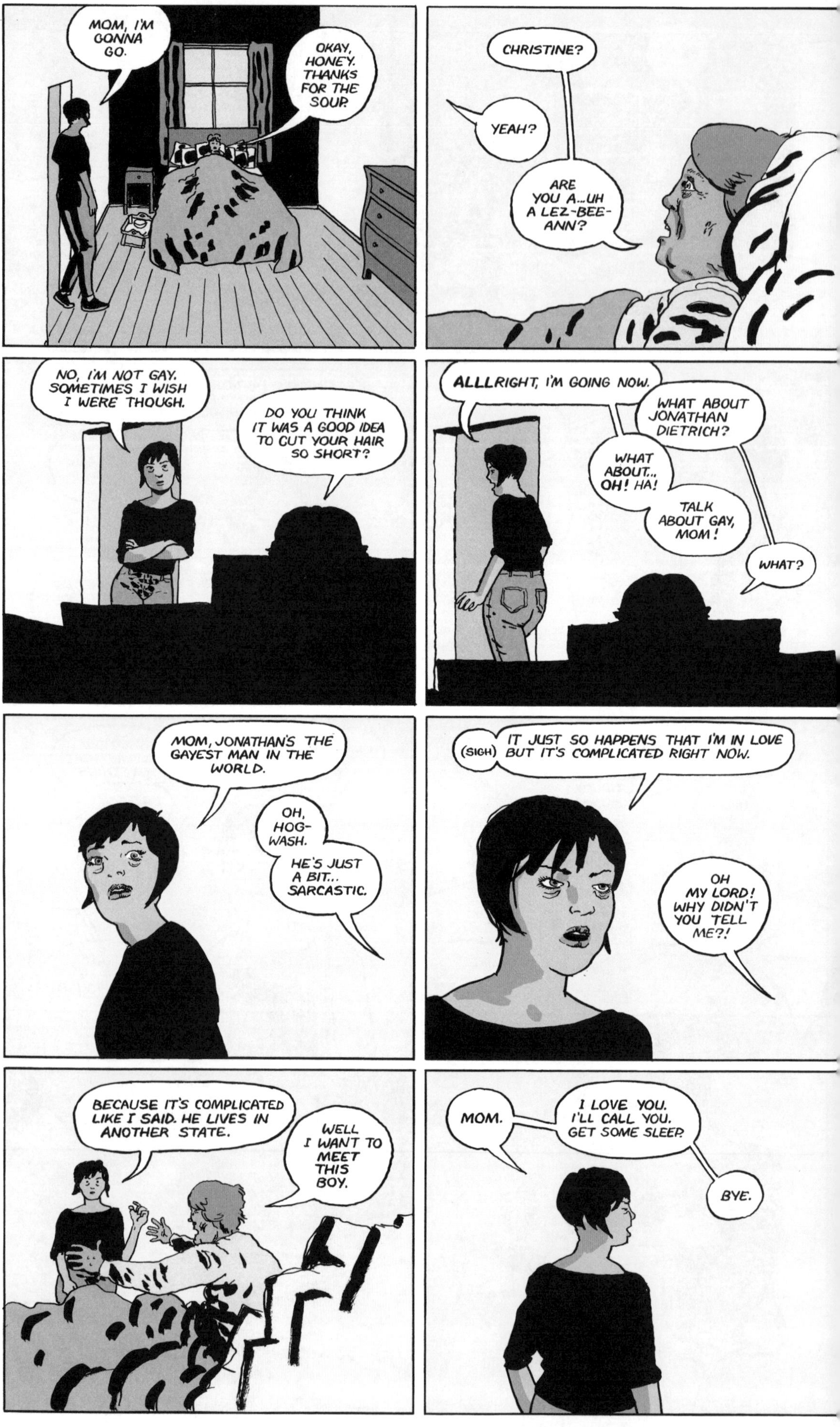
MOM, I'M GONNA GO.
OKAY, HONEY. THANKS FOR THE SOUP.
CHRISTINE?
YEAH?
ARE YOU A...UH A LEZ-BEE-ANN?
NO, I'M NOT GAY. SOMETIMES I WISH I WERE THOUGH.
DO YOU THINK IT WAS A GOOD IDEA TO CUT YOUR HAIR SO SHORT?
ALLLRIGHT, I'M GOING NOW.
WHAT ABOUT JONATHAN DIETRICH?
WHAT ABOUT... OH! HA!
TALK ABOUT GAY, MOM!
WHAT?
MOM, JONATHAN'S THE GAYEST MAN IN THE WORLD.
OH, HOG-WASH.
HE'S JUST A BIT... SARCASTIC.
(SIGH)
IT JUST SO HAPPENS THAT I'M IN LOVE BUT IT'S COMPLICATED RIGHT NOW.
OH MY LORD! WHY DIDN'T YOU TELL ME?!
BECAUSE IT'S COMPLICATED LIKE I SAID. HE LIVES IN ANOTHER STATE.
WELL I WANT TO MEET THIS BOY.
MOM.
I LOVE YOU. I'LL CALL YOU. GET SOME SLEEP.
BYE.

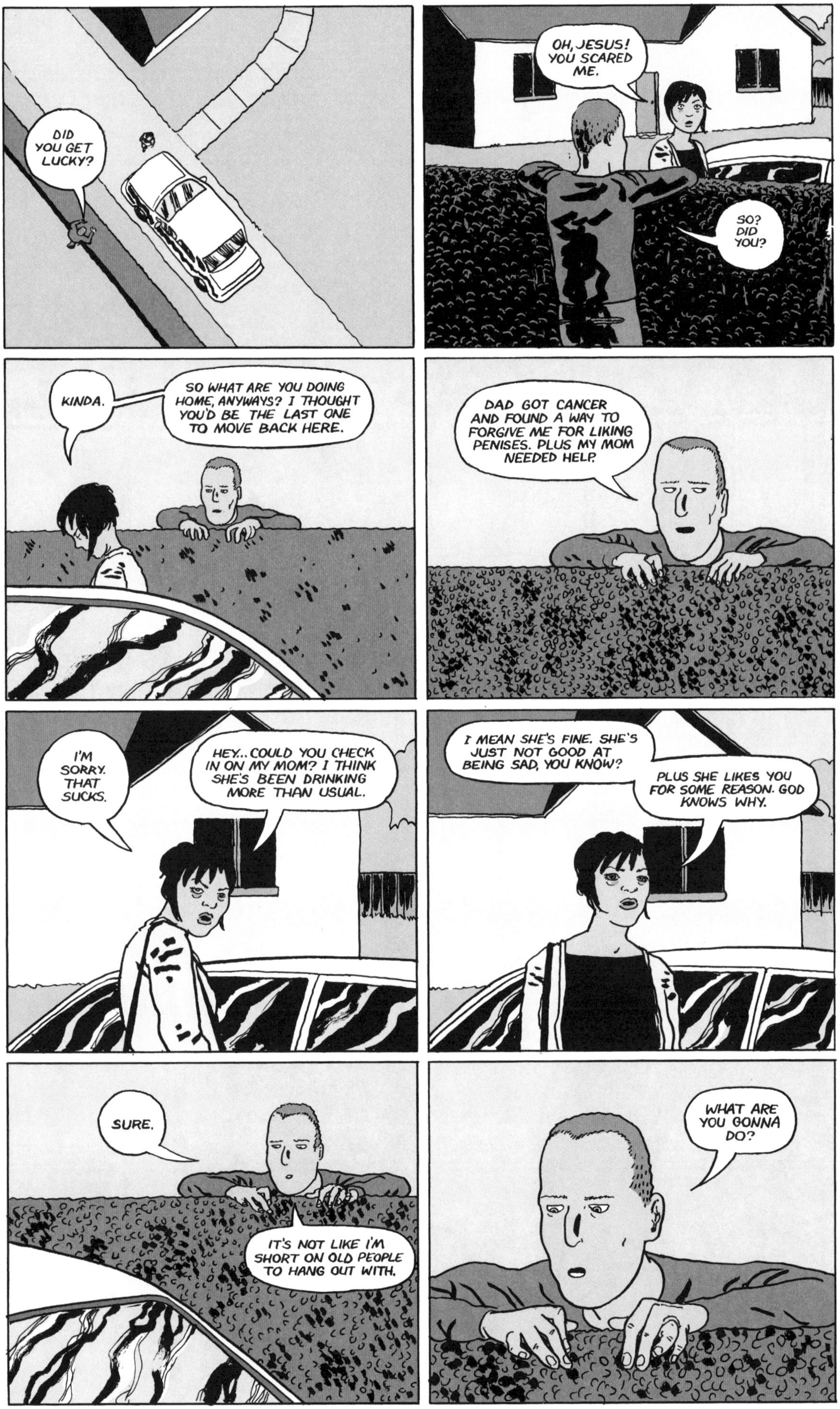
DID YOU GET LUCKY?
OH, JESUS! YOU SCARED ME.
SO? DID YOU?
KINDA.
SO WHAT ARE YOU DOING HOME, ANYWAYS? I THOUGHT YOU'D BE THE LAST ONE TO MOVE BACK HERE.
DAD GOT CANCER AND FOUND A WAY TO FORGIVE ME FOR LIKING PENISES. PLUS MY MOM NEEDED HELP.
I'M SORRY. THAT SUCKS.
HEY... COULD YOU CHECK IN ON MY MOM? I THINK SHE'S BEEN DRINKING MORE THAN USUAL.
I MEAN SHE'S FINE. SHE'S JUST NOT GOOD AT BEING SAD, YOU KNOW?
PLUS SHE LIKES YOU FOR SOME REASON. GOD KNOWS WHY.
SURE.
IT'S NOT LIKE I'M SHORT ON OLD PEOPLE TO HANG OUT WITH.
WHAT ARE YOU GONNA DO?

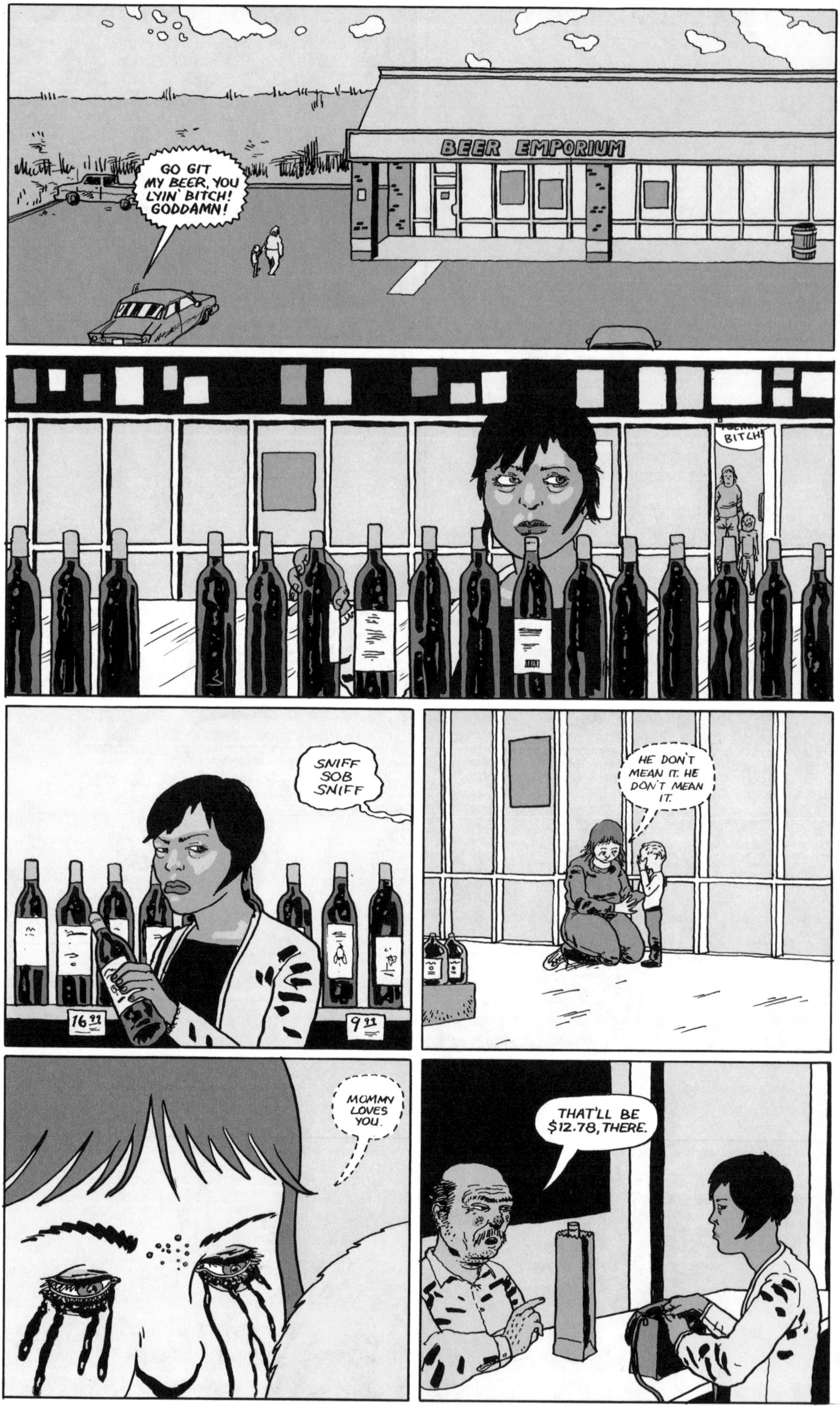
BEER EMPORIUM
GO GIT MY BEER, YOU LYIN' BITCH! GODDAMN!
BITCH!
SNIFF SOB SNIFF
16.99
9.99
HE DON'T MEAN IT. HE DON'T MEAN IT.
MOMMY LOVES YOU.
THAT'LL BE $12.78, THERE.

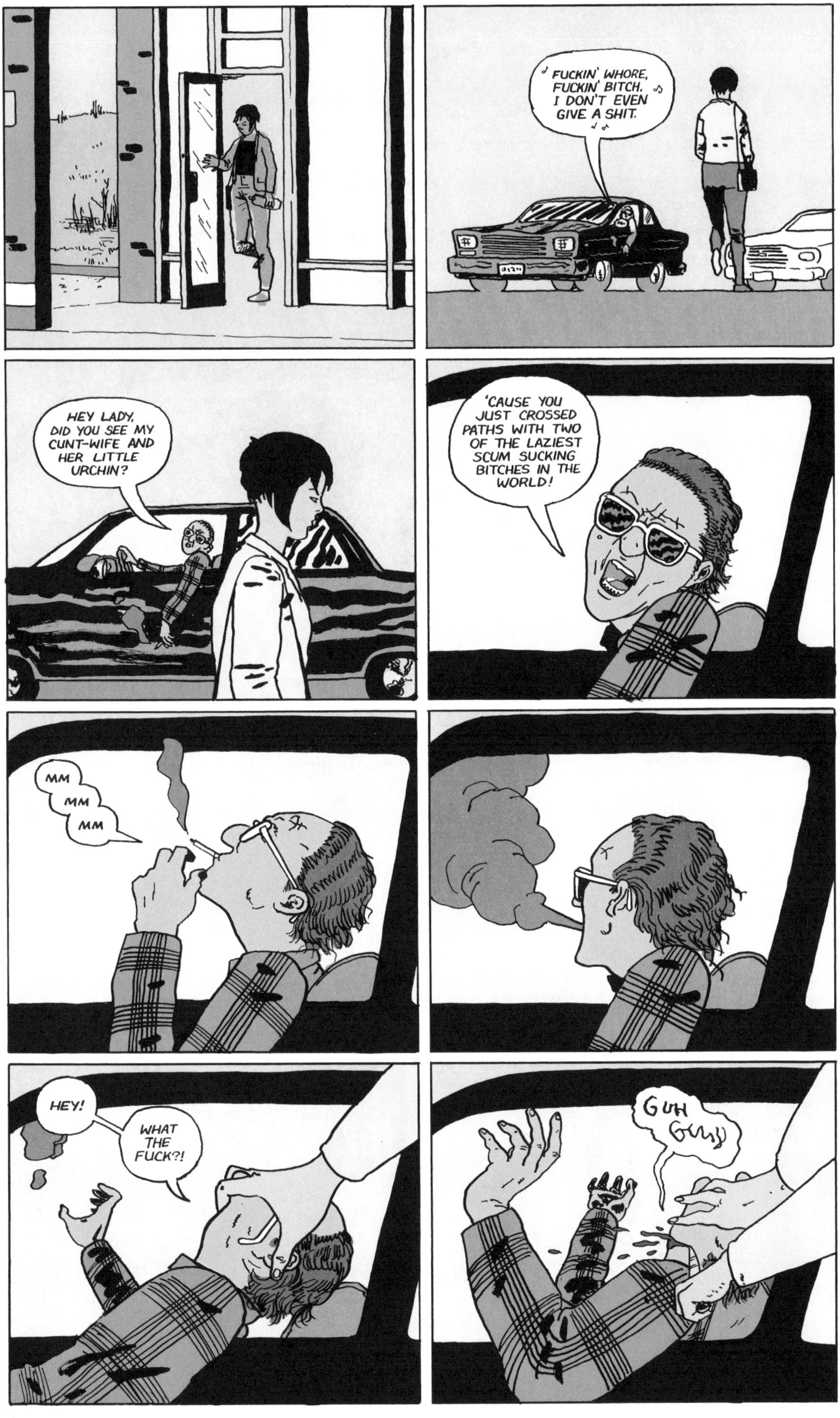
FUCKIN' WHORE, FUCKIN' BITCH. I DON'T EVEN GIVE A SHIT.
HEY LADY, DID YOU SEE MY CUNT-WIFE AND HER LITTLE URCHIN?
'CAUSE YOU JUST CROSSED PATHS WITH TWO OF THE LAZIEST SCUM SUCKING BITCHES IN THE WORLD!
MM
MM
MM
HEY!
WHAT THE FUCK?!
GUH

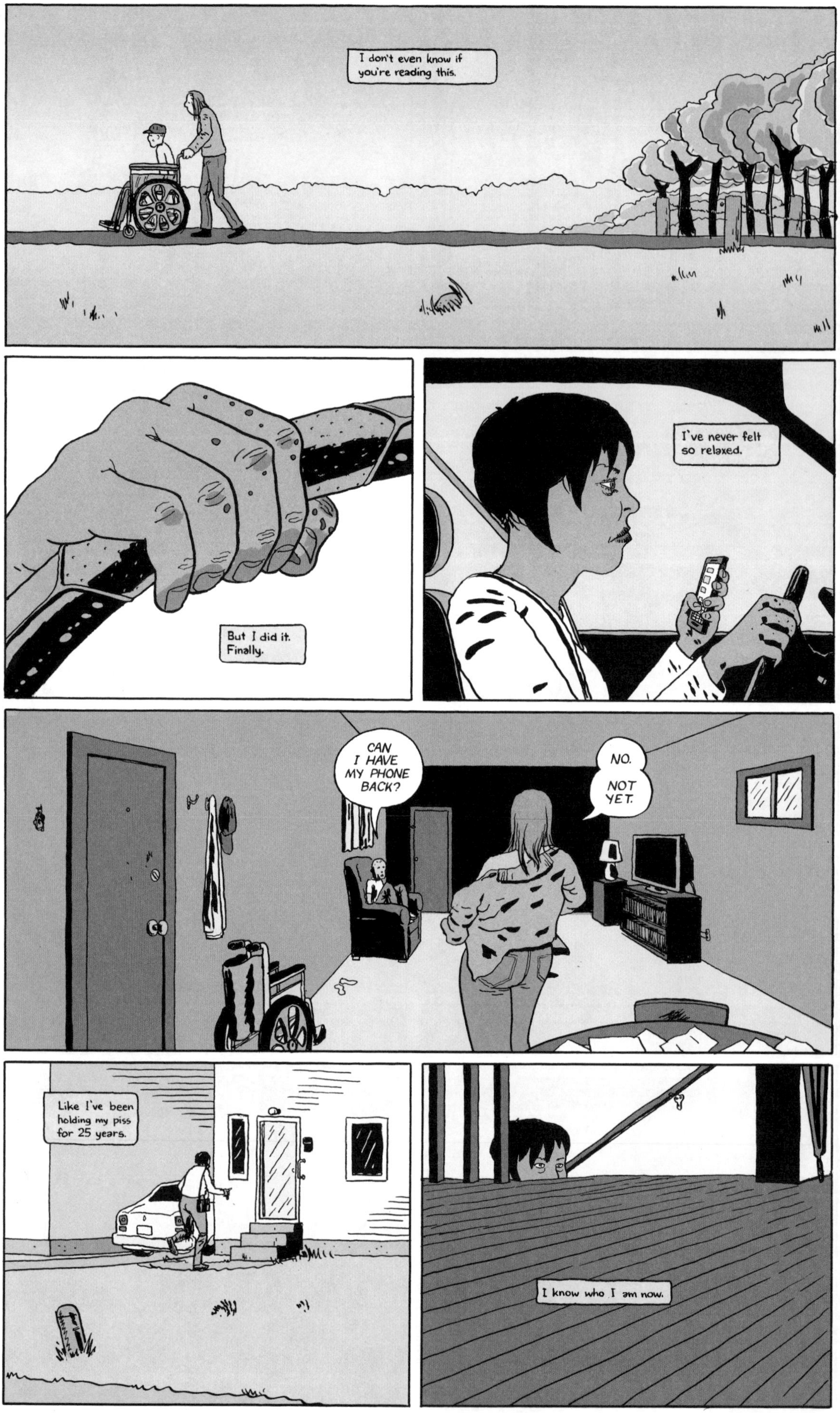

I don't even know if you're reading this.
But I did it. Finally.
I've never felt so relaxed.
CAN I HAVE MY PHONE BACK?
NO.
NOT YET.
Like I've been holding my piss for 25 years.
I know who I am now.

And you've helped show me the way, Joshua.

I want to share this with you.

CLIP
TIP
TAP

If you are ready?

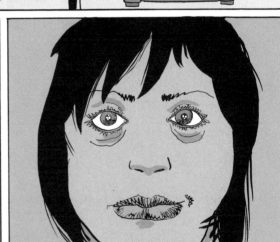

Are you my baby, Joshua? I need my baby.

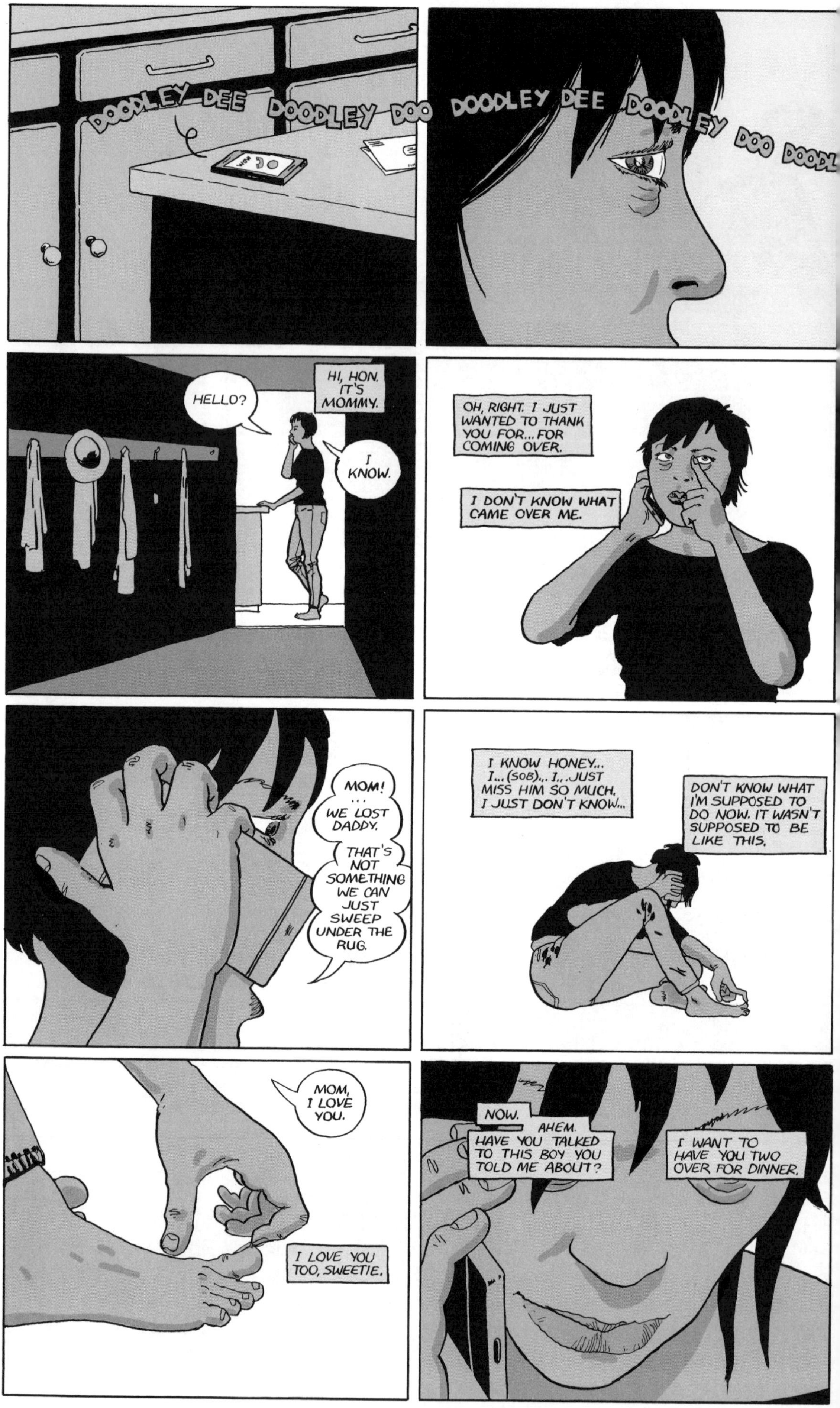
DOODLEY DEE DOODLEY DOO DOODLEY DEE DOODLEY DOO DOODL
HELLO?
HI, HON. IT'S MOMMY.
I KNOW.
OH, RIGHT. I JUST WANTED TO THANK YOU FOR... FOR COMING OVER.
I DON'T KNOW WHAT CAME OVER ME.
MOM! ... WE LOST DADDY.
THAT'S NOT SOMETHING WE CAN JUST SWEEP UNDER THE RUG.
I KNOW HONEY... I...(SOB)... I... JUST MISS HIM SO MUCH. I JUST DON'T KNOW...
DON'T KNOW WHAT I'M SUPPOSED TO DO NOW. IT WASN'T SUPPOSED TO BE LIKE THIS.
MOM, I LOVE YOU.
I LOVE YOU TOO, SWEETIE.
NOW.
AHEM.
HAVE YOU TALKED TO THIS BOY YOU TOLD ME ABOUT?
I WANT TO HAVE YOU TWO OVER FOR DINNER.

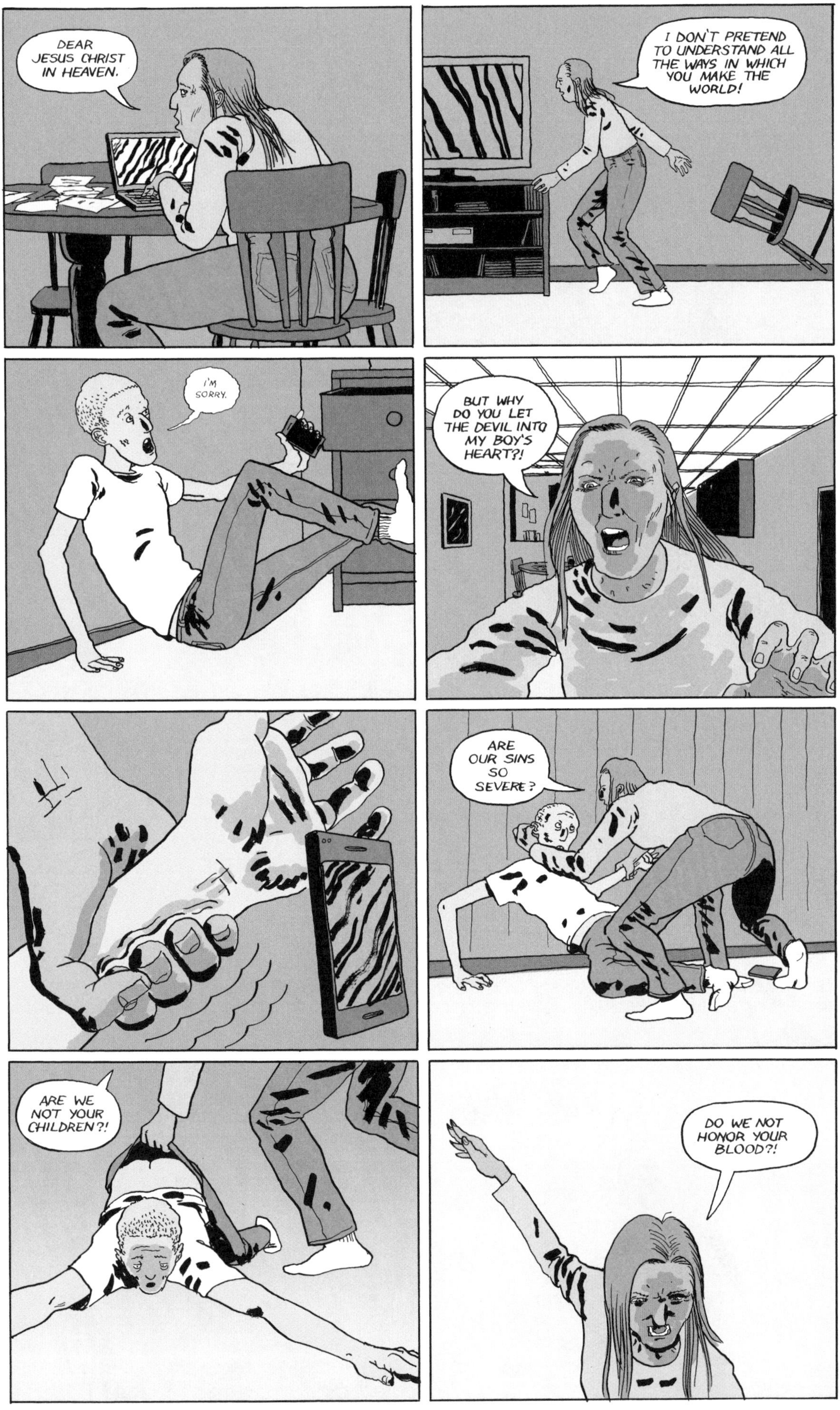
DEAR JESUS CHRIST IN HEAVEN.
I DON'T PRETEND TO UNDERSTAND ALL THE WAYS IN WHICH YOU MAKE THE WORLD!
I'M SORRY.
BUT WHY DO YOU LET THE DEVIL INTO MY BOY'S HEART?!
ARE OUR SINS SO SEVERE?
ARE WE NOT YOUR CHILDREN?!
DO WE NOT HONOR YOUR BLOOD?!

NO MOM. WE NEVER TALK ABOUT THAT STUFF.
BUT I REALLY DO LIKE HIM.
I'VE NEVER FELT. THIS WAY BEFORE.
YOU KNOW HOW YOU ASKED IF I WAS GAY? I USED TO THINK I MIGHT'VE BEEN.
BUT HE REALLY GETS ME, YOU KNOW?
I JUST WISH HE WOULD TEXT ME BACK.
OH, HONEY. MEN CAN BE REALLY SELFISH.
SOMETIMES US GIRLS NEED TO GIVE THEM A LITTLE NUDGE.

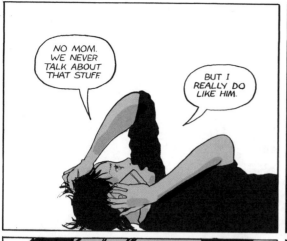

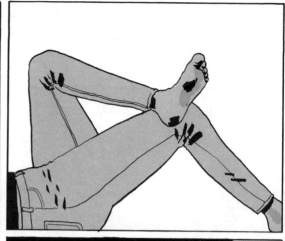

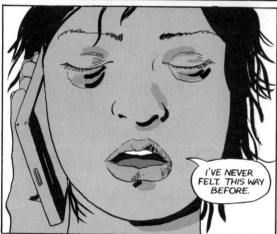

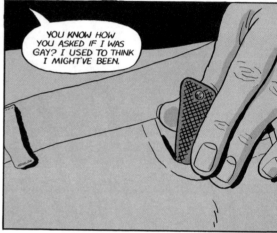

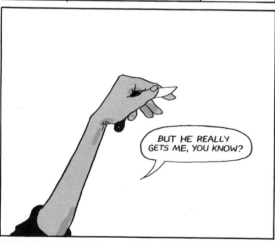

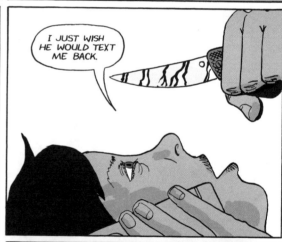

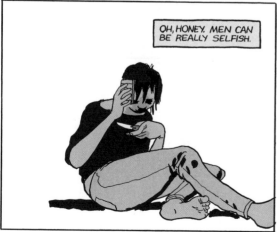

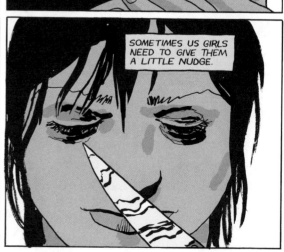

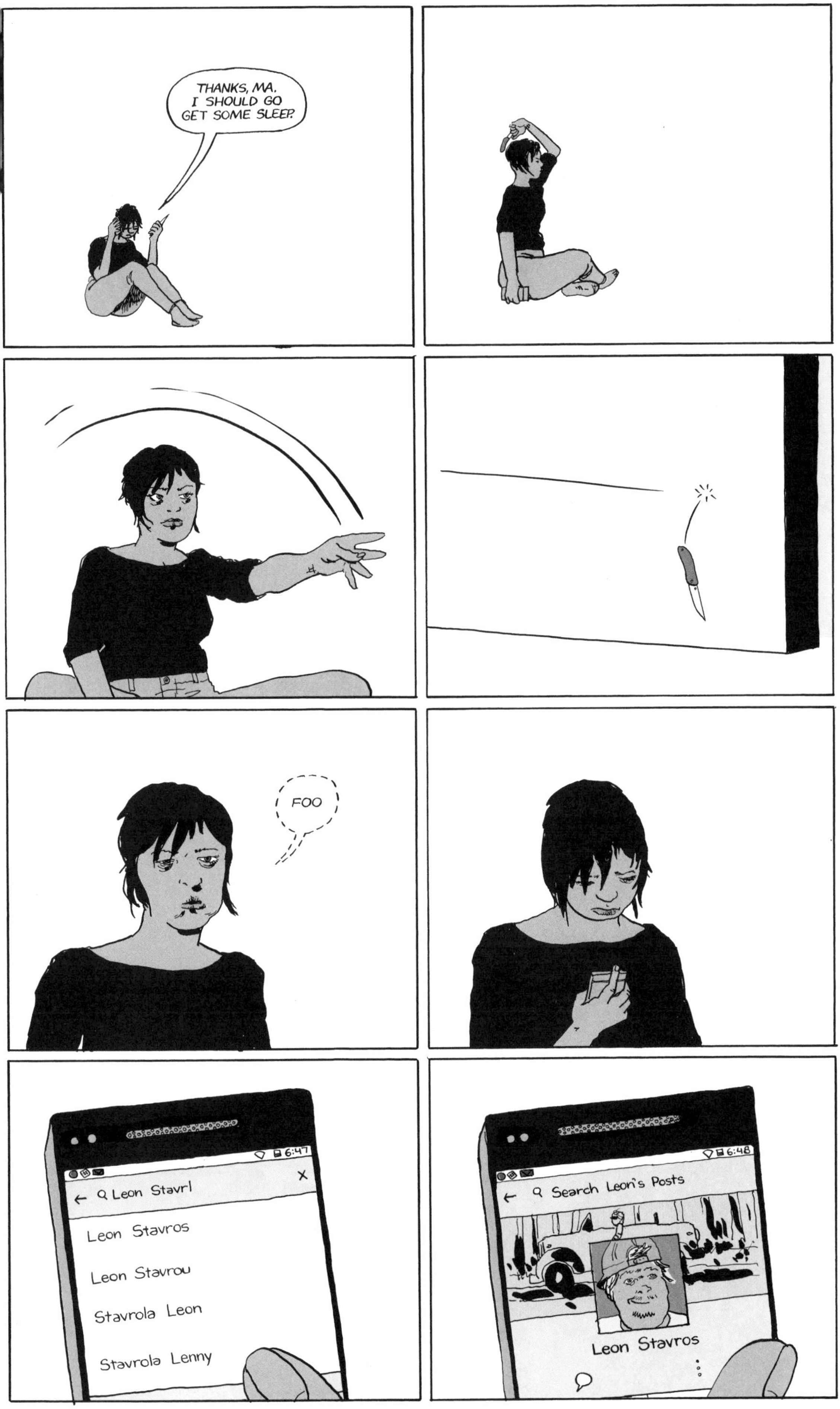
THANKS, MA. I SHOULD GO GET SOME SLEEP.
FOO
6:47
Leon Stavrl
Leon Stavros
Leon Stavrou
Stavrola Leon
Stavrola Lenny
6:48
Search Leon's Posts
Leon Stavros

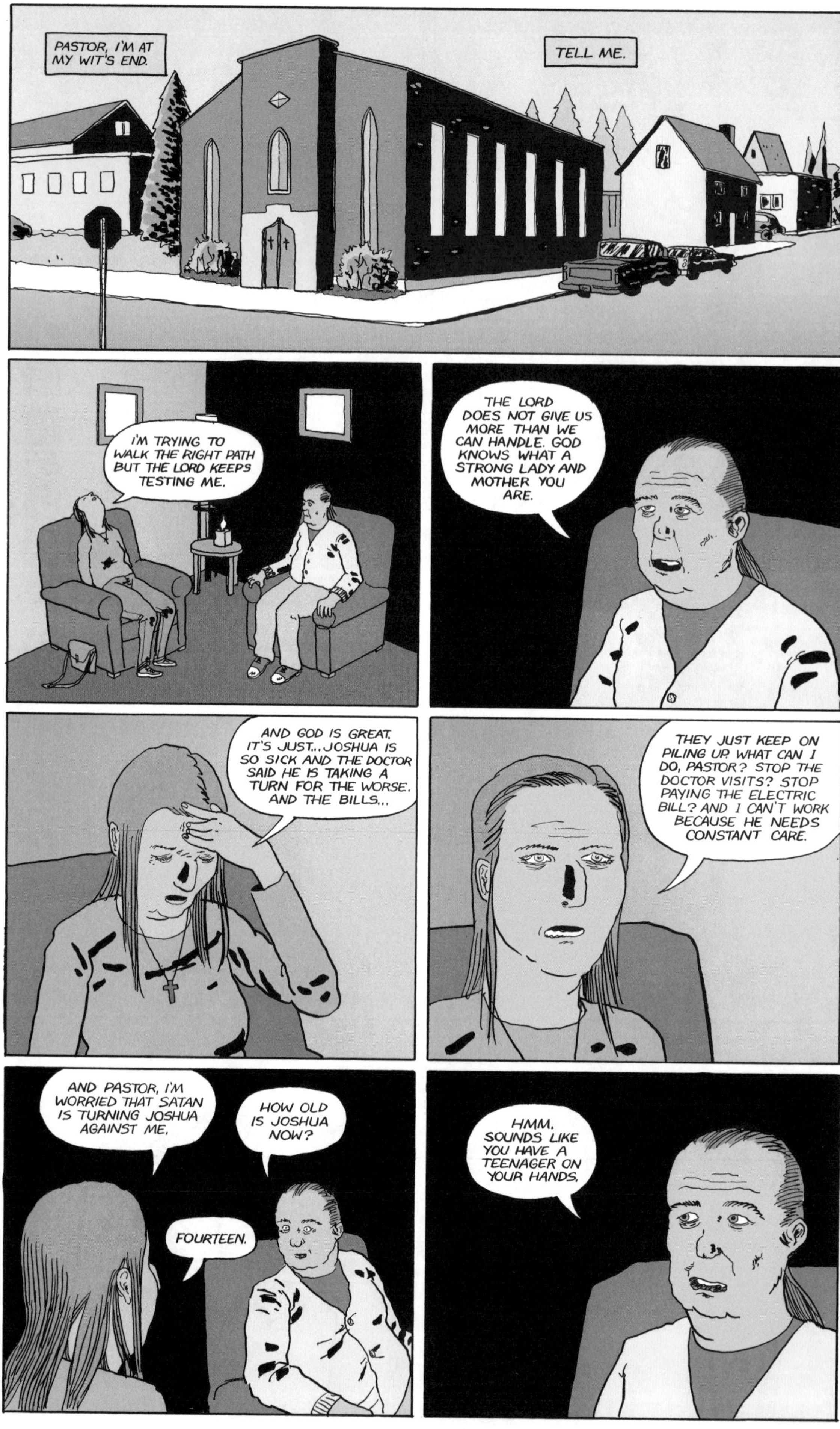
PASTOR, I'M AT MY WIT'S END.
TELL ME.
I'M TRYING TO WALK THE RIGHT PATH BUT THE LORD KEEPS TESTING ME.
THE LORD DOES NOT GIVE US MORE THAN WE CAN HANDLE. GOD KNOWS WHAT A STRONG LADY AND MOTHER YOU ARE.
AND GOD IS GREAT. IT'S JUST... JOSHUA IS SO SICK AND THE DOCTOR SAID HE IS TAKING A TURN FOR THE WORSE. AND THE BILLS...
THEY JUST KEEP ON PILING UP. WHAT CAN I DO, PASTOR? STOP THE DOCTOR VISITS? STOP PAYING THE ELECTRIC BILL? AND I CAN'T WORK BECAUSE HE NEEDS CONSTANT CARE.
AND PASTOR, I'M WORRIED THAT SATAN IS TURNING JOSHUA AGAINST ME.
HOW OLD IS JOSHUA NOW?
FOURTEEN.
HMM. SOUNDS LIKE YOU HAVE A TEENAGER ON YOUR HANDS.

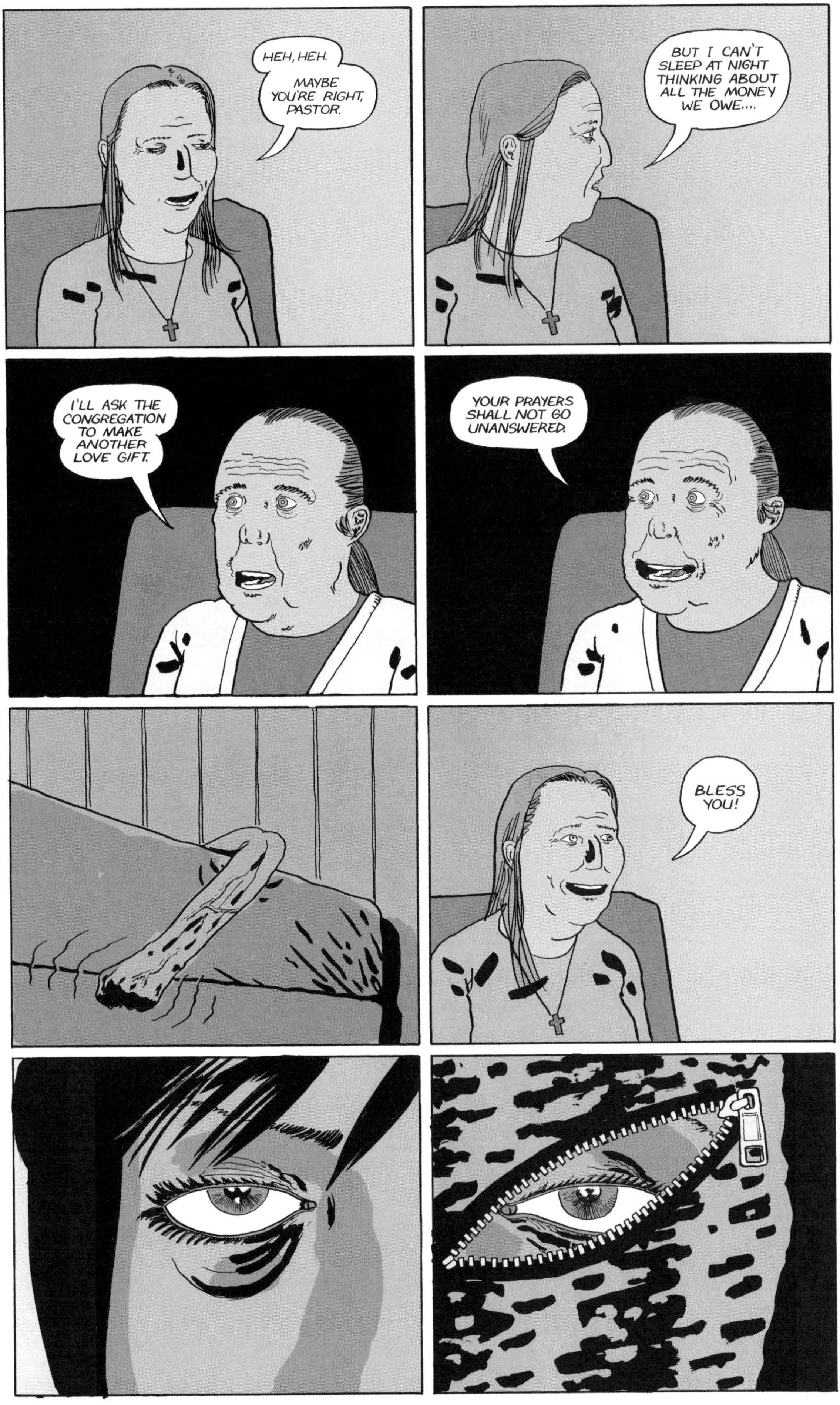
HEH, HEH.
MAYBE YOU'RE RIGHT, PASTOR.
BUT I CAN'T SLEEP AT NIGHT THINKING ABOUT ALL THE MONEY WE OWE....
I'LL ASK THE CONGREGATION TO MAKE ANOTHER LOVE GIFT.
YOUR PRAYERS SHALL NOT GO UNANSWERED.
BLESS YOU!

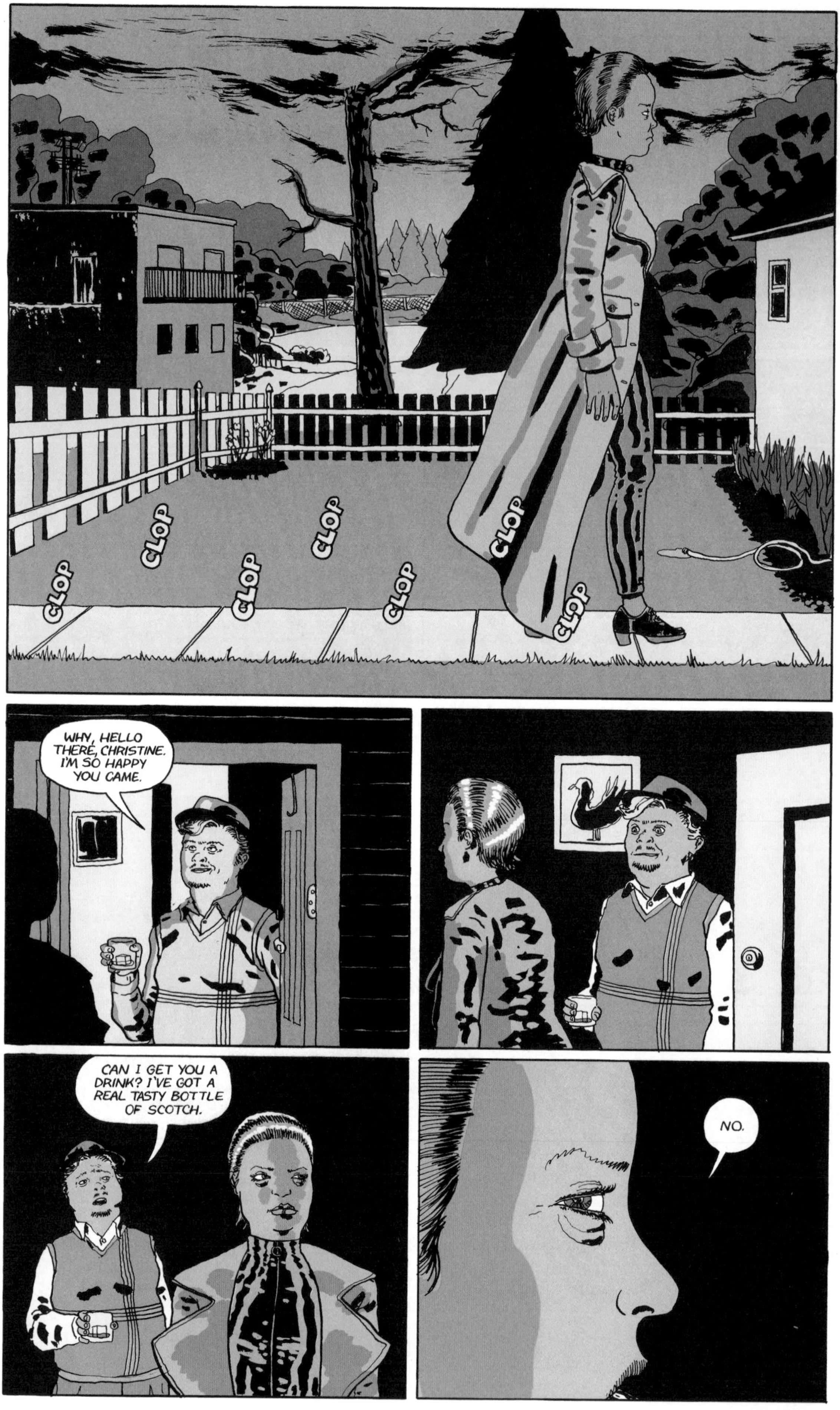
CLOP
CLOP
CLOP
CLOP
CLOP
CLOP
CLOP
WHY, HELLO THERE, CHRISTINE. I'M SO HAPPY YOU CAME.
CAN I GET YOU A DRINK? I'VE GOT A REAL TASTY BOTTLE OF SCOTCH.
NO.

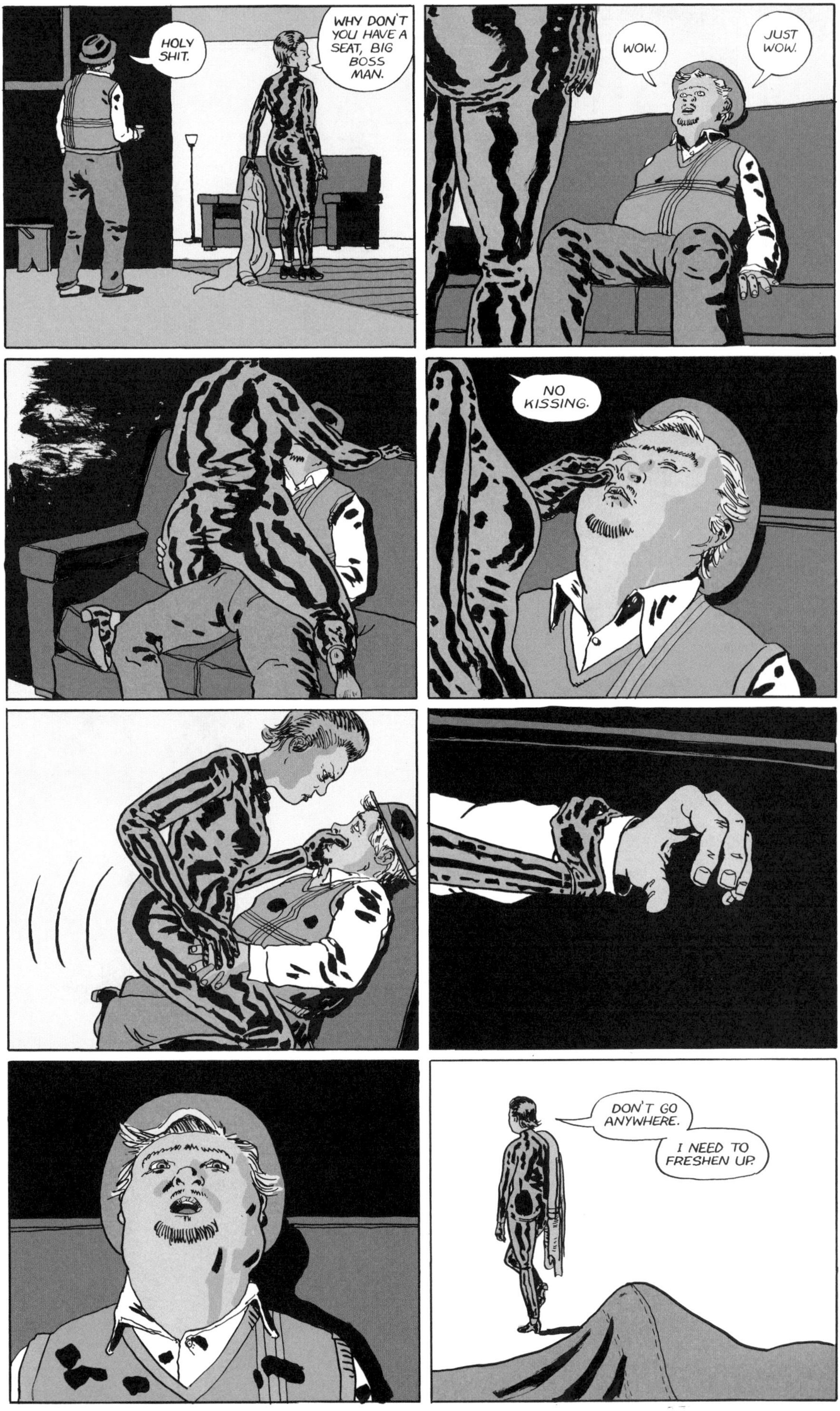
HOLY SHIT.
WHY DON'T YOU HAVE A SEAT, BIG BOSS MAN.
WOW.
JUST WOW.
NO KISSING.
DON'T GO ANYWHERE.
I NEED TO FRESHEN UP.

THERE YOU ARE.
CLOP
CLOP
CLOP
I NEEDED ANOTHER DRINKEY-POO.
SURE YOU DON'T WANT ONE?
HEY! A MASK. KINKY.
BOY. I REALLY NEEDED A BREAK FROM THE OLD BALL AND CHAIN. I LOVE DEB BUT SHE REALLY GETS UP MY ASS SOMETIMES.
Christine! I'm so sorry. My mom took my phone and laptop.
OH MY GOD!
WHAT ARE YOU DOING?!
I hate her I missed you.
I'M FIXING YOUR HAT.
I love you.

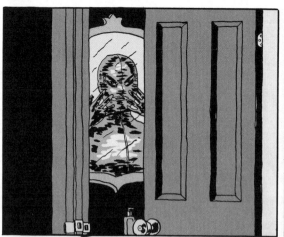

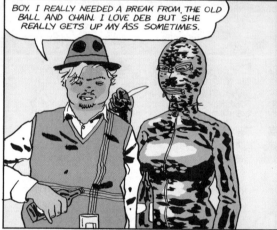

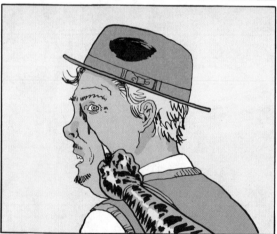

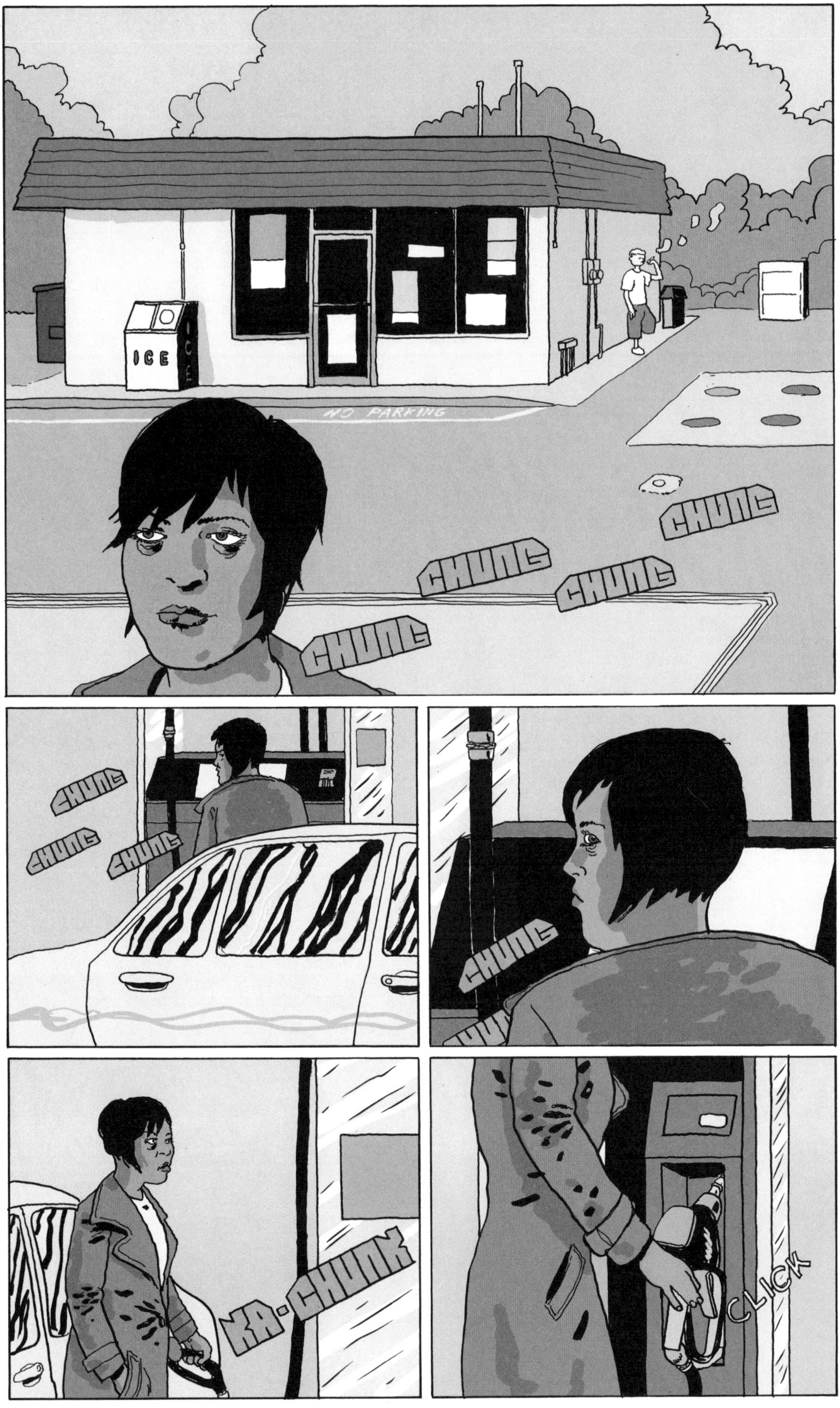
ICE
NO PARKING
CHUNG
CHUNG
CHUNG
CHUNG
CHUNG
CHUNG
CHUNG
CHUNG
KA-CHUNK
CLICK

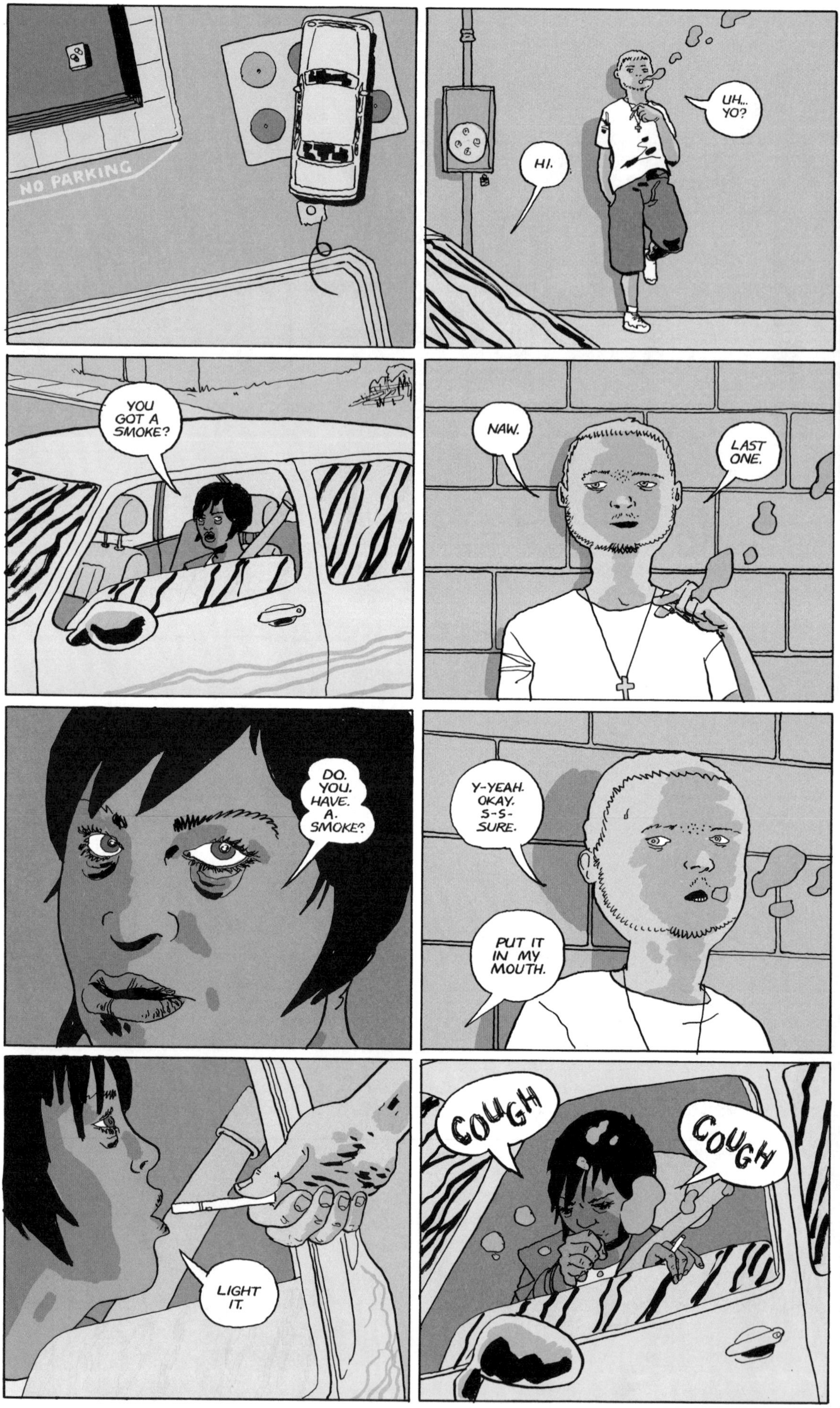
NO PARKING
UH... YO?
HI.
YOU GOT A SMOKE?
NAW.
LAST ONE.
DO. YOU. HAVE. A. SMOKE?
Y-YEAH. OKAY. S-S-SURE.
PUT IT IN MY MOUTH.
LIGHT IT.
COUGH
COUGH

WHAT THE FUCK, YO!?
COUGH
COUGH
THUMP
WHAT THE FUCK, WHAT?!
SLAM
WHAT?!
WHAT?!
'THE FUCK DO YOU THINK YOU ARE?
TAKE YOUR DICK OUT, EMINEM.
YOU'RE CRAZY, BITCH!
MY BOYS ARE GONNA FUCK YOU UP!
TAKE IT OUT NOW.
NOW TELL ME EVERY-ONE YOU'VE TERRORIZED WITH THAT THING.
ZIIIIIIIIIIP
PLEASE... STOP. PLEASE.
TELL ME.

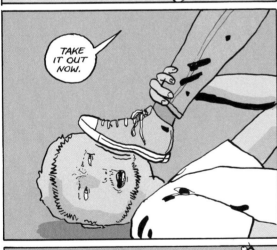

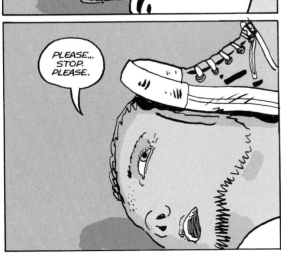

JUST TANYA.
WHO'S TANYA?
MY- MY SHORTY.
IS THAT ALL? ANYONE ELSE?
NO.
NO ONE ELSE.
DO YOU WANT TO FUCK ME?
YES?
SORRY.

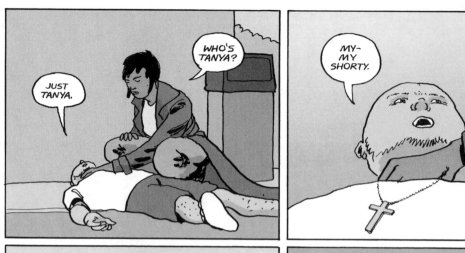

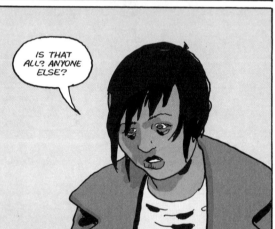

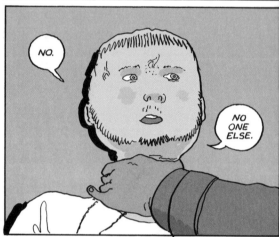

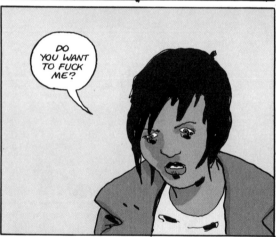

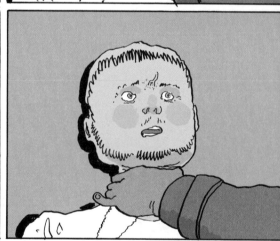

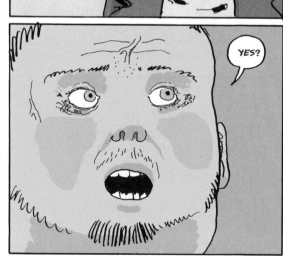

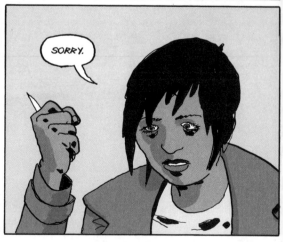

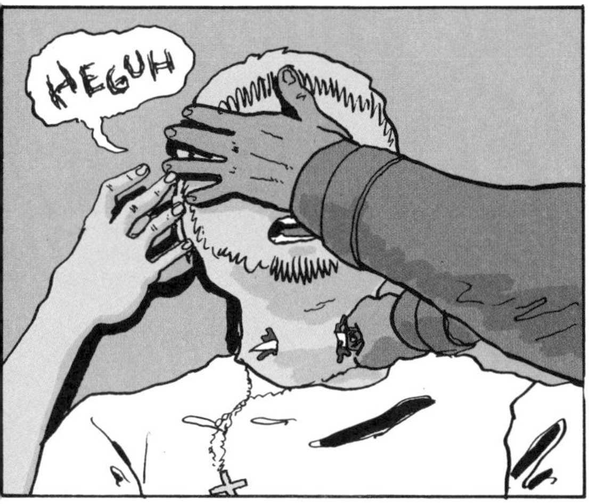
HEGUH

3

WANDERING BLADE

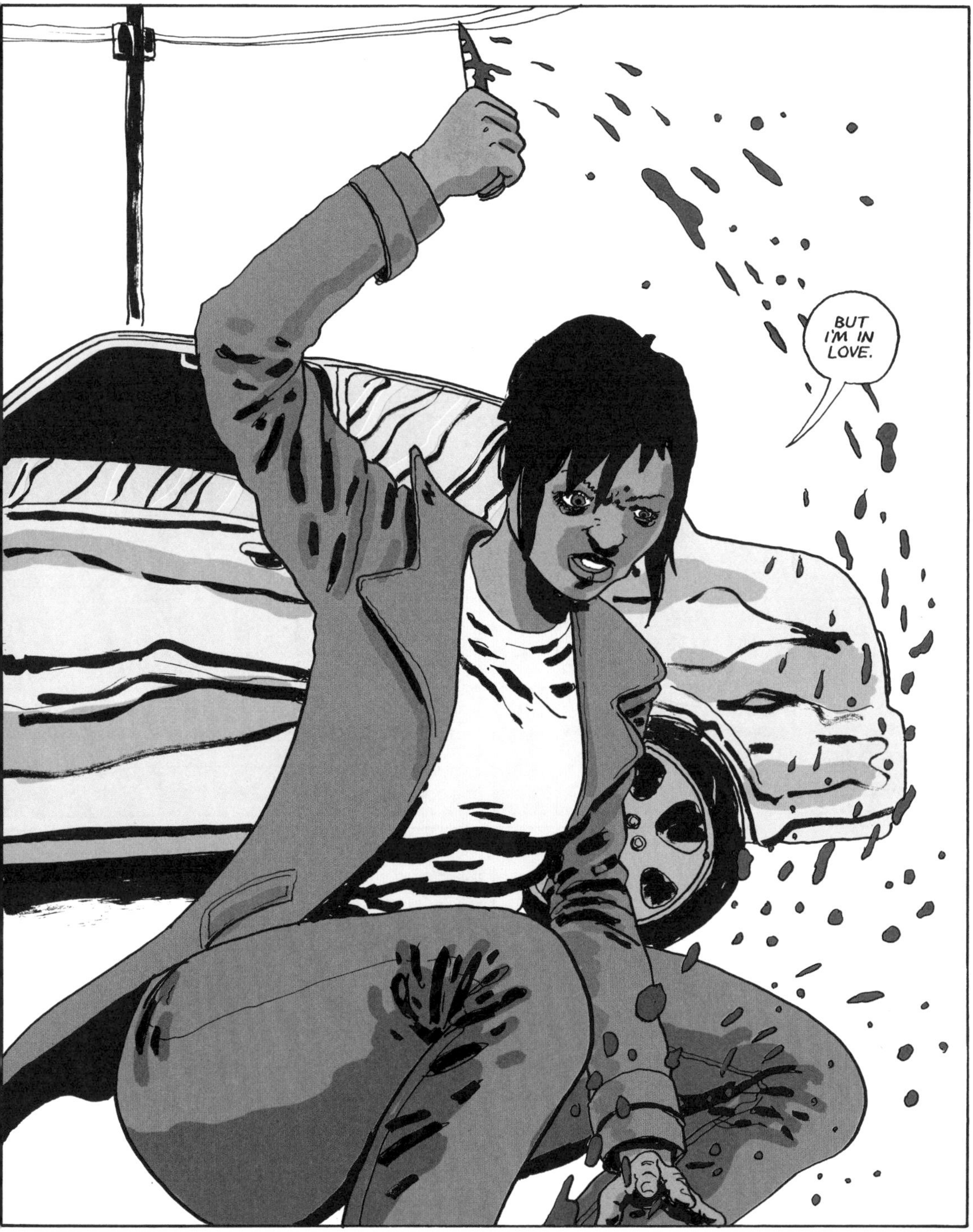
BUT I'M IN LOVE.

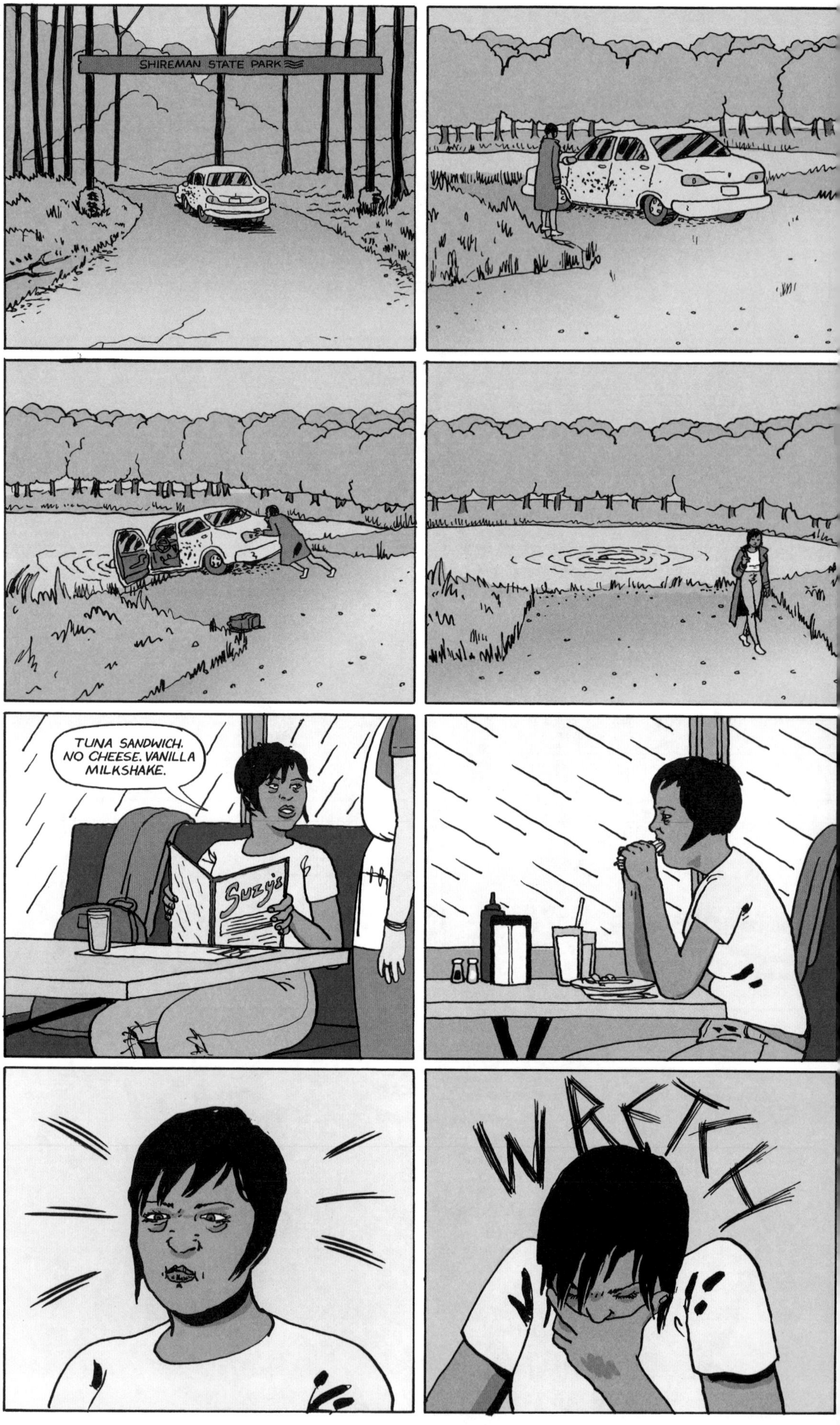
SHIREMAN STATE PARK
TUNA SANDWICH. NO CHEESE. VANILLA MILKSHAKE.
Suzy's

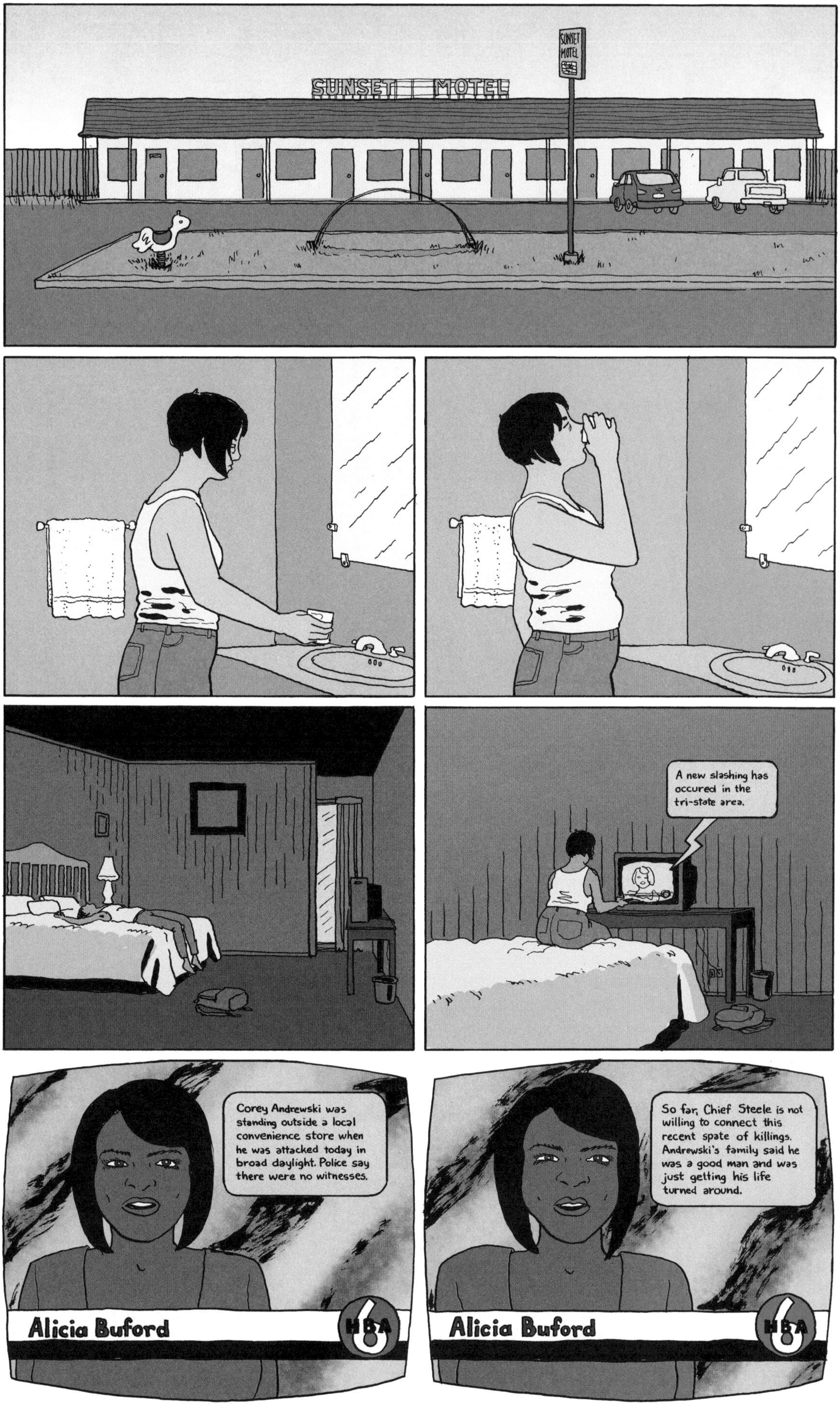
SUNSET MOTEL
SUNSET MOTEL
A new slashing has occured in the tri-state area.
Corey Andrewski was standing outside a local convenience store when he was attacked today in broad daylight. Police say there were no witnesses.
Alicia Buford
HBA 6
So far, Chief Steele is not willing to connect this recent spate of killings. Andrewski's family said he was a good man and was just getting his life turned around.
Alicia Buford
HBA 6

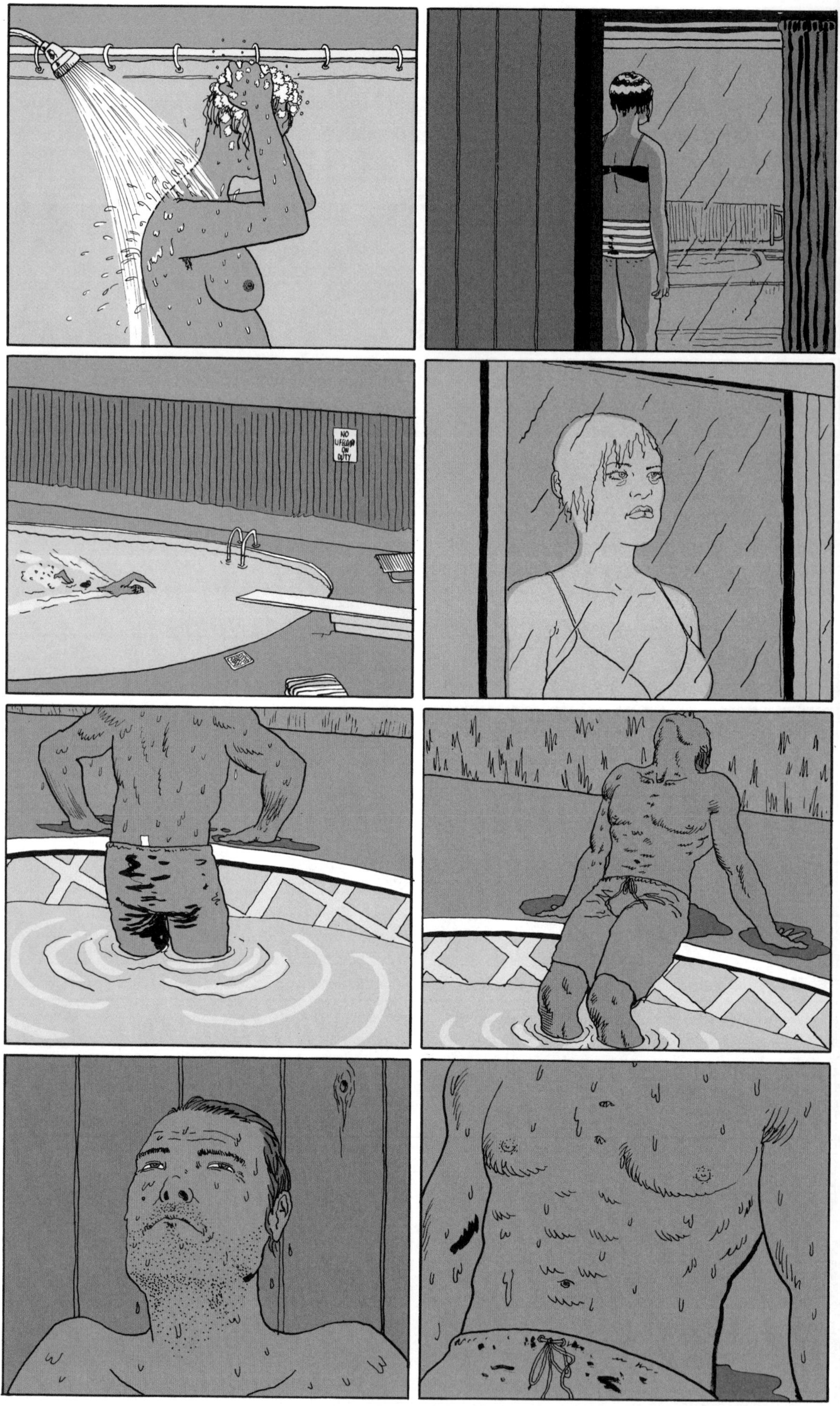
NO
ON
DUTY

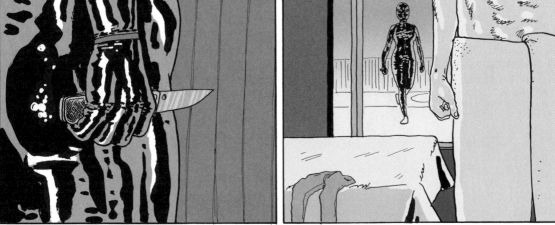

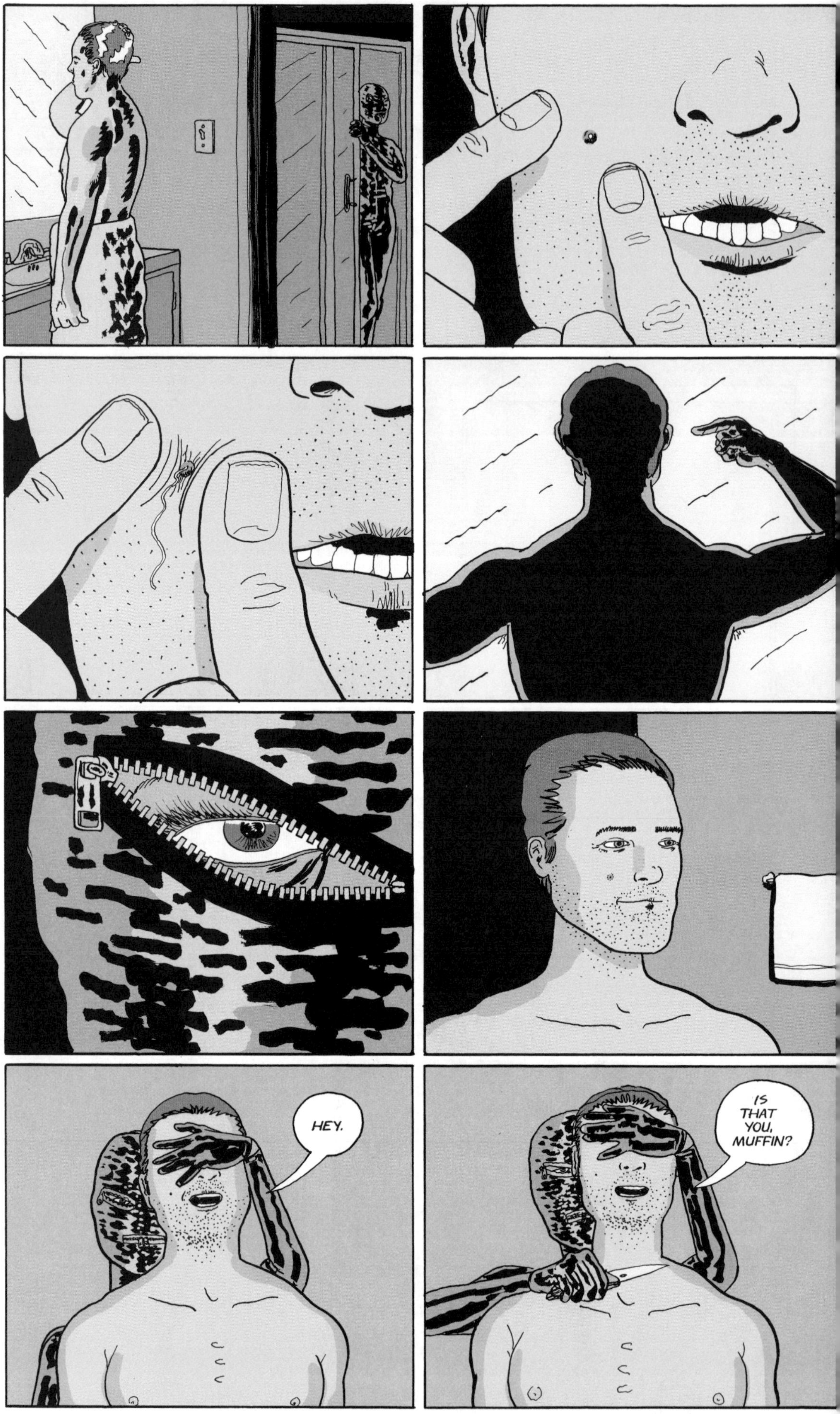
HEY.
IS THAT YOU, MUFFIN?

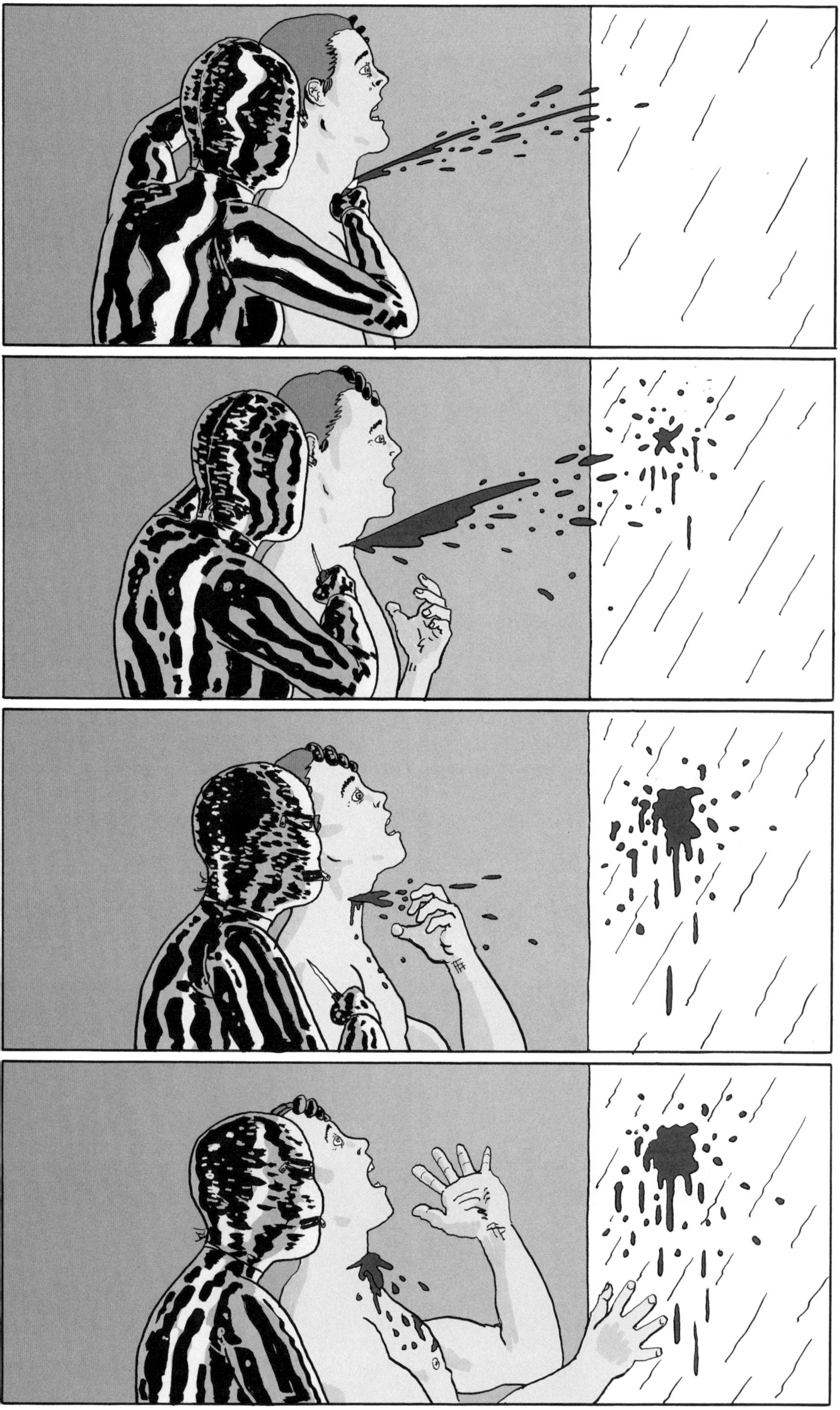

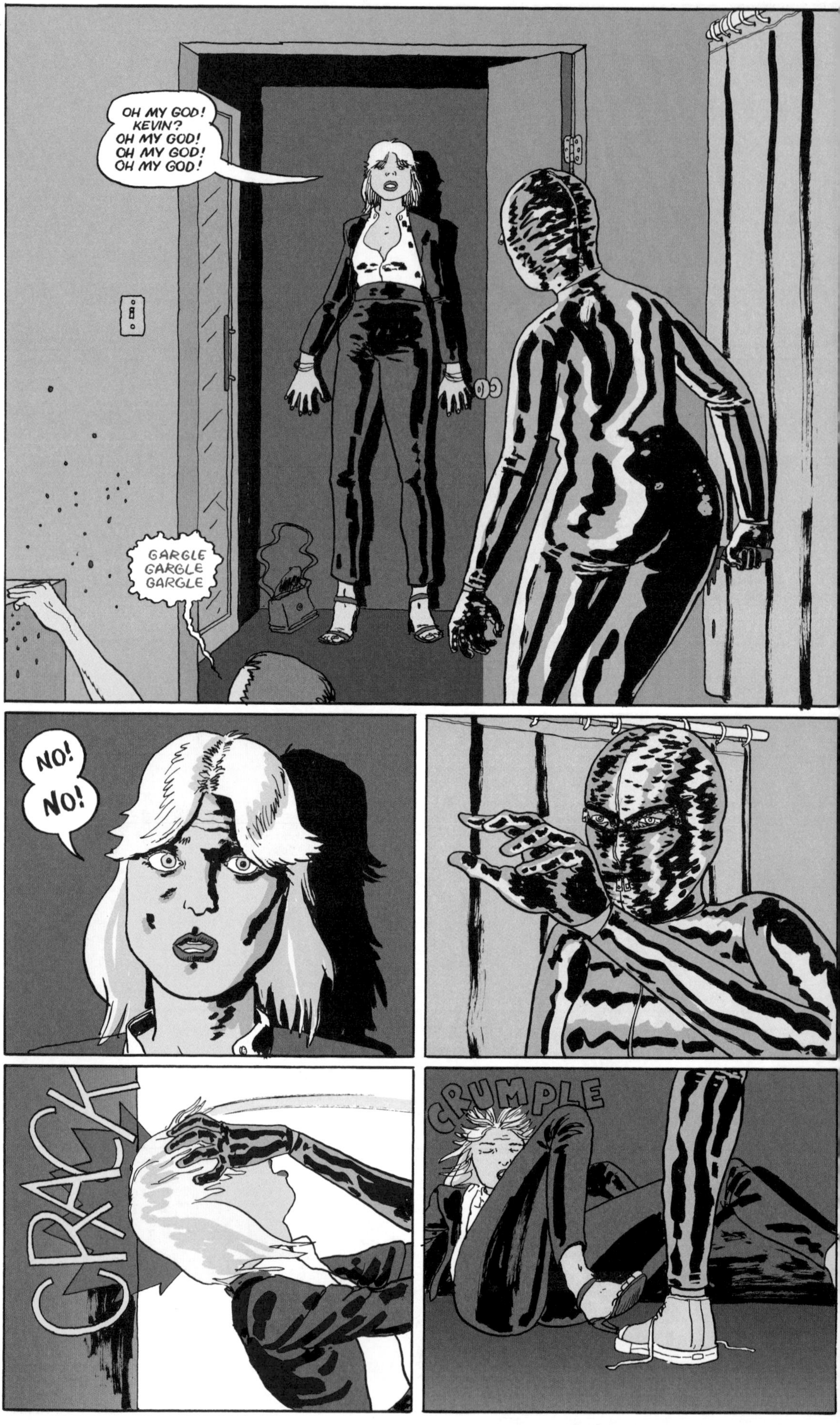
OH MY GOD!
KEVIN?
OH MY GOD!
OH MY GOD!
OH MY GOD!
GARGLE
GARGLE
GARGLE
NO!
NO!
CRACK
CRUMPLE

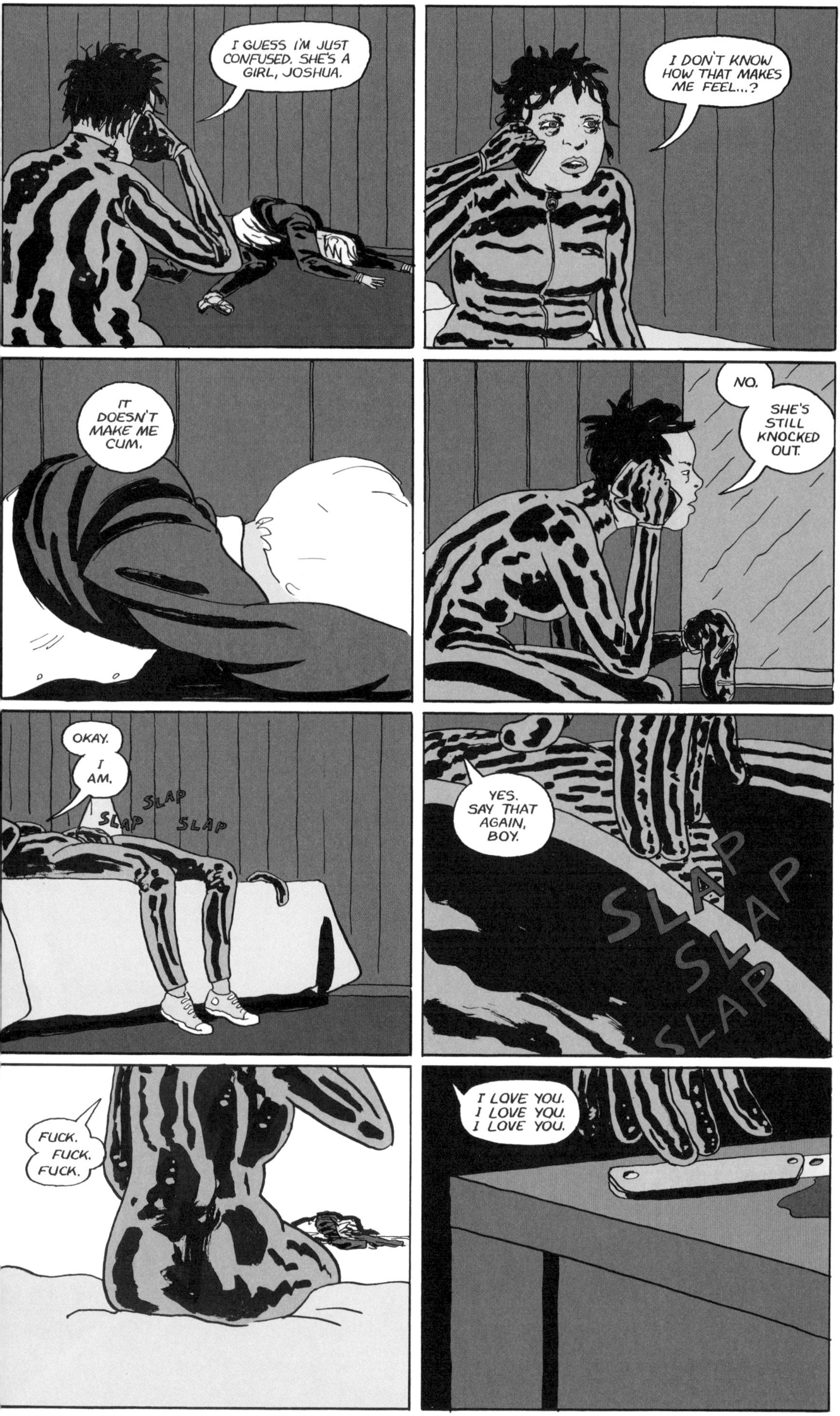
I GUESS I'M JUST CONFUSED. SHE'S A GIRL, JOSHUA.
I DON'T KNOW HOW THAT MAKES ME FEEL...?
IT DOESN'T MAKE ME CUM.
NO.
SHE'S STILL KNOCKED OUT.
OKAY.
I AM.
SLAP SLAP SLAP
YES. SAY THAT AGAIN, BOY.
SLAP SLAP SLAP
FUCK. FUCK. FUCK.
I LOVE YOU. I LOVE YOU. I LOVE YOU.

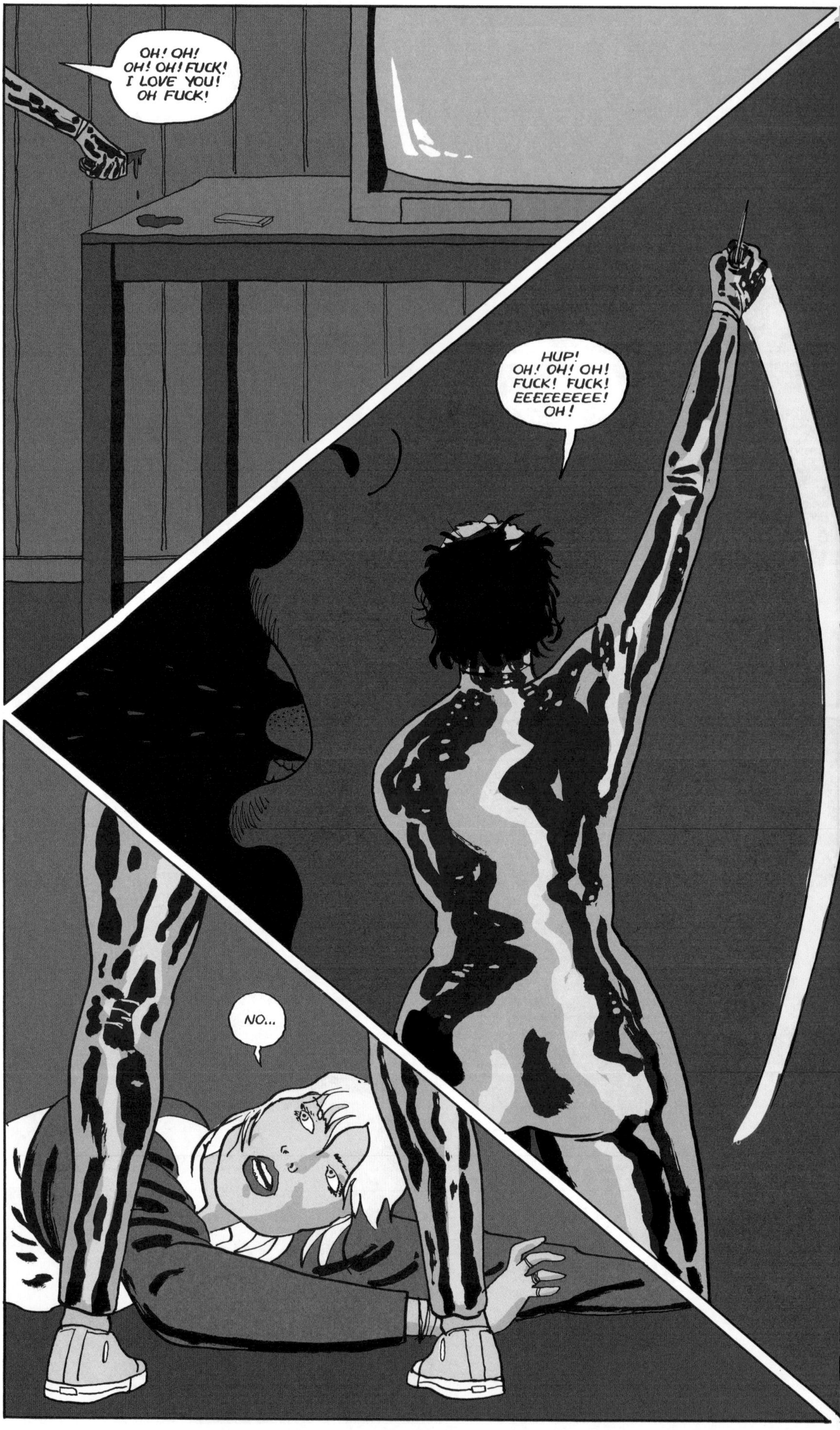
OH! OH!
OH! OH! FUCK!
I LOVE YOU!
OH FUCK!
HUP!
OH! OH! OH!
FUCK! FUCK!
EEEEEEEEE!
OH!
NO...

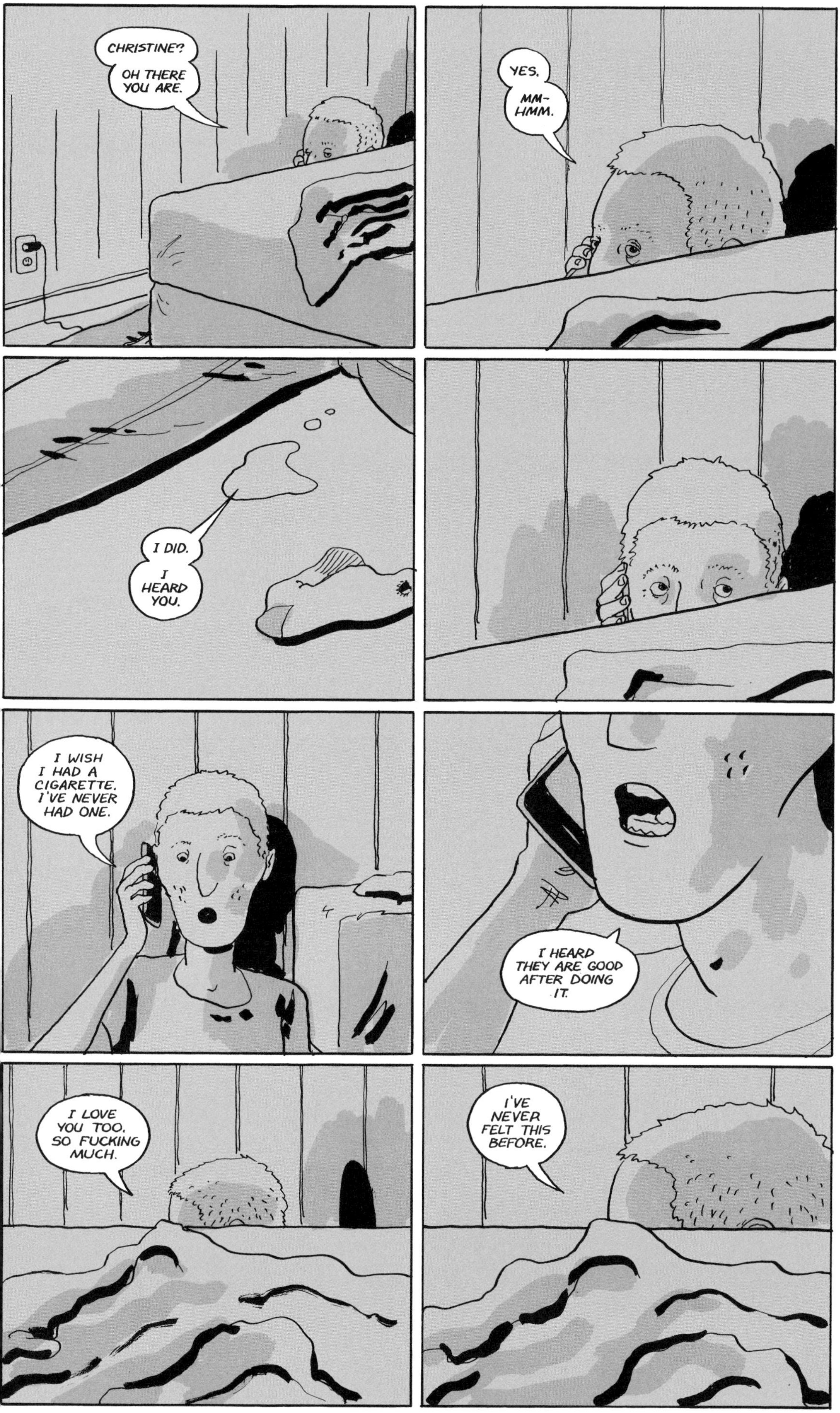
CHRISTINE?
OH THERE YOU ARE.
YES.
MM-HMM.
I DID.
I HEARD YOU.
I WISH I HAD A CIGARETTE. I'VE NEVER HAD ONE.
I HEARD THEY ARE GOOD AFTER DOING IT.
I LOVE YOU TOO, SO FUCKING MUCH.
I'VE NEVER FELT THIS BEFORE.

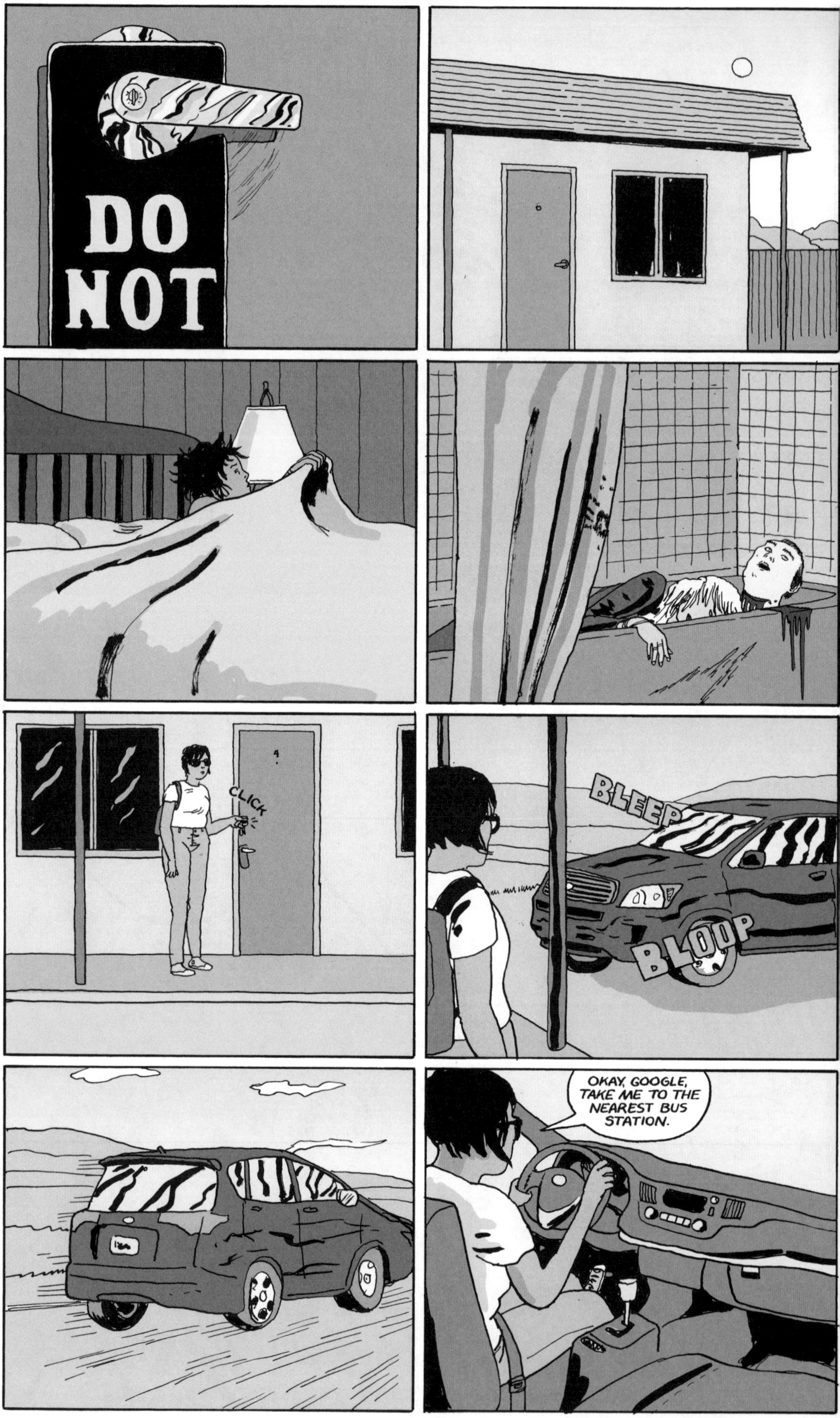
DO
NOT
CLICK
BLEEP
BLOOP
OKAY, GOOGLE, TAKE ME TO THE NEAREST BUS STATION.

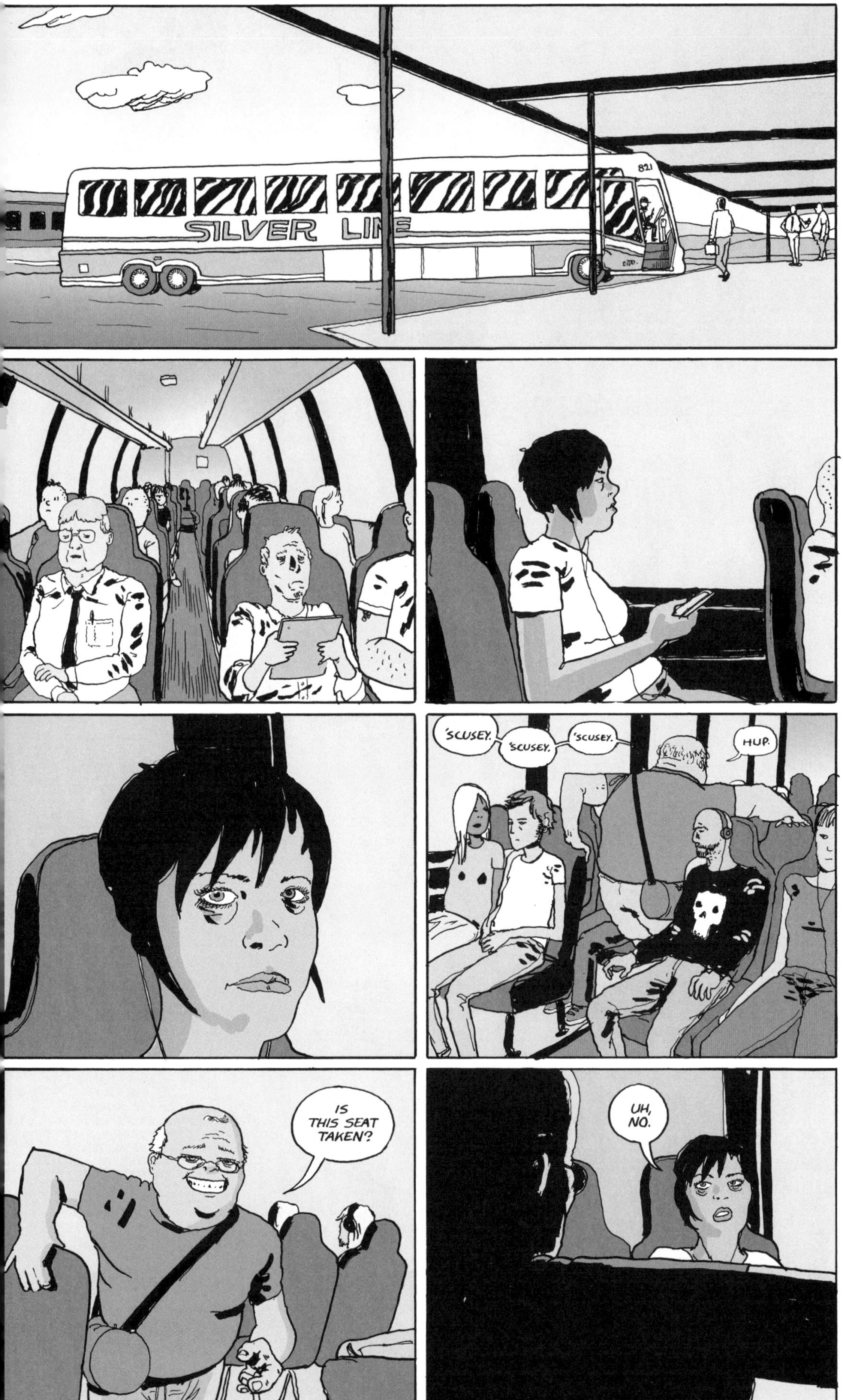
SILVER LINE
821
'SCUSEY.
'SCUSEY.
'SCUSEY.
HUP.
IS THIS SEAT TAKEN?
UH, NO.

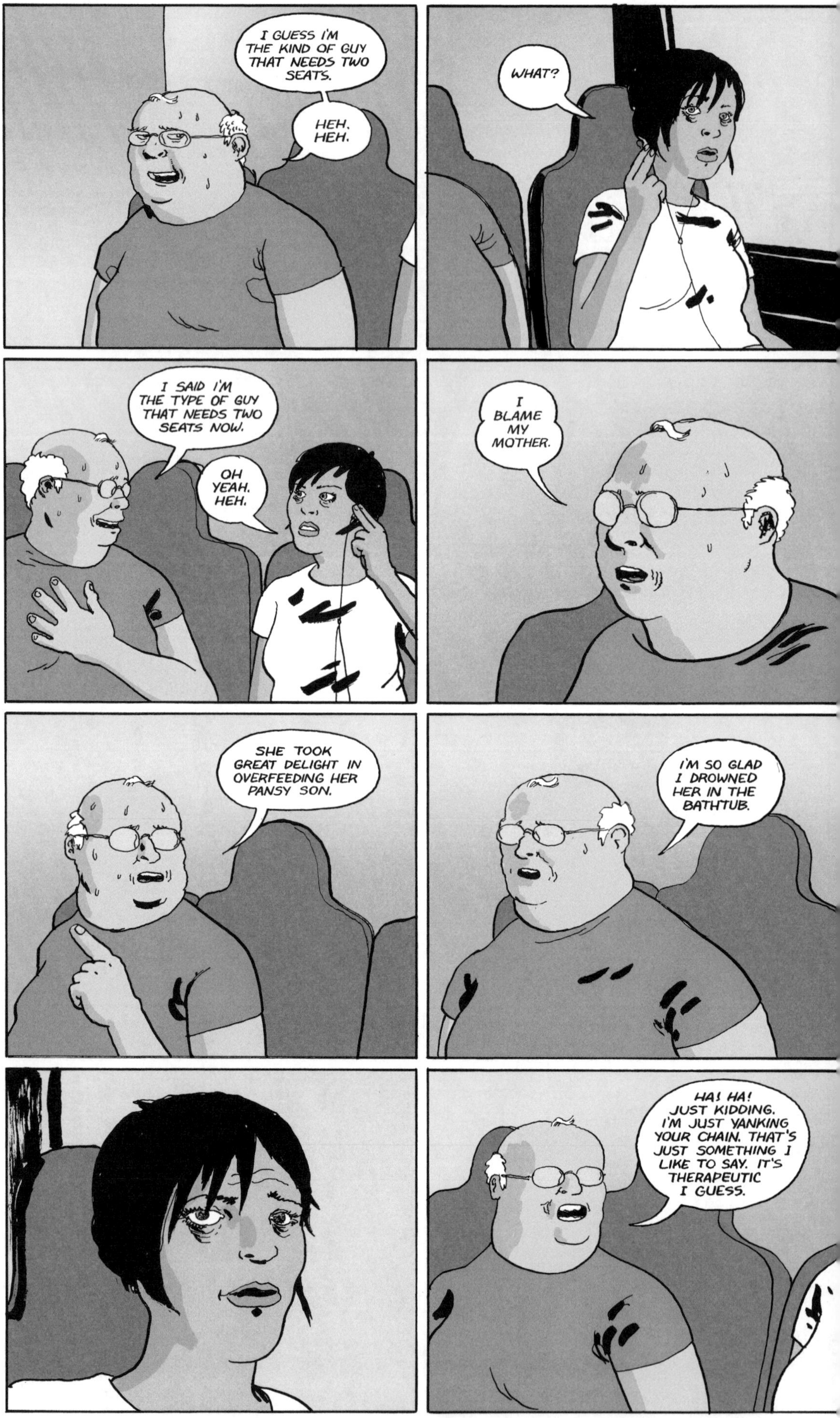
I GUESS I'M THE KIND OF GUY THAT NEEDS TWO SEATS.
HEH. HEH.
WHAT?
I SAID I'M THE TYPE OF GUY THAT NEEDS TWO SEATS NOW.
OH YEAH. HEH.
I BLAME MY MOTHER.
SHE TOOK GREAT DELIGHT IN OVERFEEDING HER PANSY SON.
I'M SO GLAD I DROWNED HER IN THE BATHTUB.
HA! HA! JUST KIDDING. I'M JUST YANKING YOUR CHAIN. THAT'S JUST SOMETHING I LIKE TO SAY. IT'S THERAPEUTIC I GUESS.

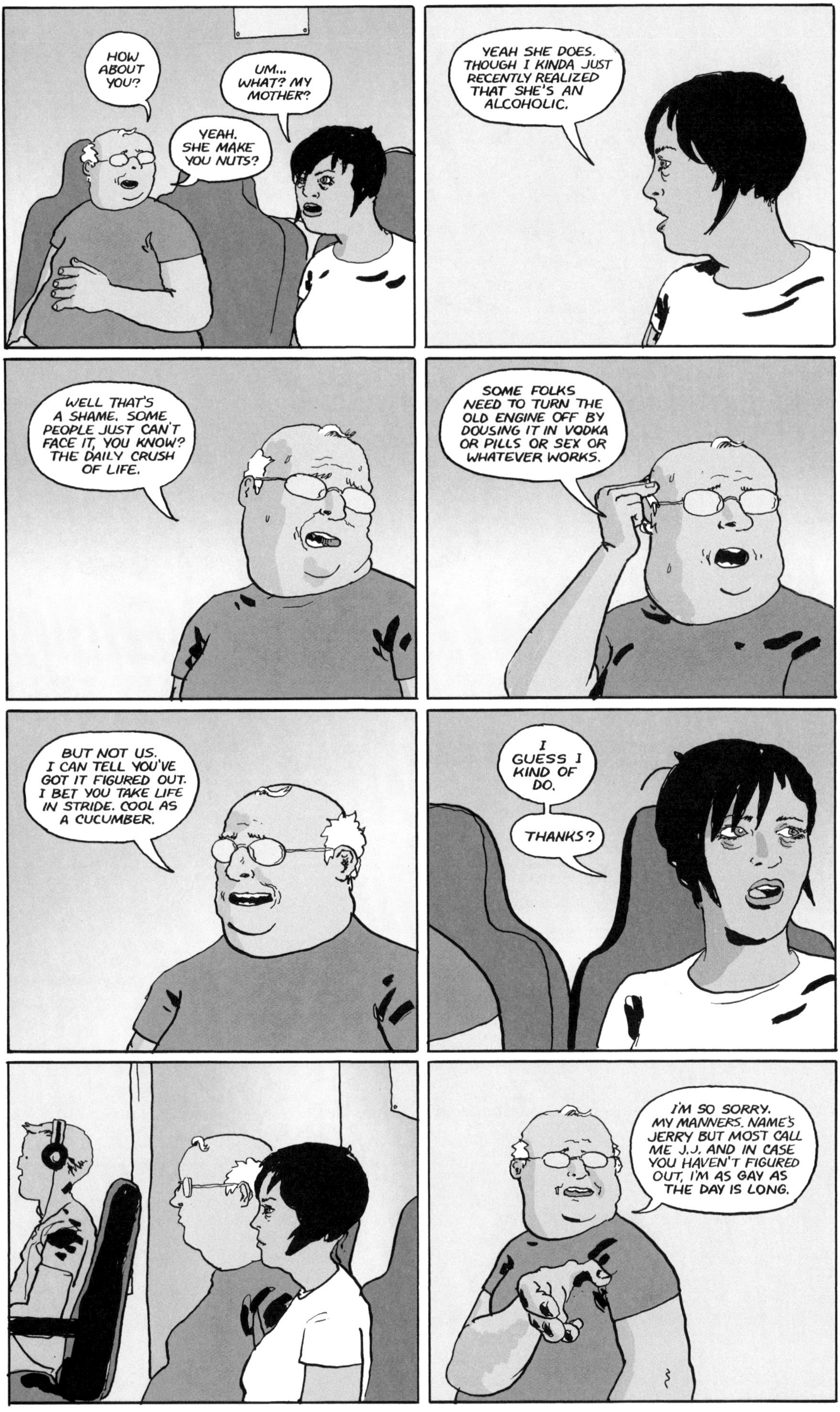
HOW ABOUT YOU?
UM... WHAT? MY MOTHER?
YEAH. SHE MAKE YOU NUTS?
YEAH SHE DOES. THOUGH I KINDA JUST RECENTLY REALIZED THAT SHE'S AN ALCOHOLIC.
WELL THAT'S A SHAME. SOME PEOPLE JUST CAN'T FACE IT, YOU KNOW? THE DAILY CRUSH OF LIFE.
SOME FOLKS NEED TO TURN THE OLD ENGINE OFF BY DOUSING IT IN VODKA OR PILLS OR SEX OR WHATEVER WORKS.
BUT NOT US. I CAN TELL YOU'VE GOT IT FIGURED OUT. I BET YOU TAKE LIFE IN STRIDE. COOL AS A CUCUMBER.
I GUESS I KIND OF DO.
THANKS?
I'M SO SORRY. MY MANNERS. NAME'S JERRY BUT MOST CALL ME J.J. AND IN CASE YOU HAVEN'T FIGURED OUT, I'M AS GAY AS THE DAY IS LONG.

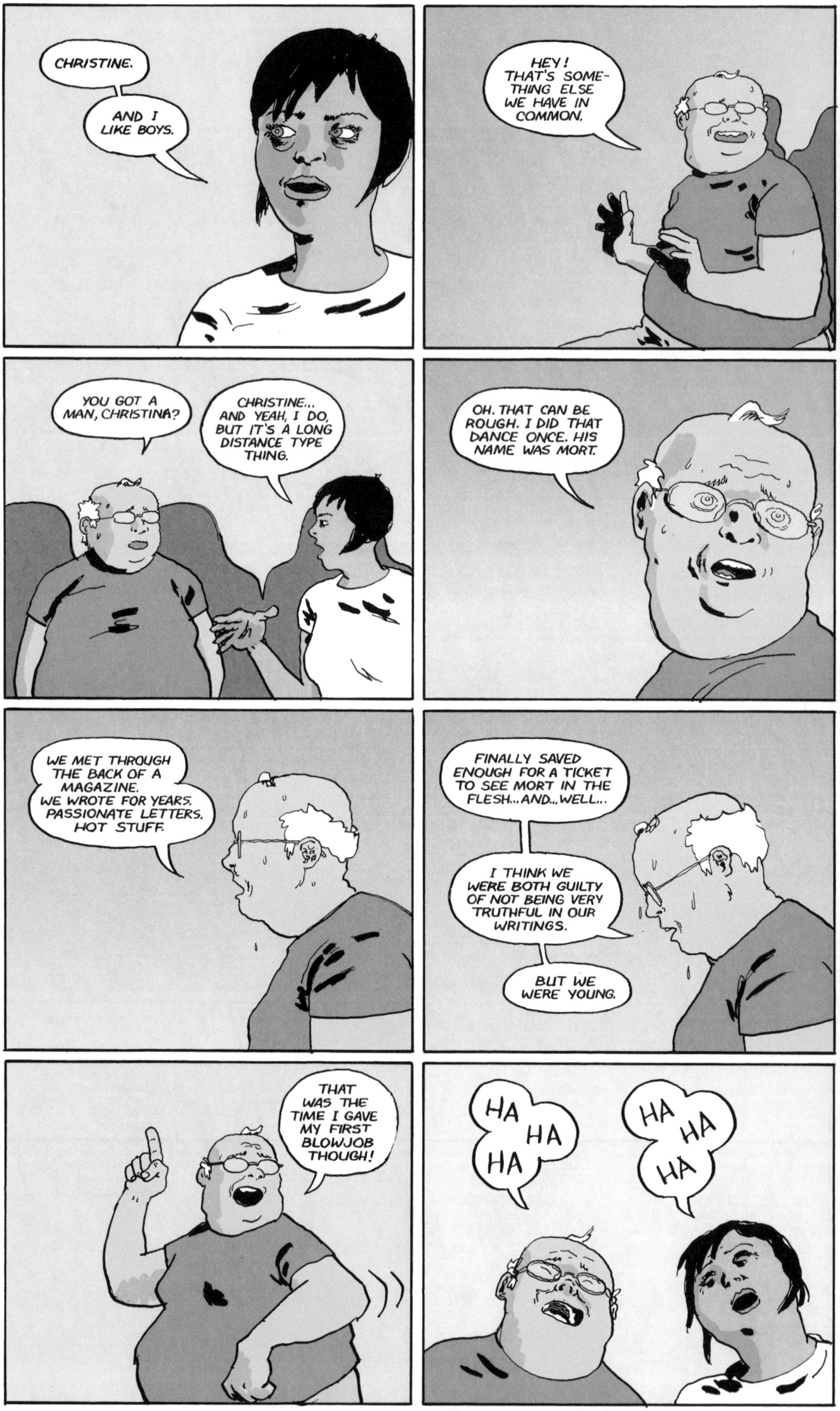
CHRISTINE.
AND I LIKE BOYS.
HEY! THAT'S SOME-THING ELSE WE HAVE IN COMMON.
YOU GOT A MAN, CHRISTINA?
CHRISTINE... AND YEAH, I DO, BUT IT'S A LONG DISTANCE TYPE THING.
OH. THAT CAN BE ROUGH. I DID THAT DANCE ONCE. HIS NAME WAS MORT.
WE MET THROUGH THE BACK OF A MAGAZINE. WE WROTE FOR YEARS. PASSIONATE LETTERS. HOT STUFF.
FINALLY SAVED ENOUGH FOR A TICKET TO SEE MORT IN THE FLESH... AND... WELL...
I THINK WE WERE BOTH GUILTY OF NOT BEING VERY TRUTHFUL IN OUR WRITINGS.
BUT WE WERE YOUNG.
THAT WAS THE TIME I GAVE MY FIRST BLOWJOB THOUGH!
HA HA HA
HA HA HA

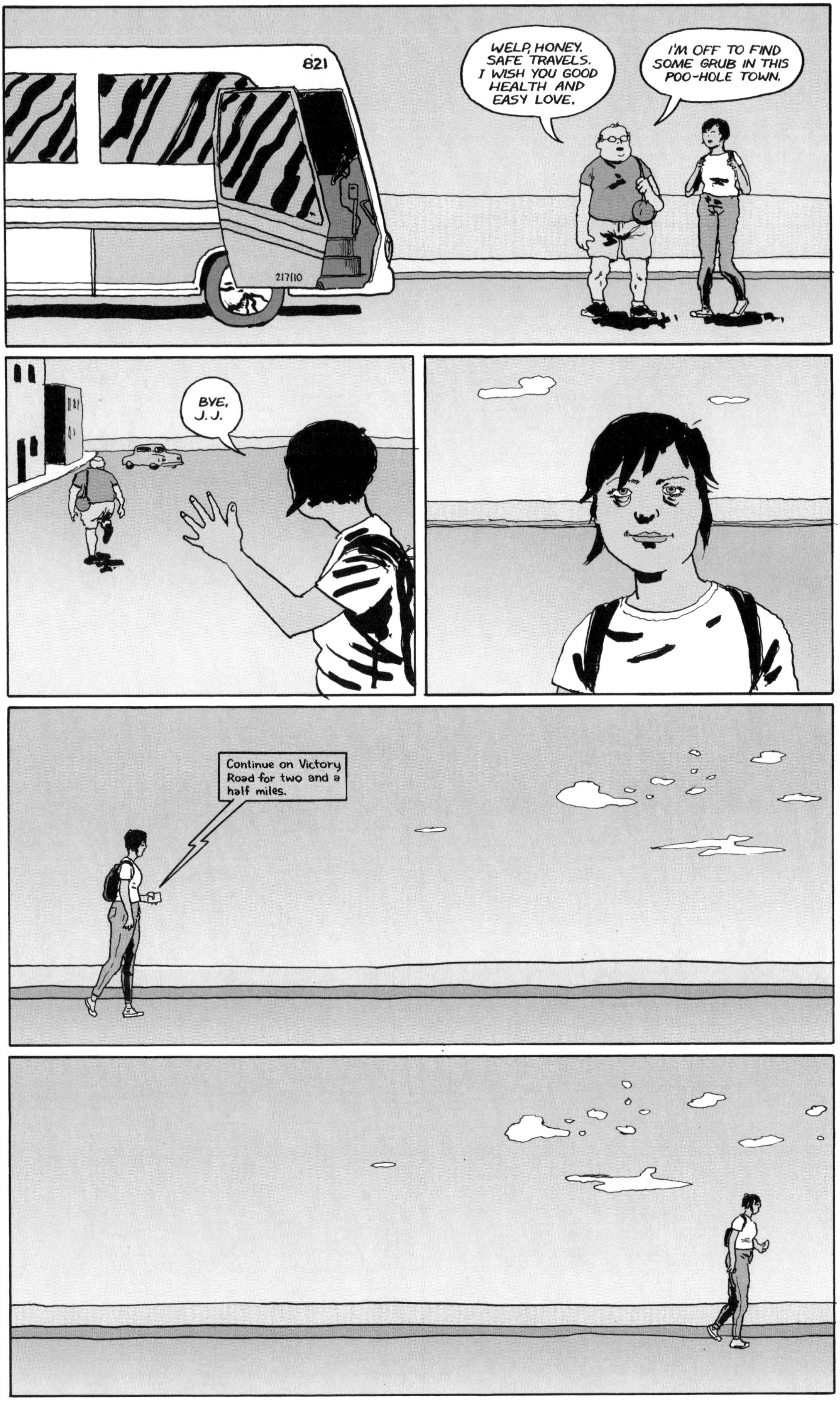
821
217110
WELP, HONEY. SAFE TRAVELS. I WISH YOU GOOD HEALTH AND EASY LOVE.
I'M OFF TO FIND SOME GRUB IN THIS POO-HOLE TOWN.
BYE, J. J.
Continue on Victory Road for two and a half miles.

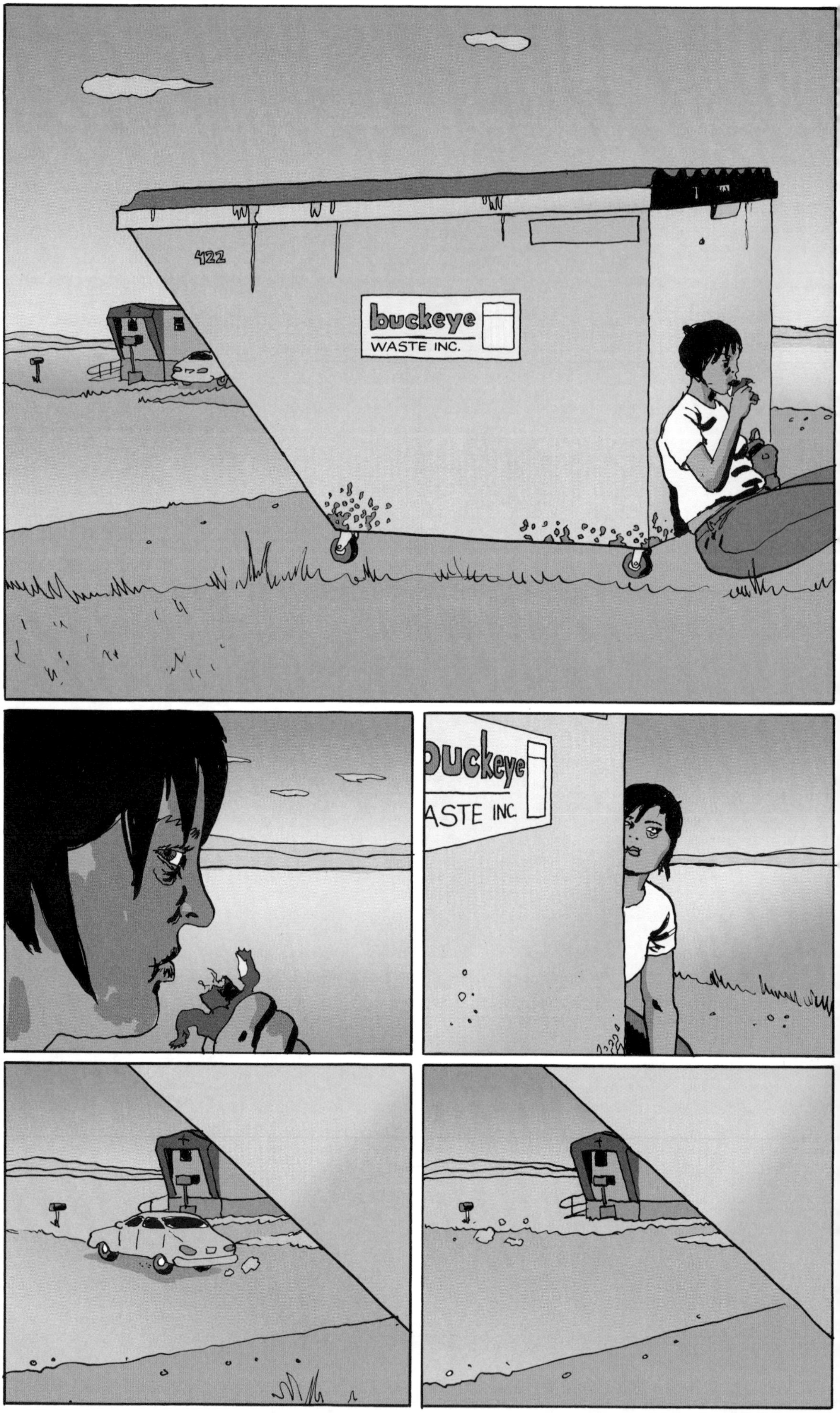
422
buckeye
WASTE INC.
buckeye
ASTE INC.

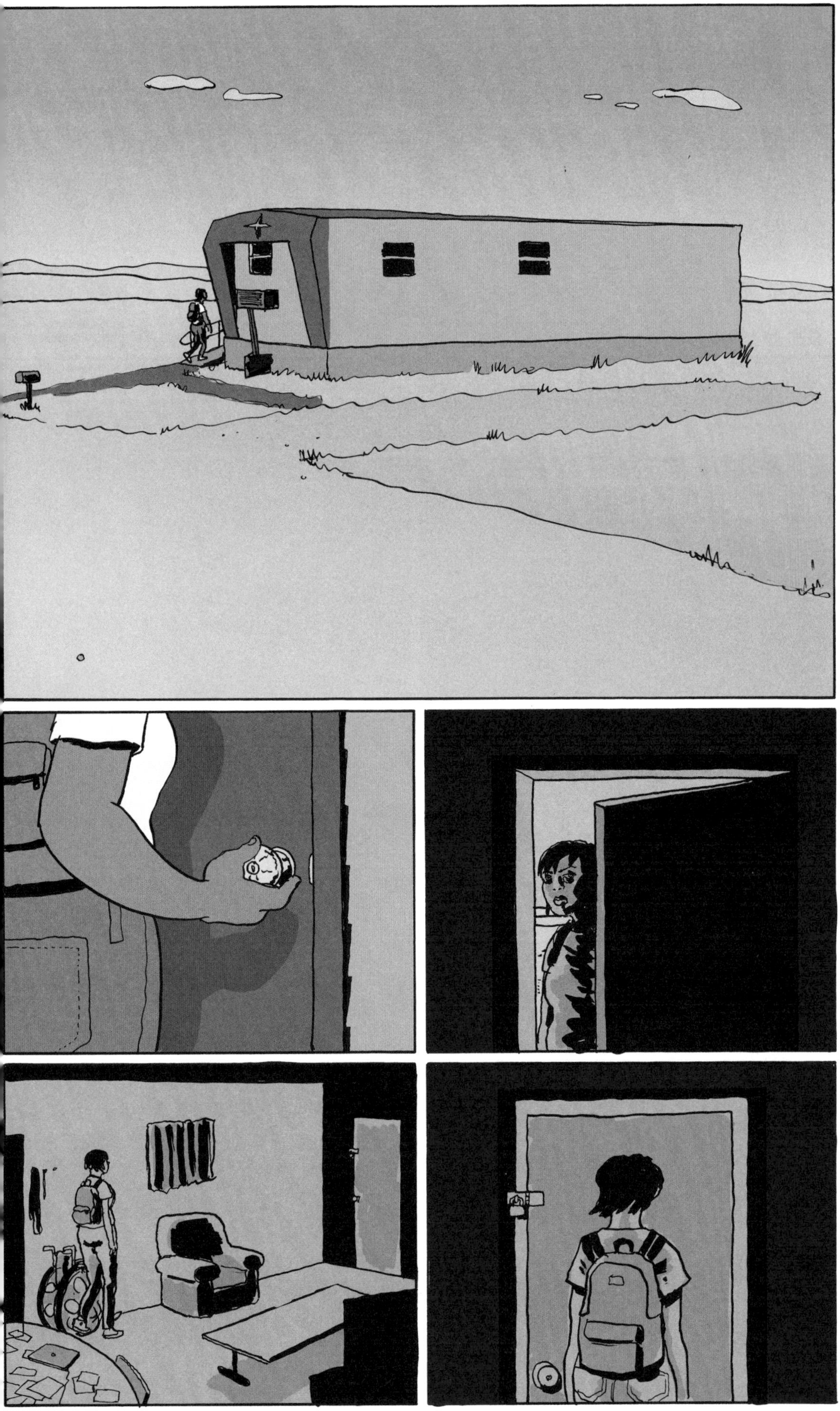

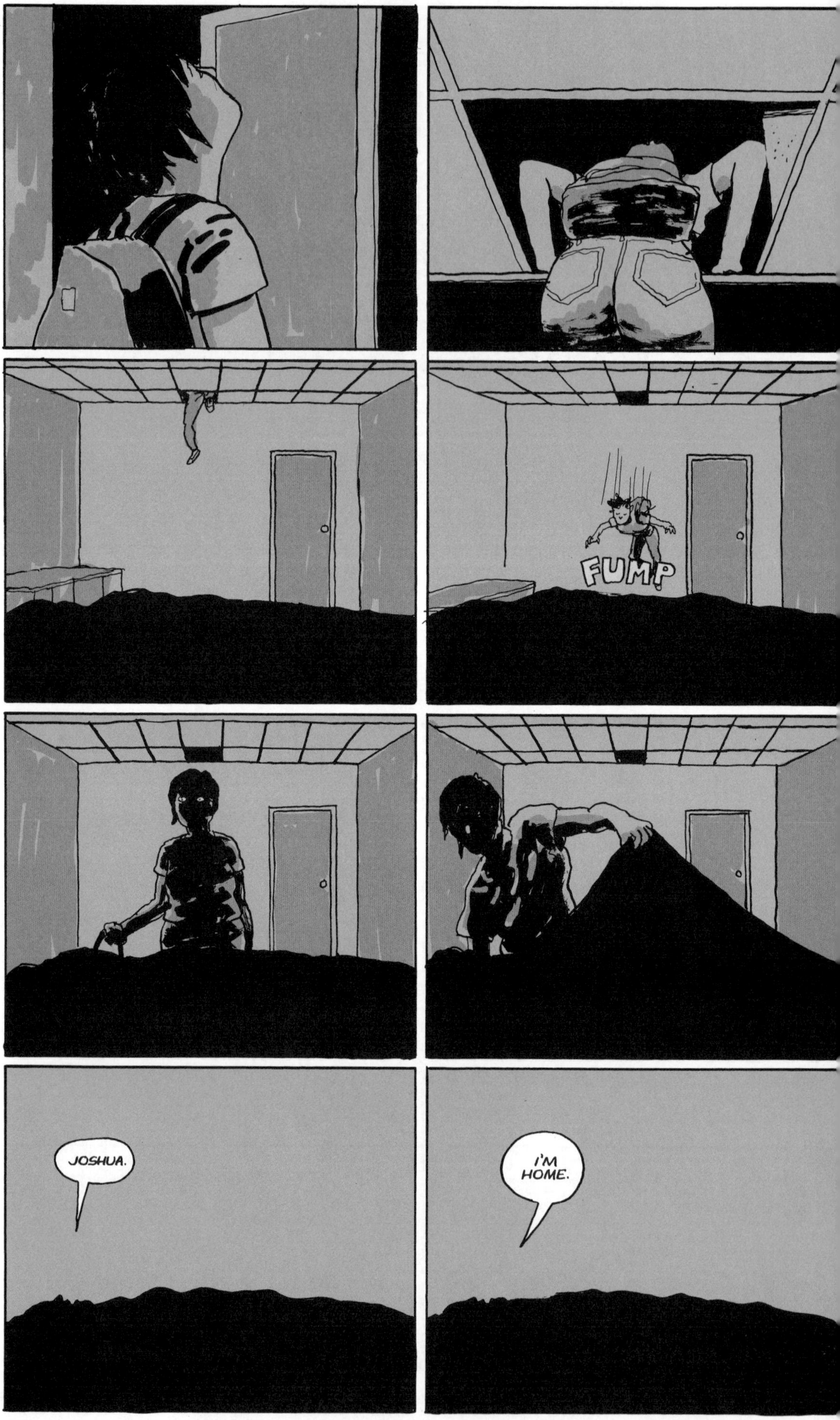
FUMP
JOSHUA.
I'M HOME.

YOU SHOULD NOT HAVE COME HERE.
I MEAN, I'M GLAD THAT YOU DID, GIRL.
BUT I WASN'T QUITE READY FOR YOU.

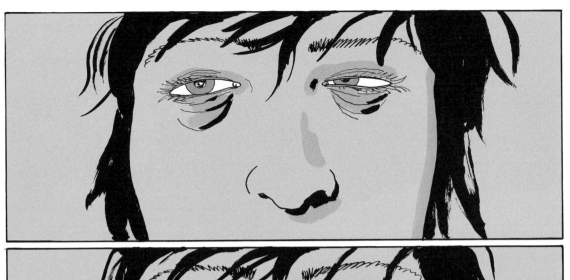

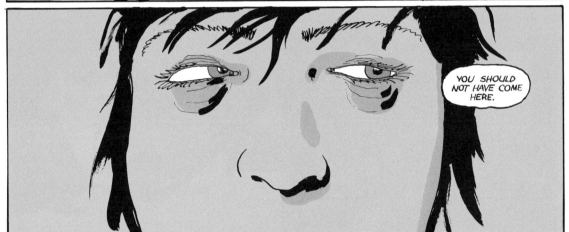

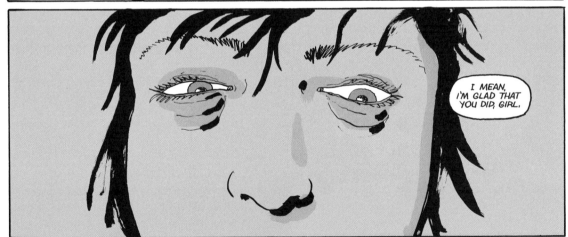

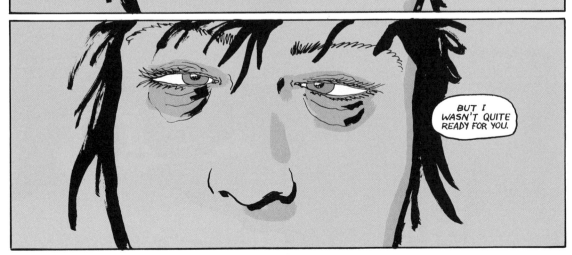

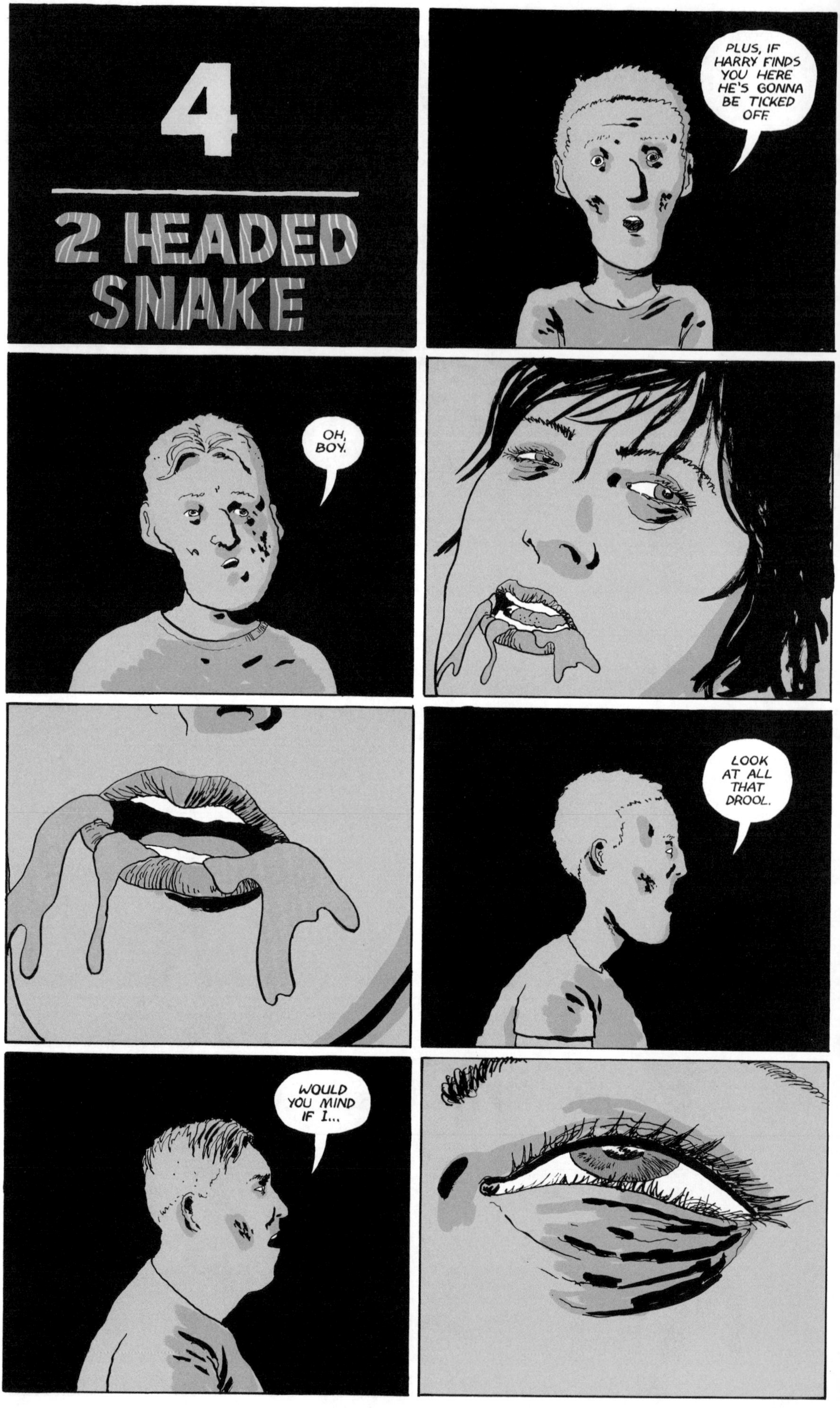
4
2 HEADED SNAKE
PLUS, IF HARRY FINDS YOU HERE HE'S GONNA BE TICKED OFF.
OH, BOY.
LOOK AT ALL THAT DROOL.
WOULD YOU MIND IF I...

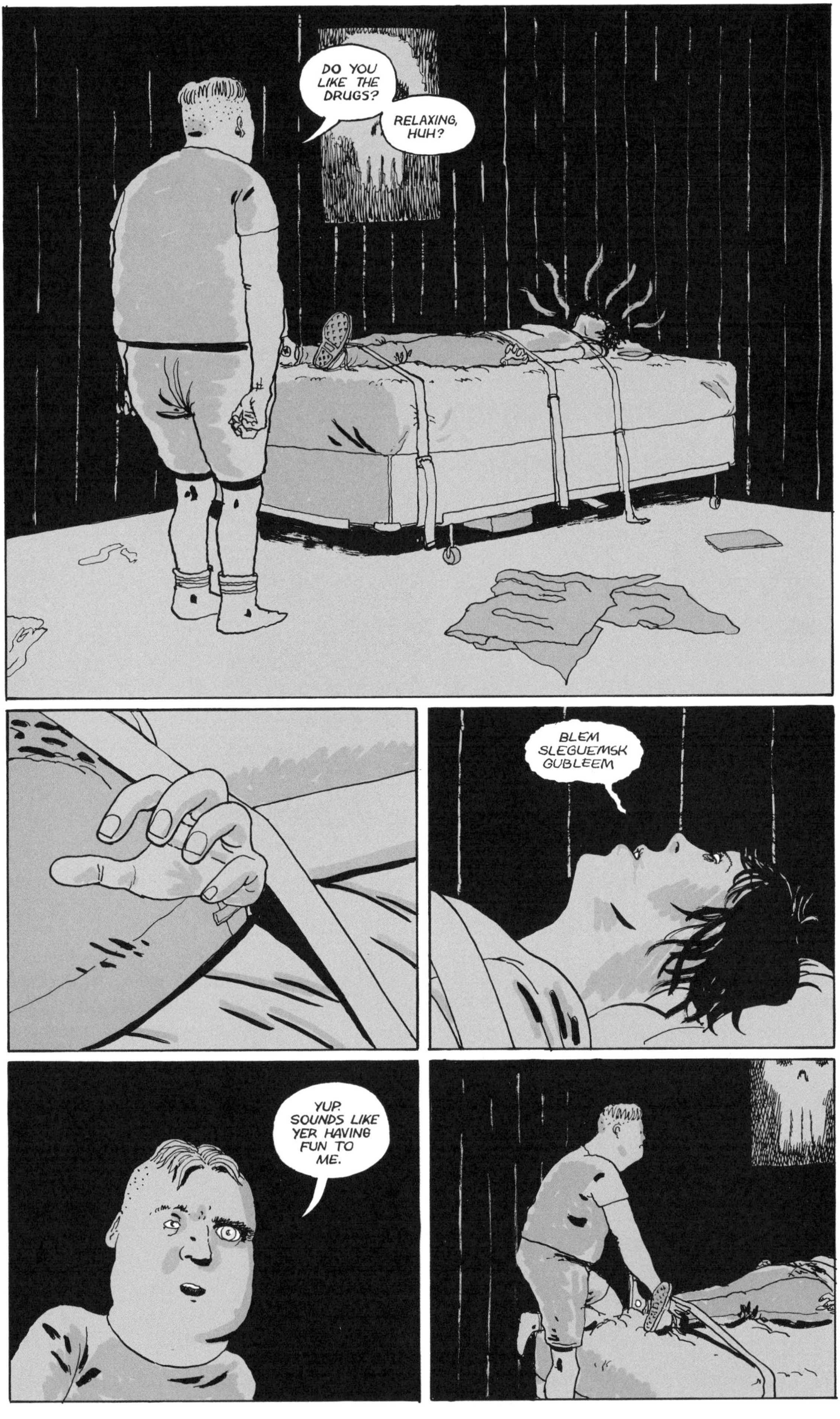
DO YOU LIKE THE DRUGS?
RELAXING, HUH?
BLEM SLEGUEMSK GUBLEEM
YUP. SOUNDS LIKE YER HAVING FUN TO ME.

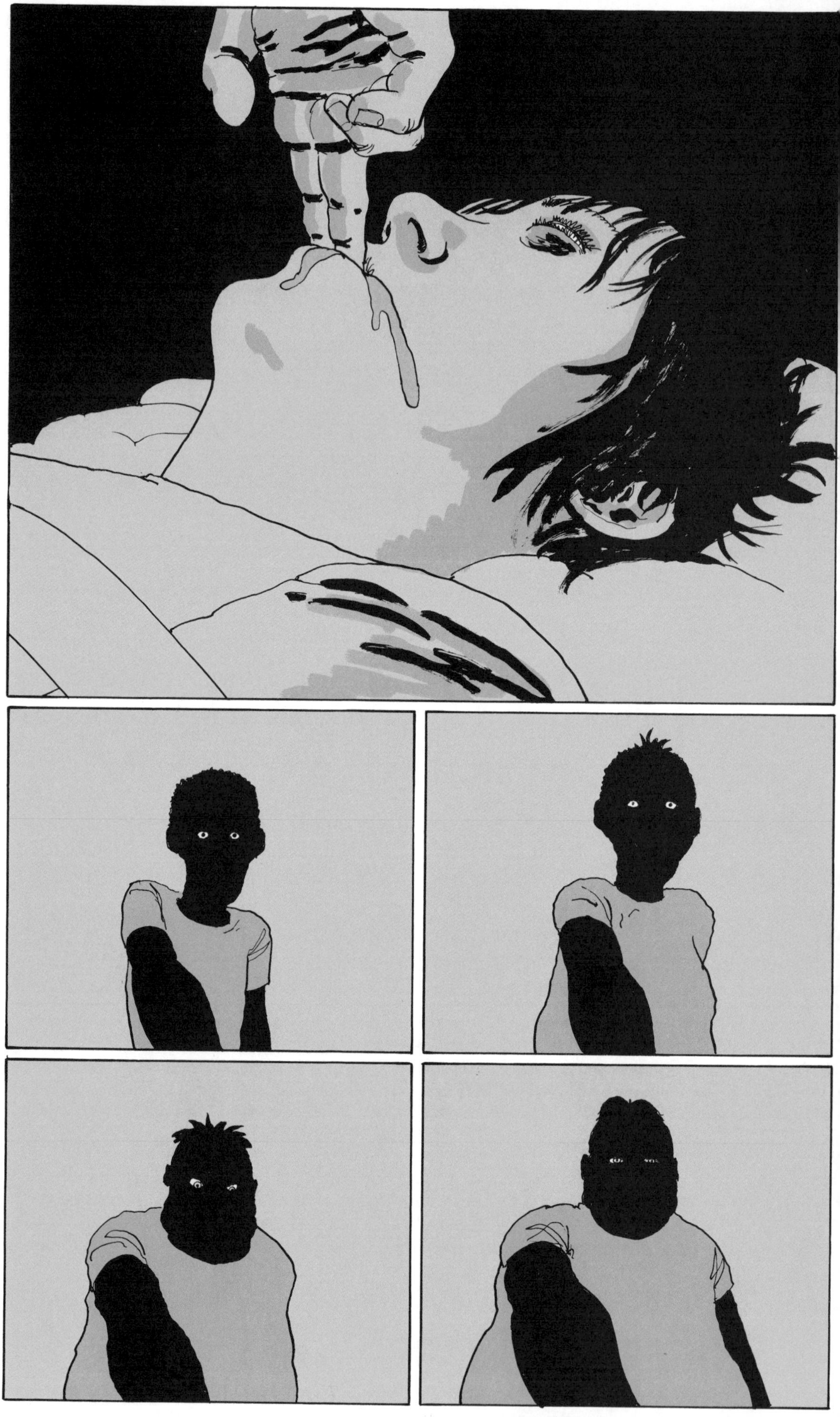

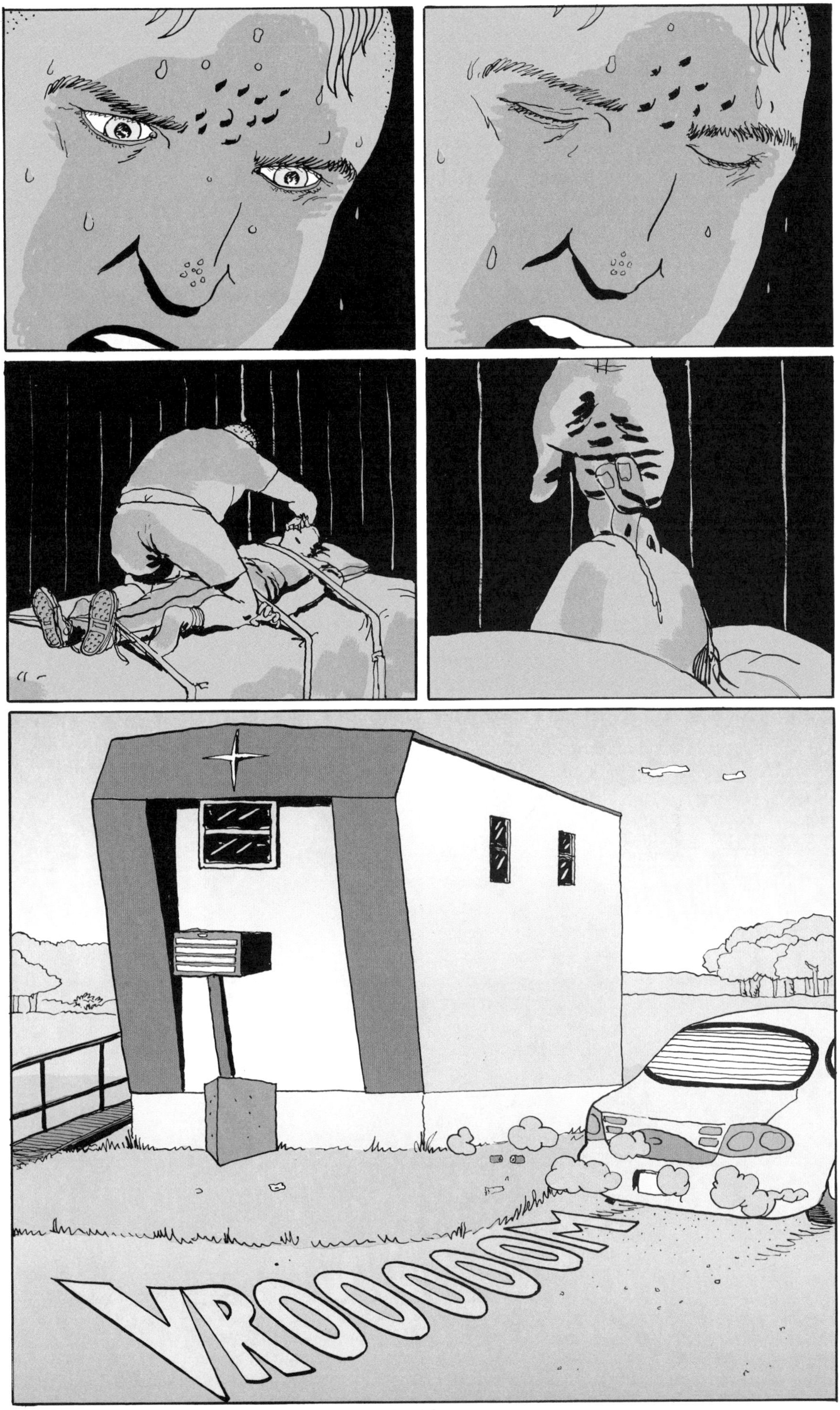
VROOOOOM

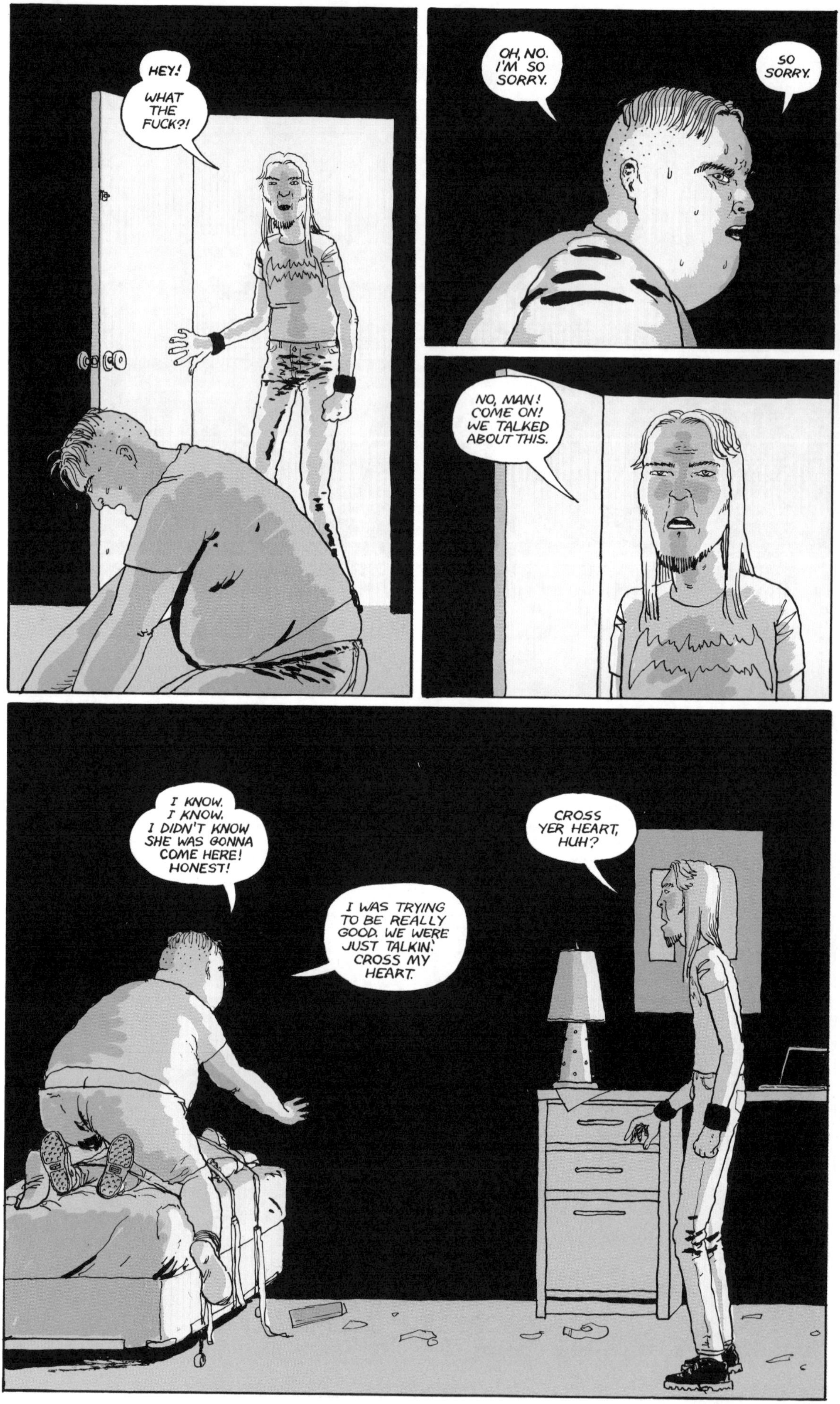
HEY!
WHAT THE FUCK?!
OH, NO. I'M SO SORRY.
SO SORRY.
NO, MAN! COME ON! WE TALKED ABOUT THIS.
I KNOW. I KNOW. I DIDN'T KNOW SHE WAS GONNA COME HERE! HONEST!
I WAS TRYING TO BE REALLY GOOD. WE WERE JUST TALKIN'. CROSS MY HEART.
CROSS YER HEART, HUH?

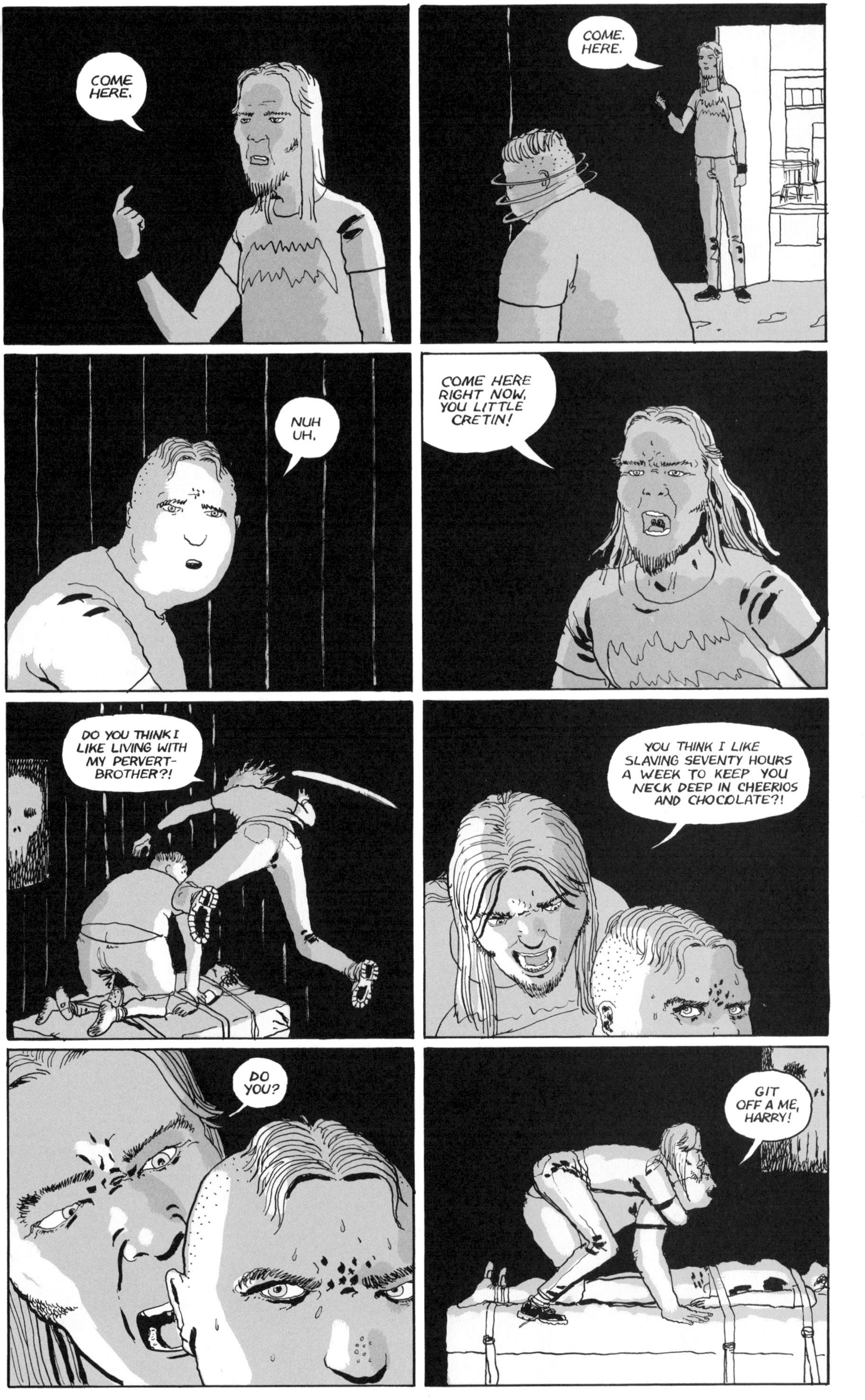
COME HERE.
COME. HERE.
NUH UH.
COME HERE RIGHT NOW, YOU LITTLE CRETIN!
DO YOU THINK I LIKE LIVING WITH MY PERVERT-BROTHER?!
YOU THINK I LIKE SLAVING SEVENTY HOURS A WEEK TO KEEP YOU NECK DEEP IN CHEERIOS AND CHOCOLATE?!
DO YOU?
GIT OFF A ME, HARRY!

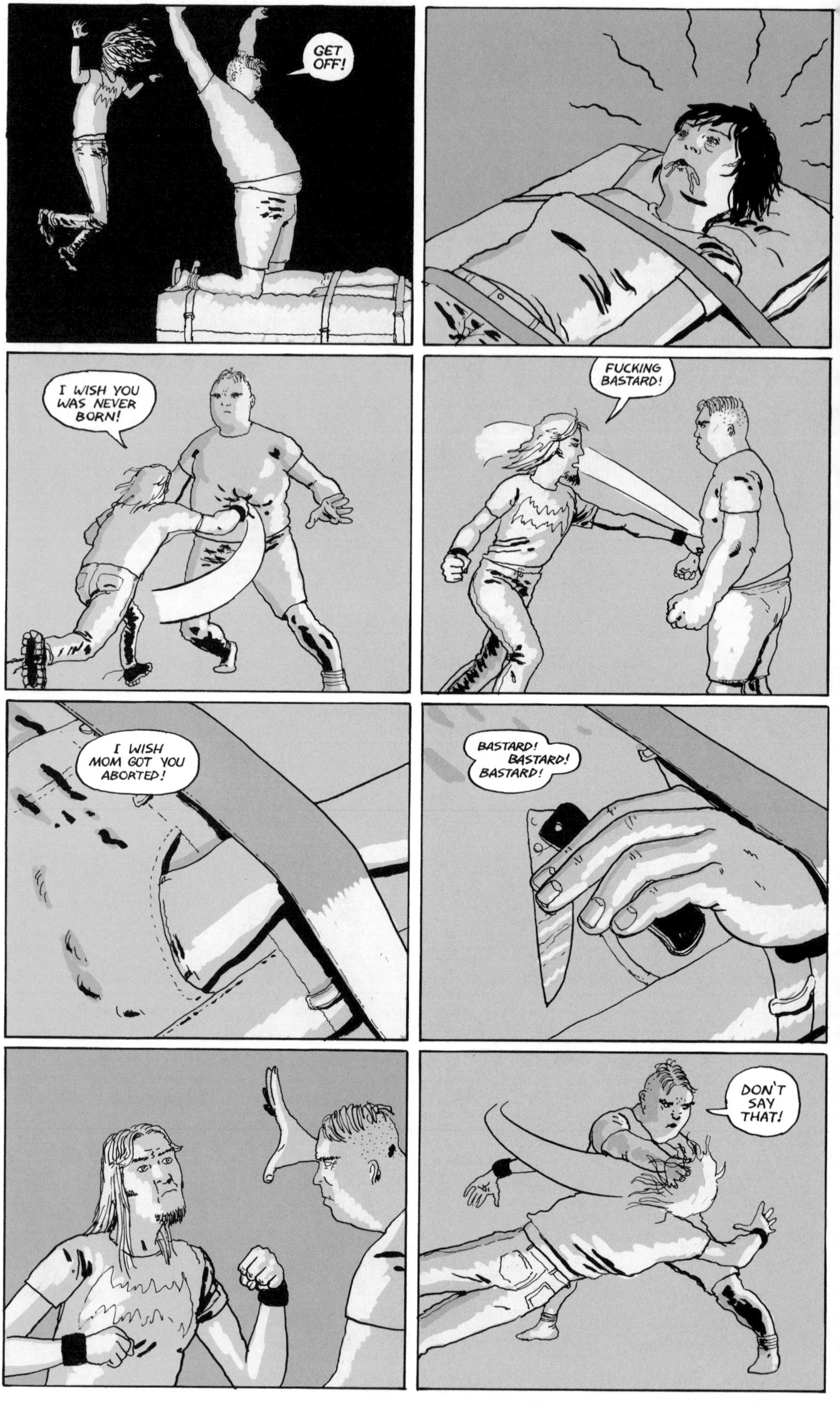
GET OFF!
I WISH YOU WAS NEVER BORN!
FUCKING BASTARD!
I WISH MOM GOT YOU ABORTED!
BASTARD! BASTARD! BASTARD!
DON'T SAY THAT!

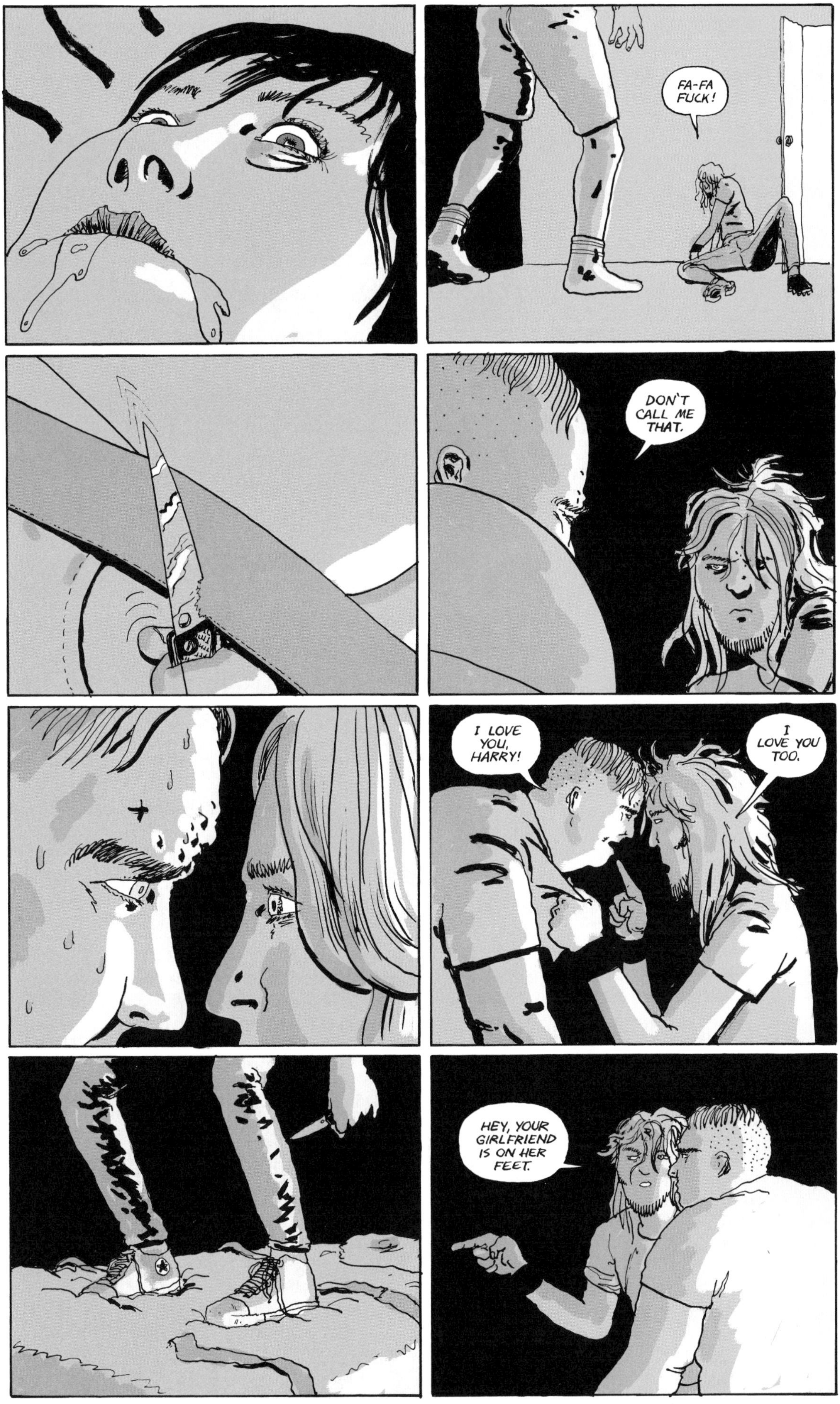
FA-FA FUCK!
DON'T CALL ME THAT.
I LOVE YOU, HARRY!
I LOVE YOU TOO.
HEY, YOUR GIRLFRIEND IS ON HER FEET.

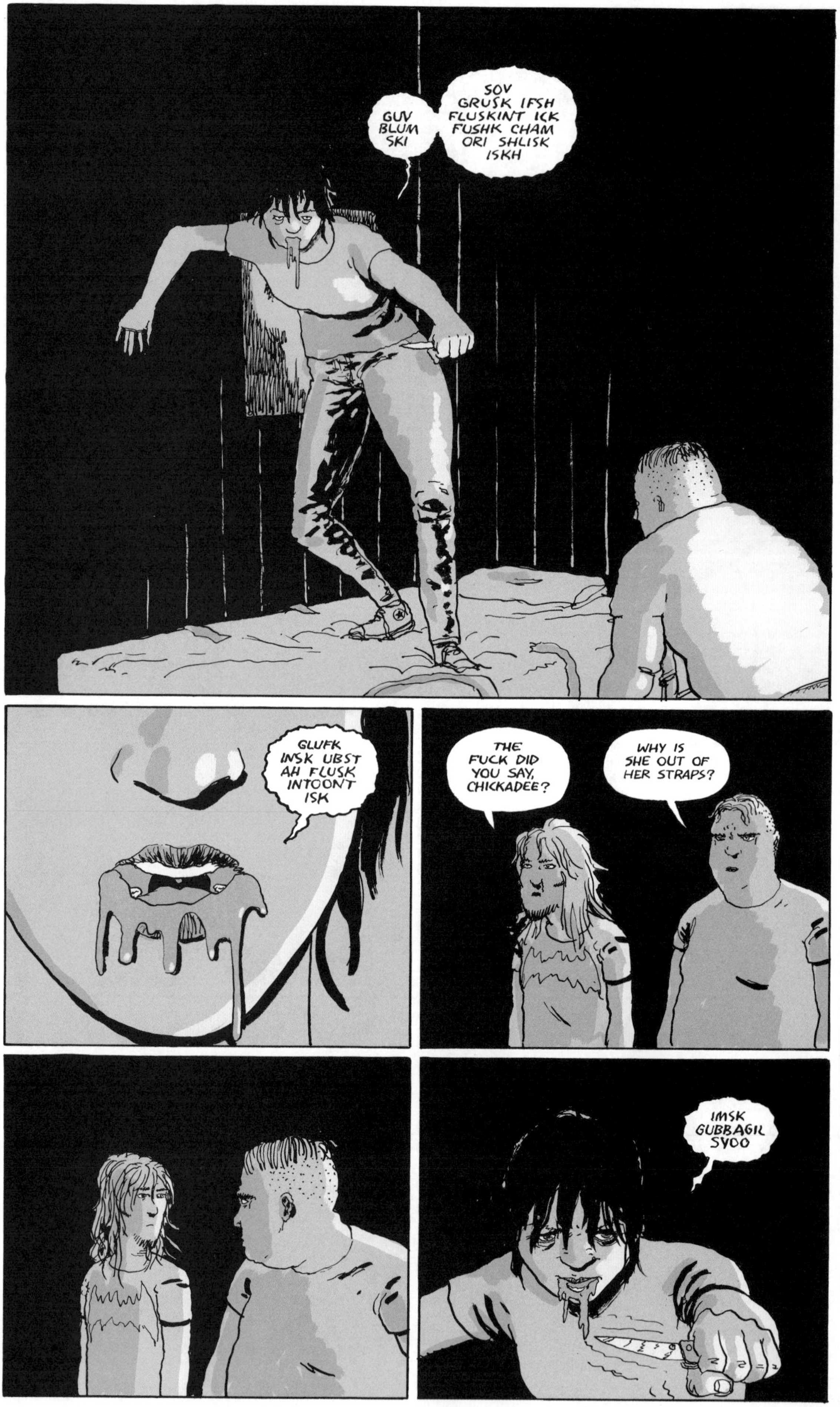
GUV BLUM SKI
SOV GRUSK IFSH FLUSKINT ICK FUSHK CHAM ORI SHLISK ISKH
GLUFK INSK UBST AH FLUSK INTOONT ISK
THE FUCK DID YOU SAY, CHICKADEE?
WHY IS SHE OUT OF HER STRAPS?
IMSK GUBBAGIL SYOO

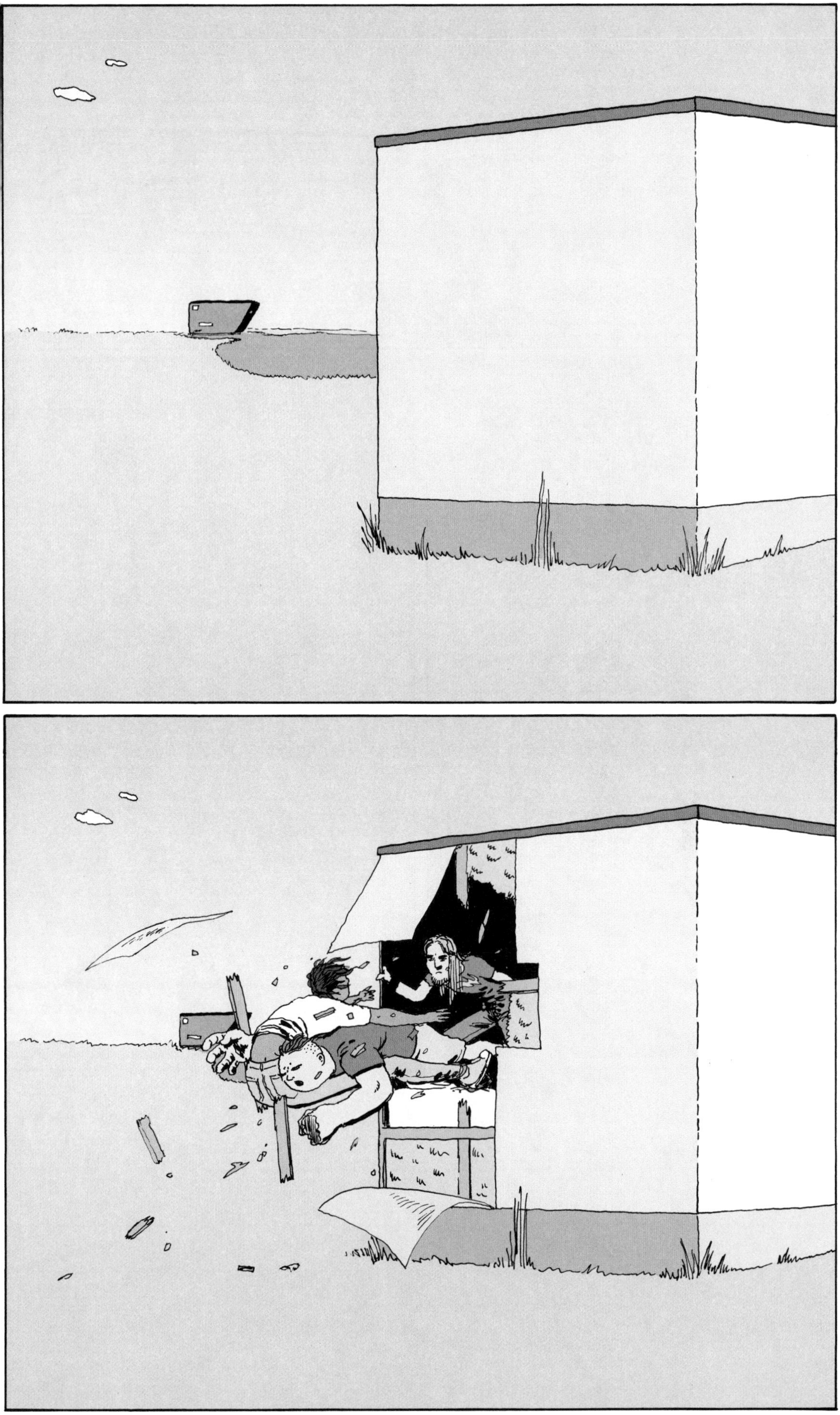

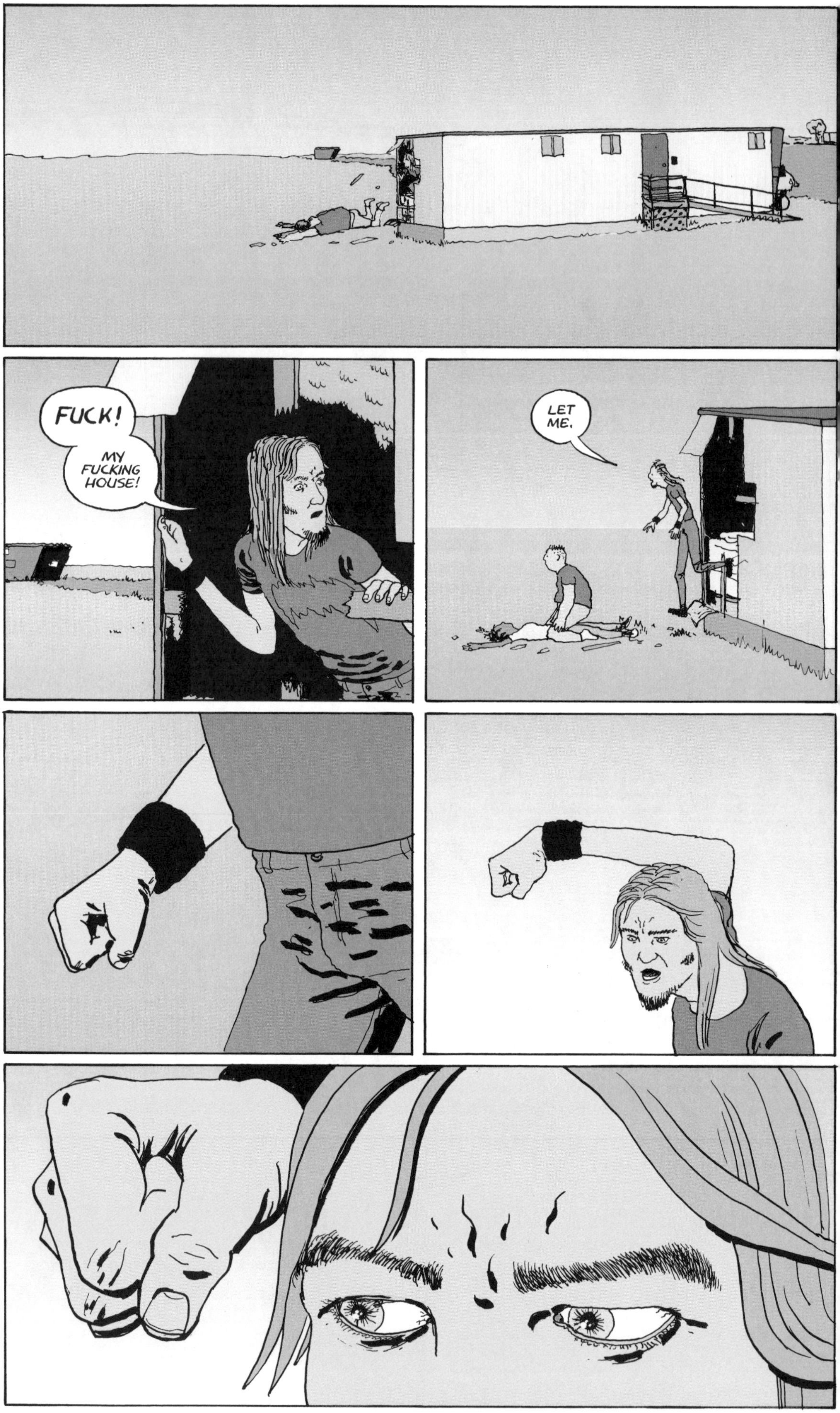
FUCK!
MY FUCKING HOUSE!
LET ME.

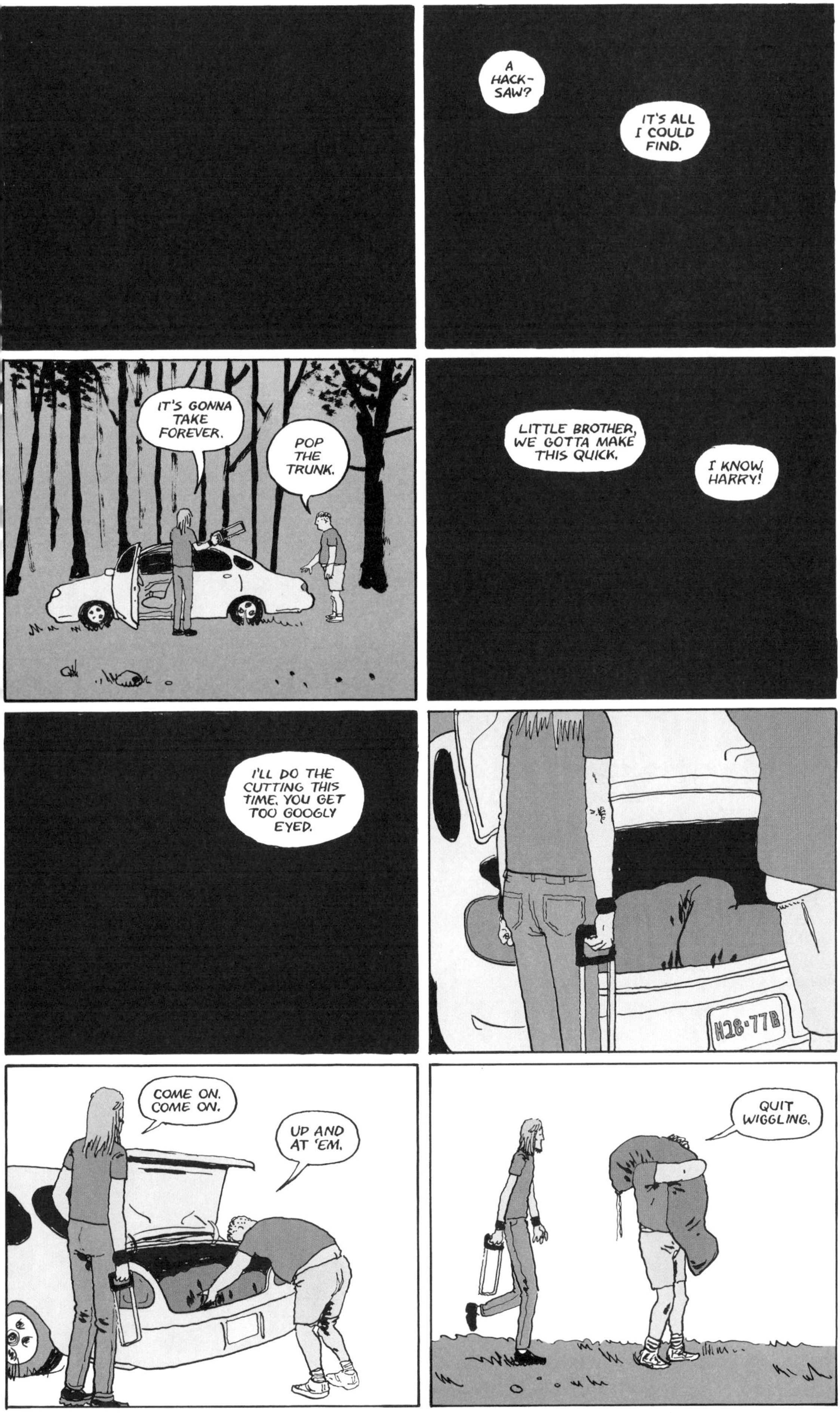
A HACK-SAW?
IT'S ALL I COULD FIND.
IT'S GONNA TAKE FOREVER.
POP THE TRUNK.
LITTLE BROTHER, WE GOTTA MAKE THIS QUICK.
I KNOW, HARRY!
I'LL DO THE CUTTING THIS TIME. YOU GET TOO GOOGLY EYED.
H28·77B
COME ON. COME ON.
UP AND AT 'EM.
QUIT WIGGLING.

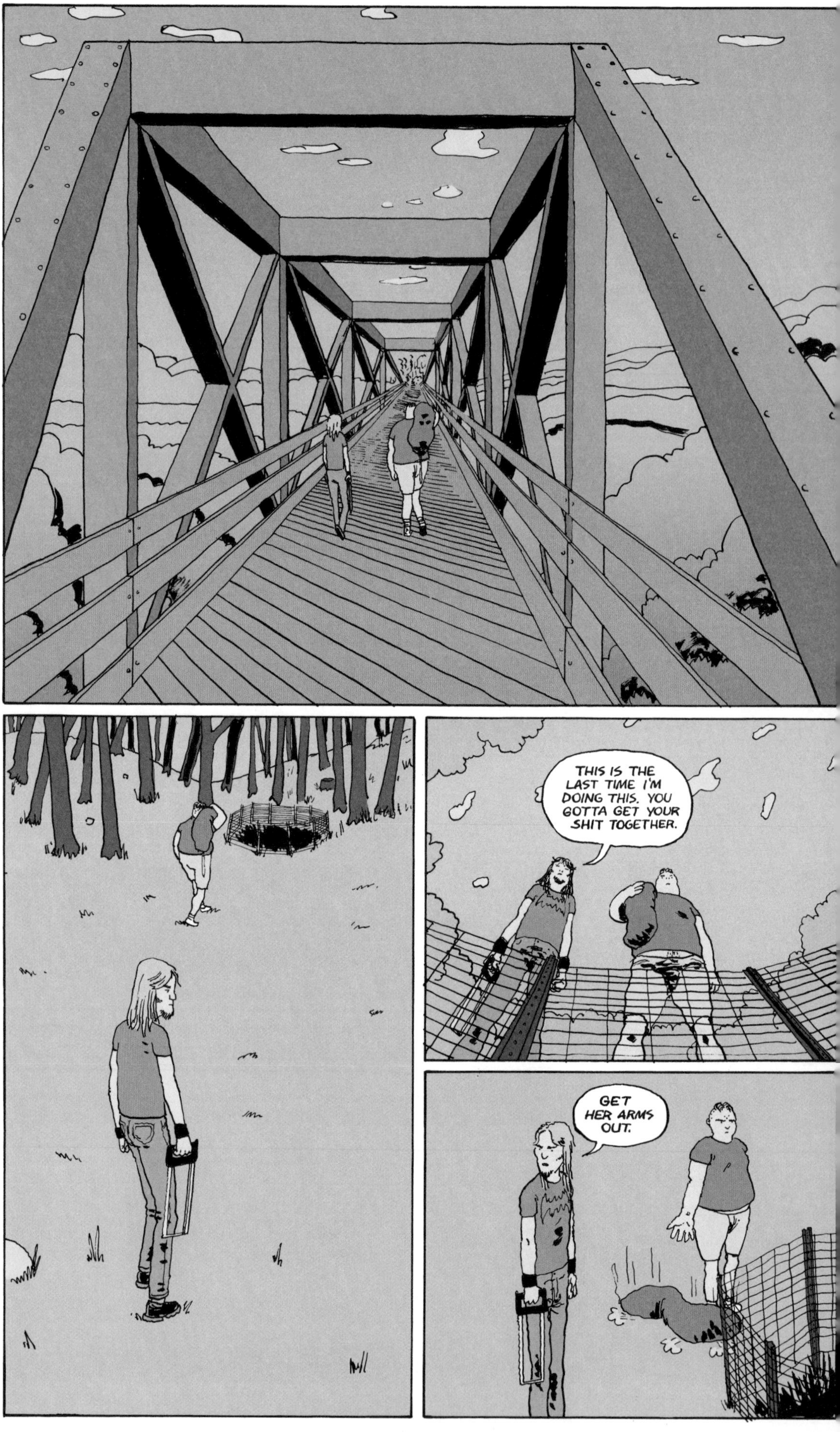
THIS IS THE LAST TIME I'M DOING THIS. YOU GOTTA GET YOUR SHIT TOGETHER.
GET HER ARMS OUT.

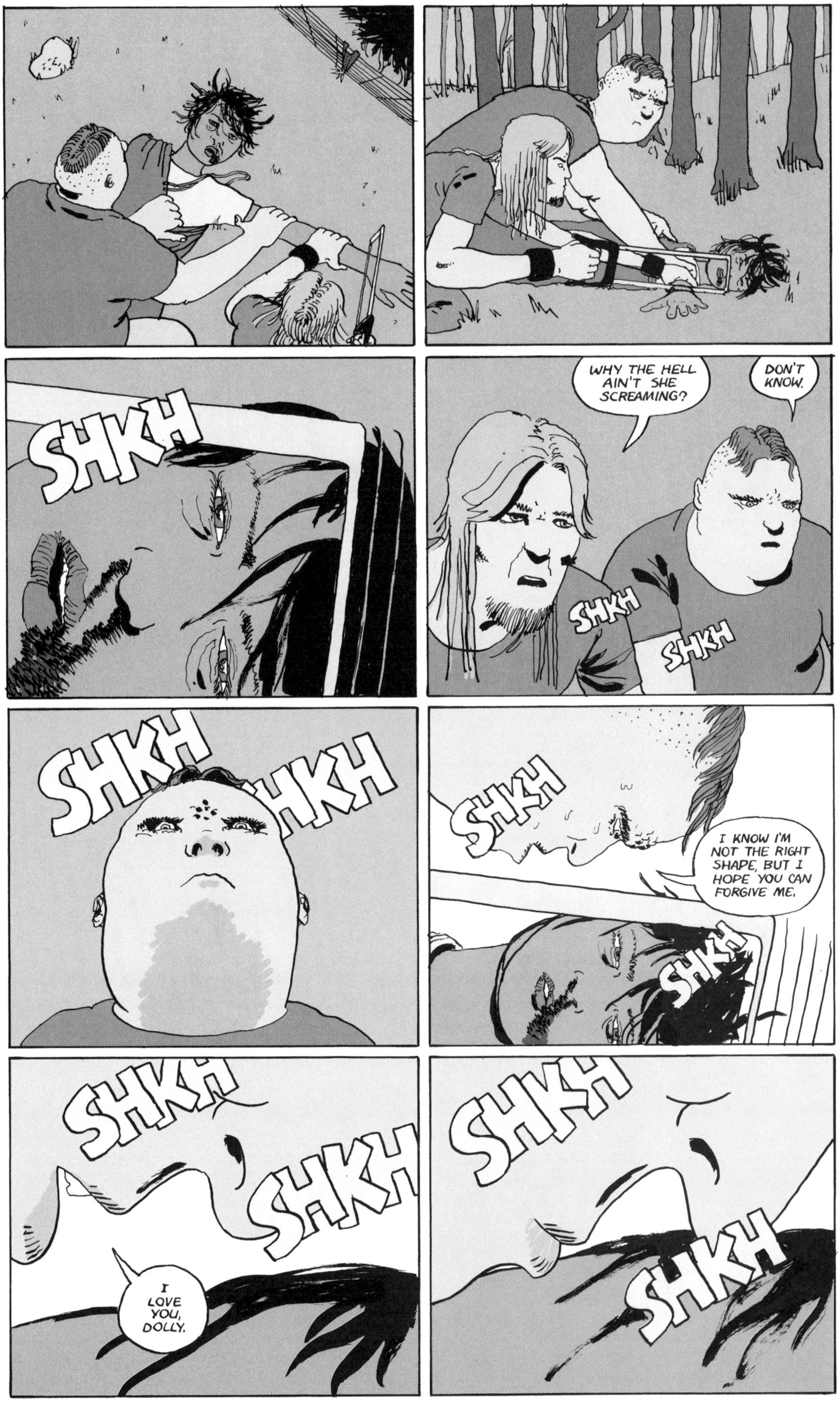
SHKH
WHY THE HELL AIN'T SHE SCREAMING?
DON'T KNOW.
SHKH
SHKH
SHKH
SHKH
SHKH
I KNOW I'M NOT THE RIGHT SHAPE, BUT I HOPE YOU CAN FORGIVE ME.
SHKH
SHKH
SHKH
I LOVE YOU, DOLLY.
SHKH
SHKH

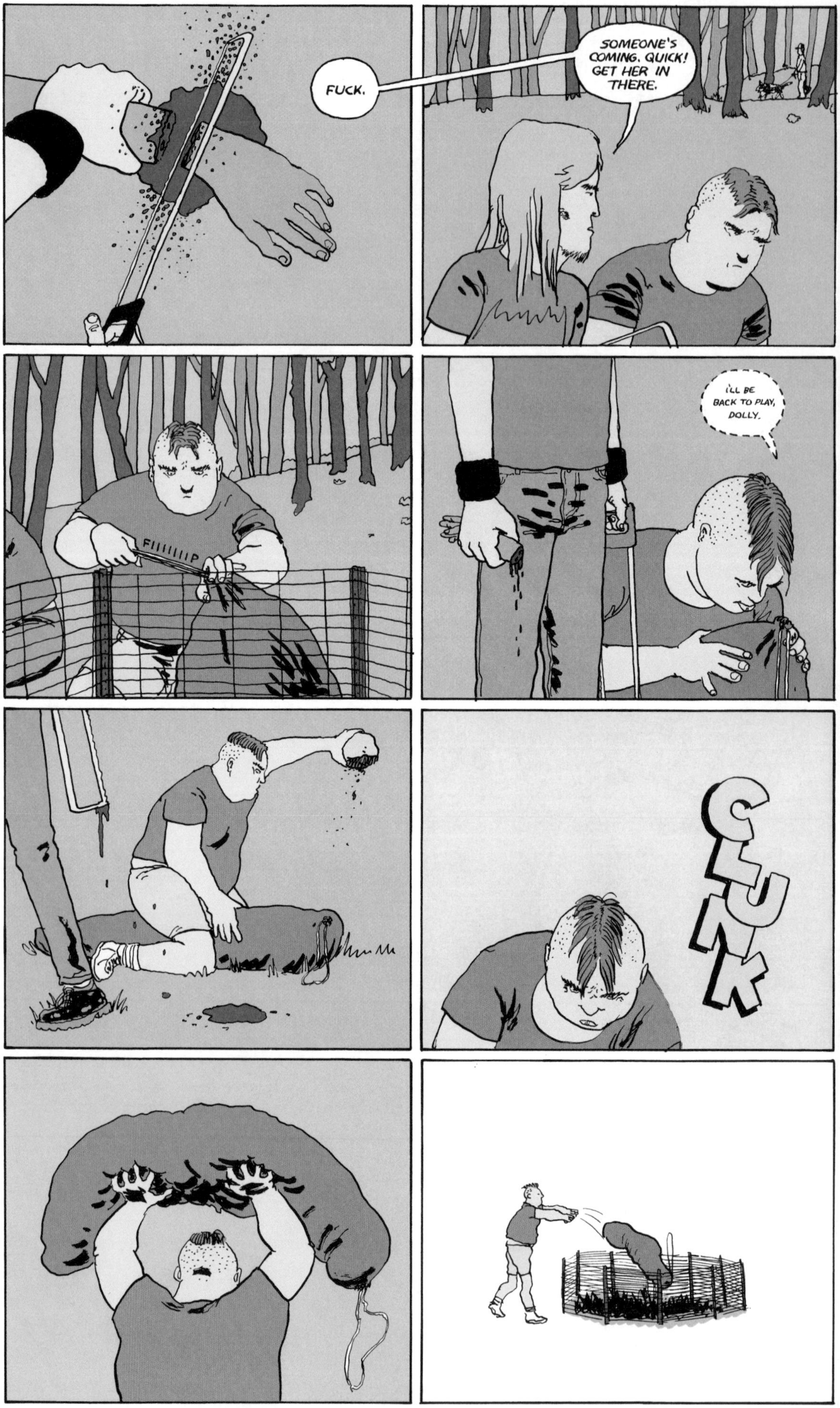
FUCK.
SOMEONE'S COMING. QUICK! GET HER IN THERE.
FIIIIIIP
I'LL BE BACK TO PLAY, DOLLY.
CLUNK

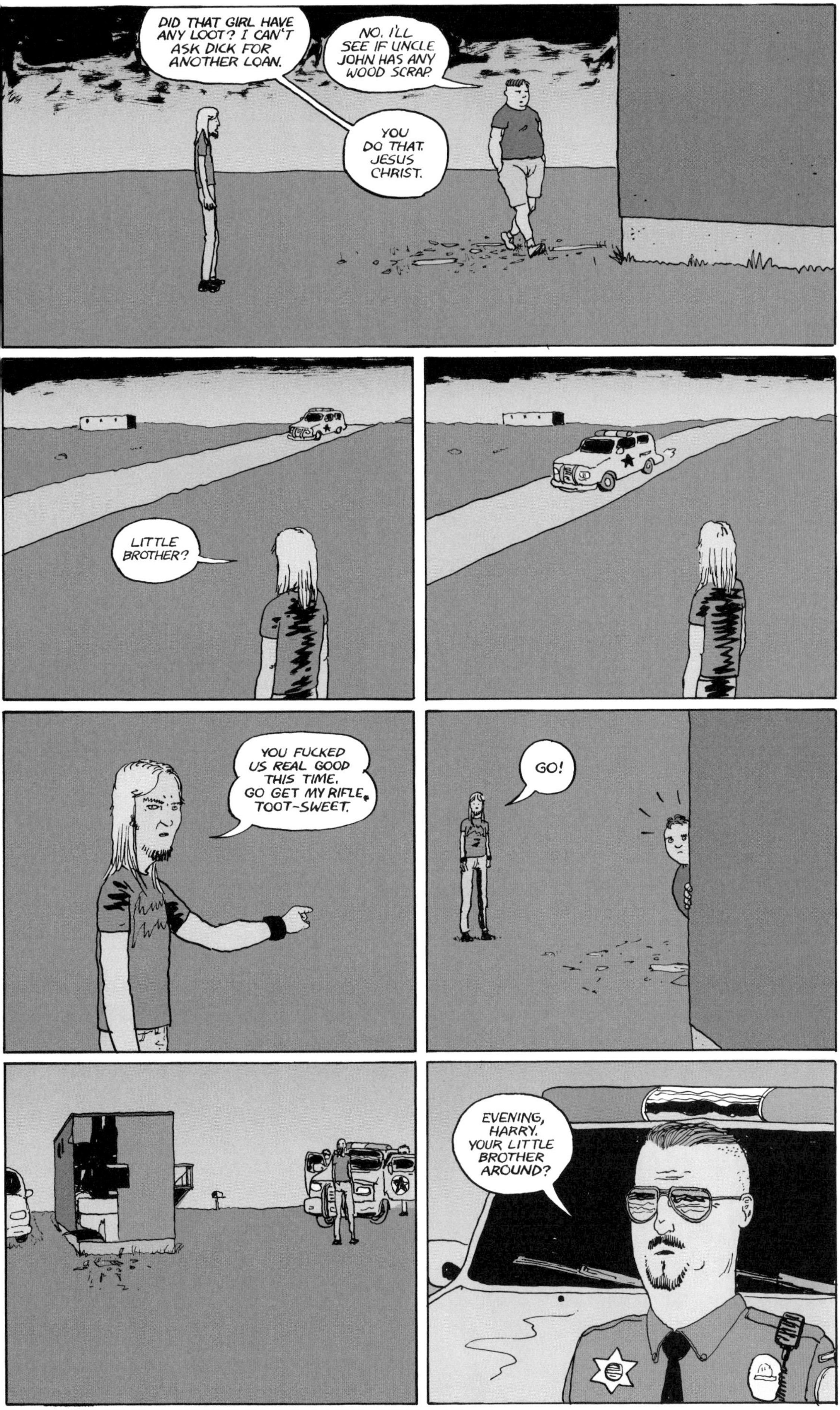

DID THAT GIRL HAVE ANY LOOT? I CAN'T ASK DICK FOR ANOTHER LOAN.
NO. I'LL SEE IF UNCLE JOHN HAS ANY WOOD SCRAP.
YOU DO THAT. JESUS CHRIST.
LITTLE BROTHER?
YOU FUCKED US REAL GOOD THIS TIME. GO GET MY RIFLE. TOOT-SWEET.
GO!
EVENING, HARRY. YOUR LITTLE BROTHER AROUND?

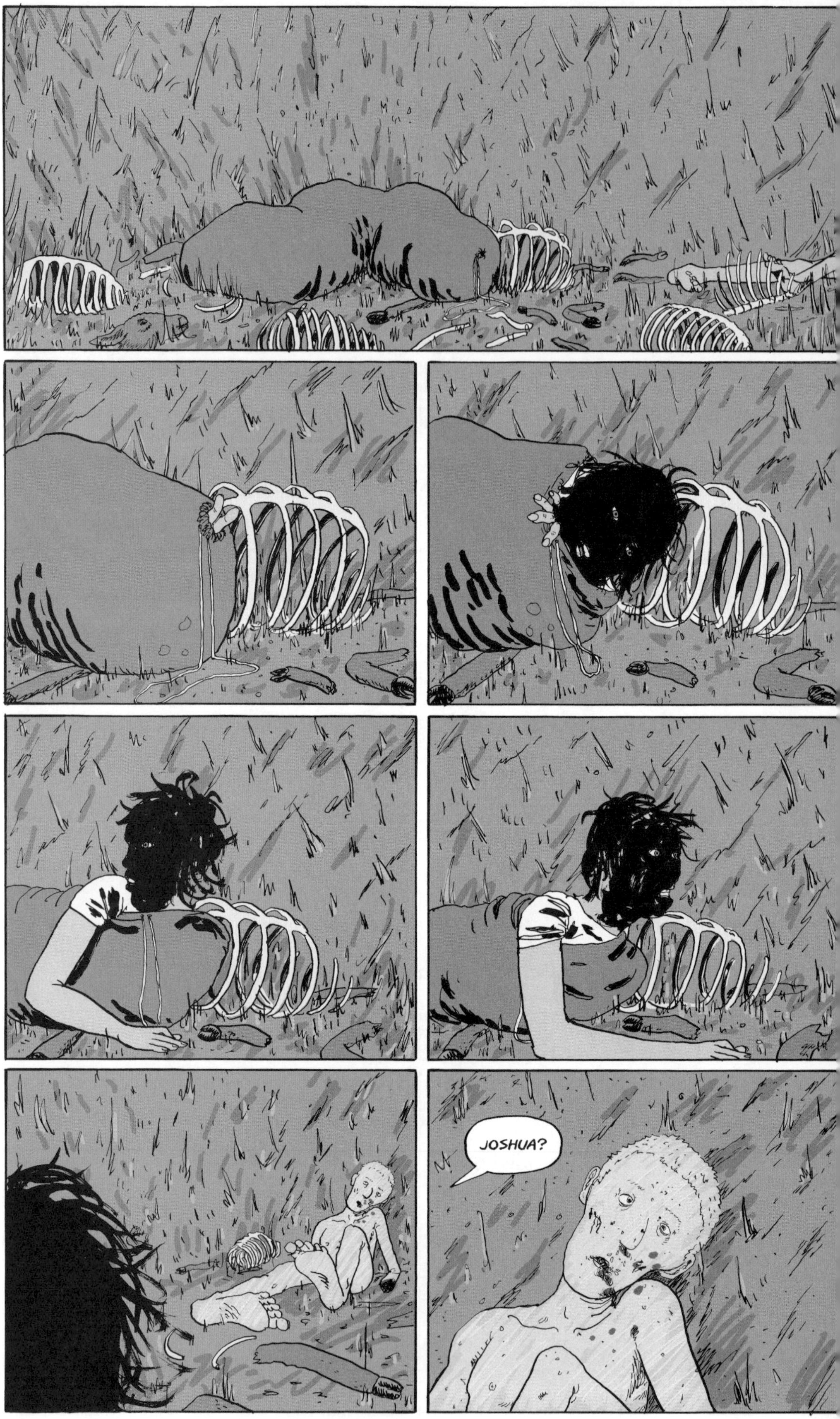
JOSHUA?

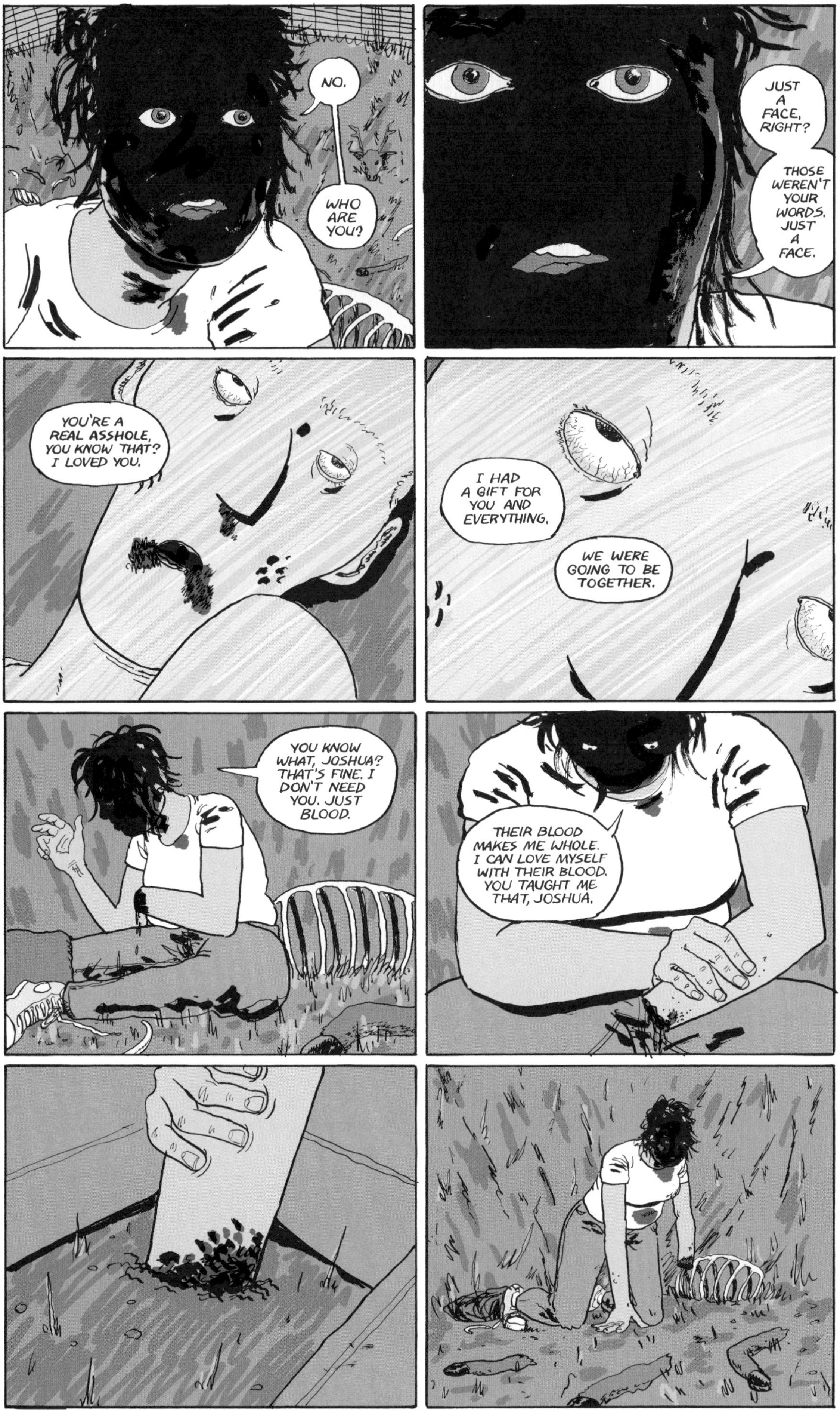
NO.
WHO ARE YOU?
JUST A FACE, RIGHT?
THOSE WEREN'T YOUR WORDS. JUST A FACE.
YOU'RE A REAL ASSHOLE, YOU KNOW THAT? I LOVED YOU.
I HAD A GIFT FOR YOU AND EVERYTHING.
WE WERE GOING TO BE TOGETHER.
YOU KNOW WHAT, JOSHUA? THAT'S FINE. I DON'T NEED YOU. JUST BLOOD.
THEIR BLOOD MAKES ME WHOLE. I CAN LOVE MYSELF WITH THEIR BLOOD. YOU TAUGHT ME THAT, JOSHUA.

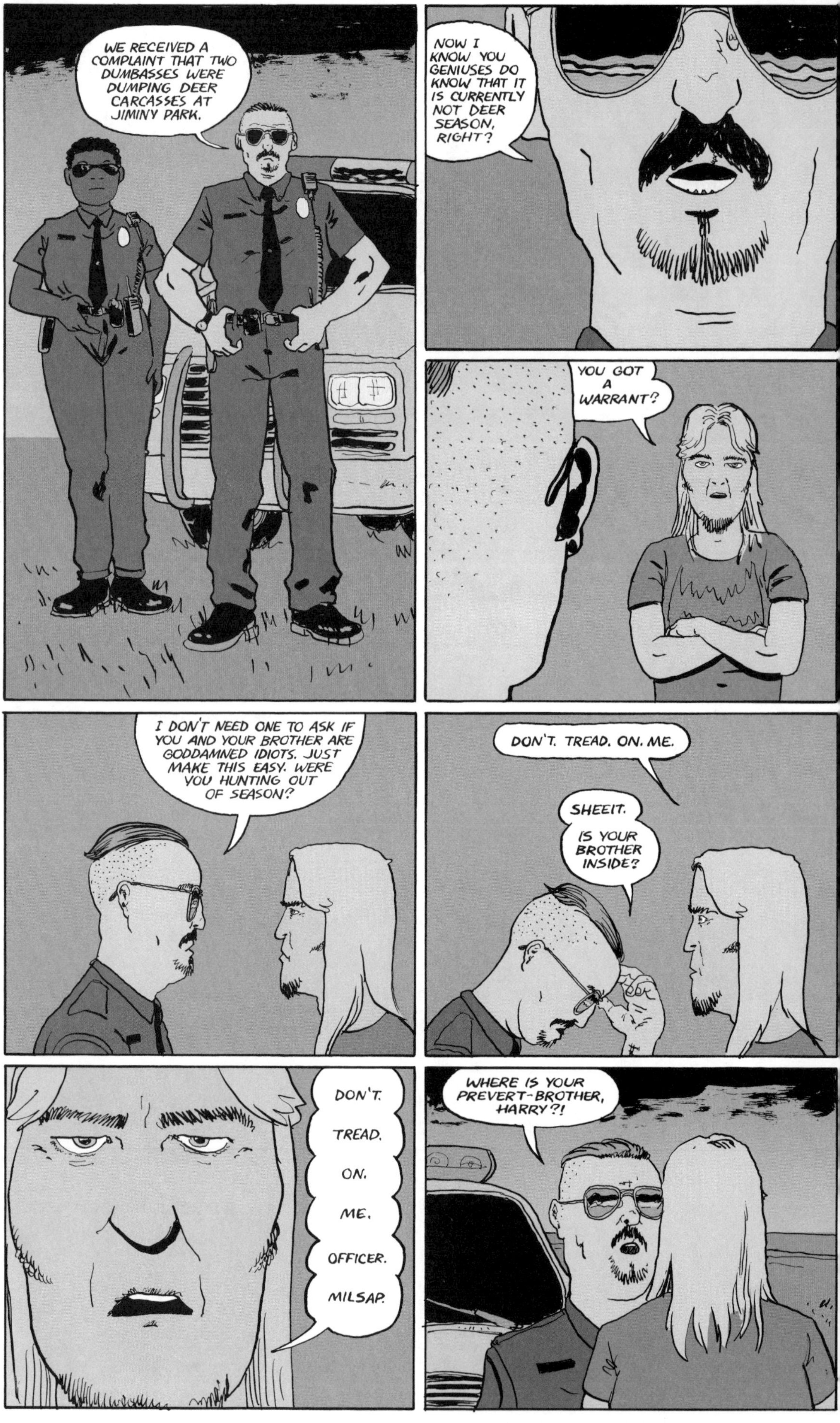
WE RECEIVED A COMPLAINT THAT TWO DUMBASSES WERE DUMPING DEER CARCASSES AT JIMINY PARK.
NOW I KNOW YOU GENIUSES DO KNOW THAT IT IS CURRENTLY NOT DEER SEASON, RIGHT?
YOU GOT A WARRANT?
I DON'T NEED ONE TO ASK IF YOU AND YOUR BROTHER ARE GODDAMNED IDIOTS. JUST MAKE THIS EASY. WERE YOU HUNTING OUT OF SEASON?
DON'T. TREAD. ON. ME.
SHEEIT.
IS YOUR BROTHER INSIDE?
DON'T.
TREAD.
ON.
ME.
OFFICER.
MILSAP.
WHERE IS YOUR PREVERT-BROTHER, HARRY?!

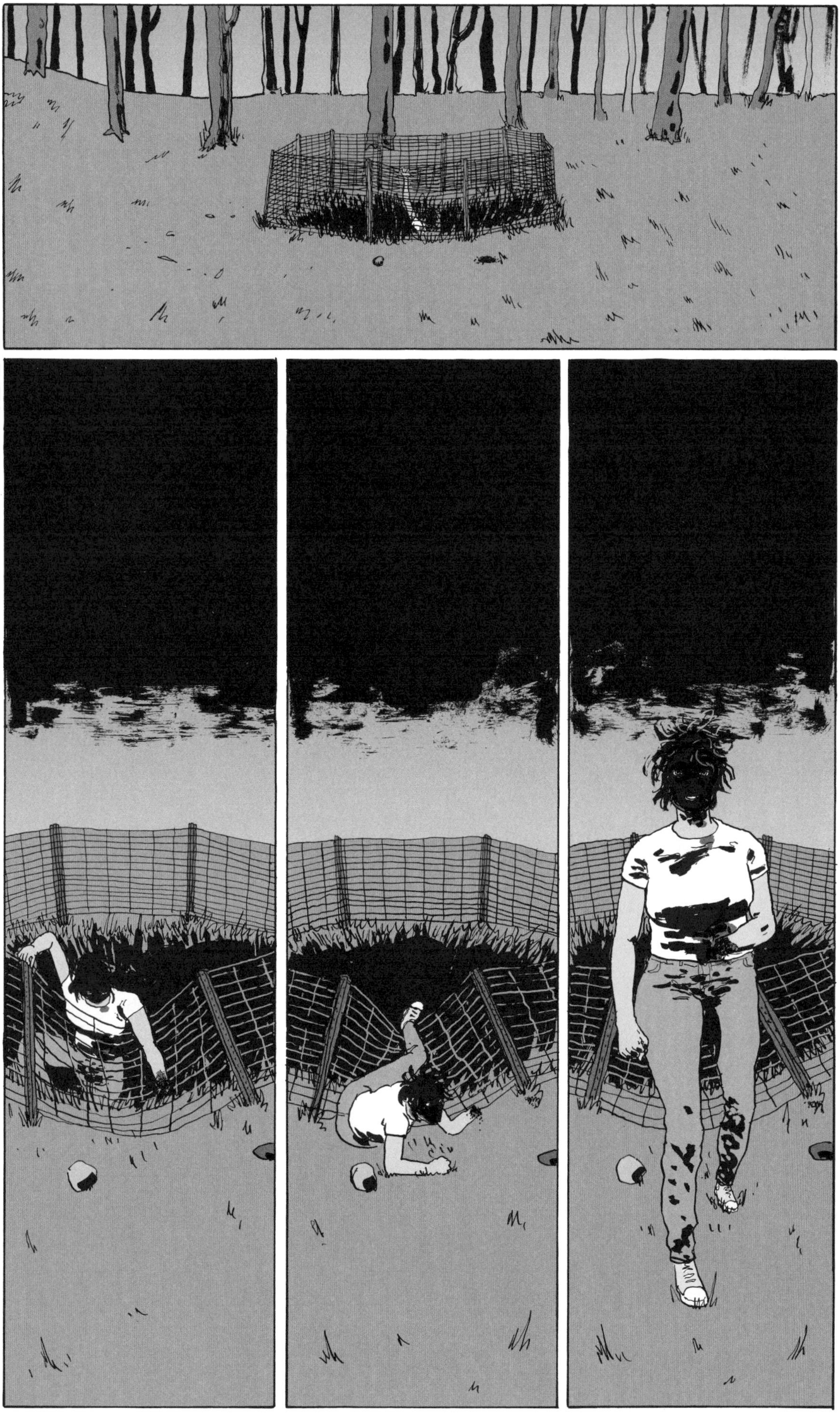

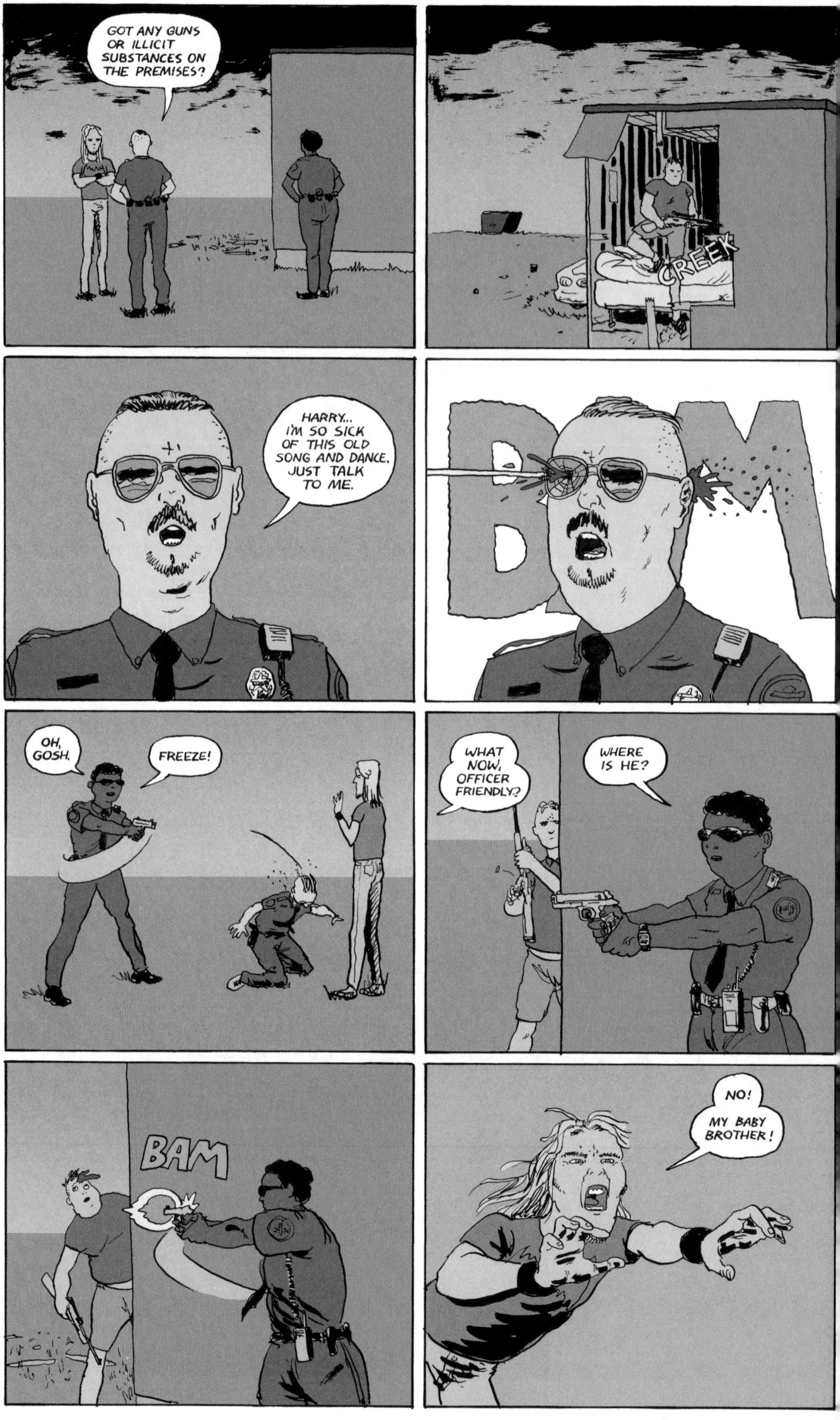
GOT ANY GUNS OR ILLICIT SUBSTANCES ON THE PREMISES?
CREEK
HARRY... I'M SO SICK OF THIS OLD SONG AND DANCE. JUST TALK TO ME.
OH, GOSH.
FREEZE!
WHAT NOW, OFFICER FRIENDLY?
WHERE IS HE?
BAM
NO!
MY BABY BROTHER!

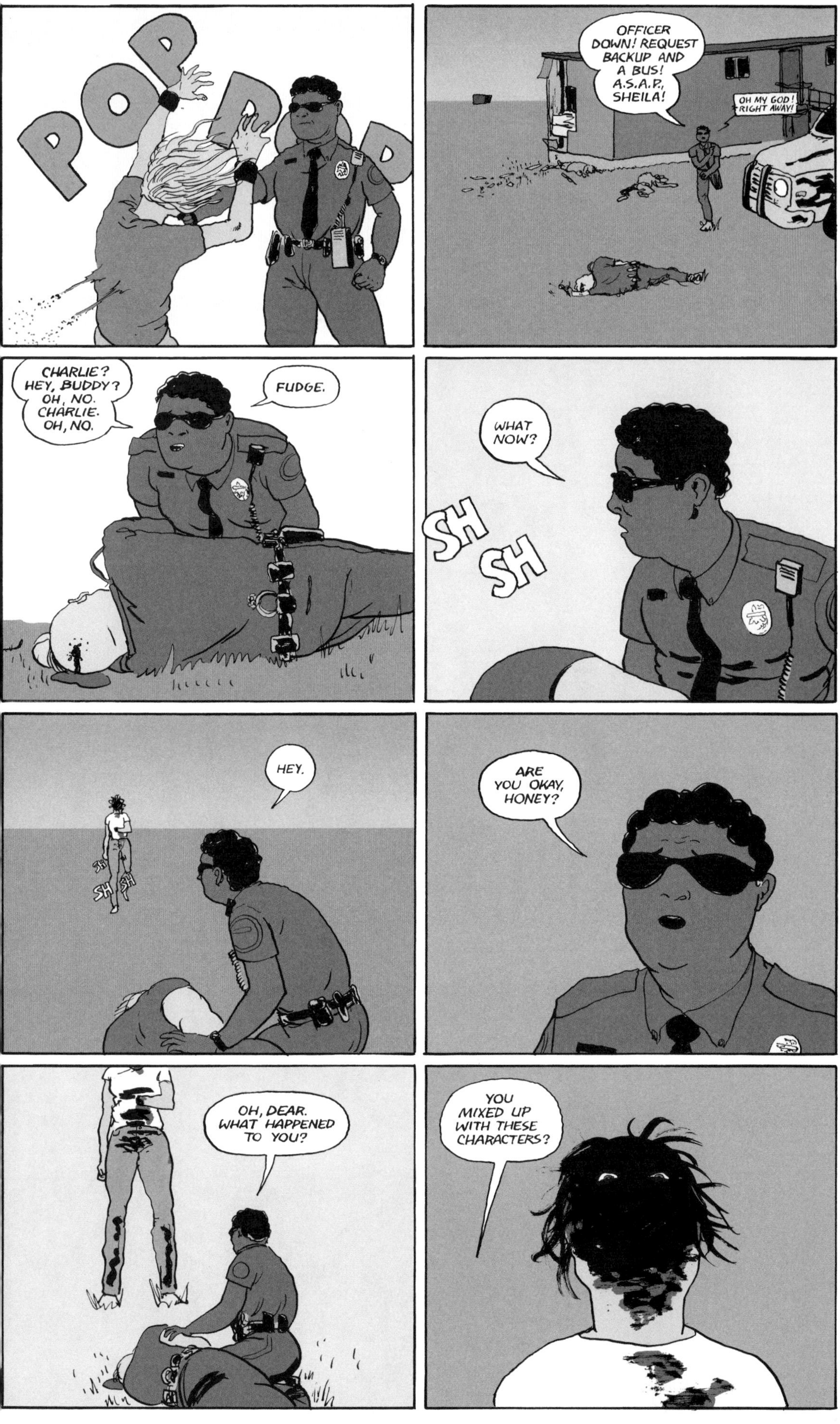
POP
POP
POP
OFFICER DOWN! REQUEST BACKUP AND A BUS! A.S.A.P., SHEILA!
OH MY GOD! RIGHT AWAY!
CHARLIE? HEY, BUDDY? OH, NO. CHARLIE. OH, NO.
FUDGE.
WHAT NOW?
SH
SH
HEY.
SH
SH
SH
ARE YOU OKAY, HONEY?
OH, DEAR. WHAT HAPPENED TO YOU?
YOU MIXED UP WITH THESE CHARACTERS?

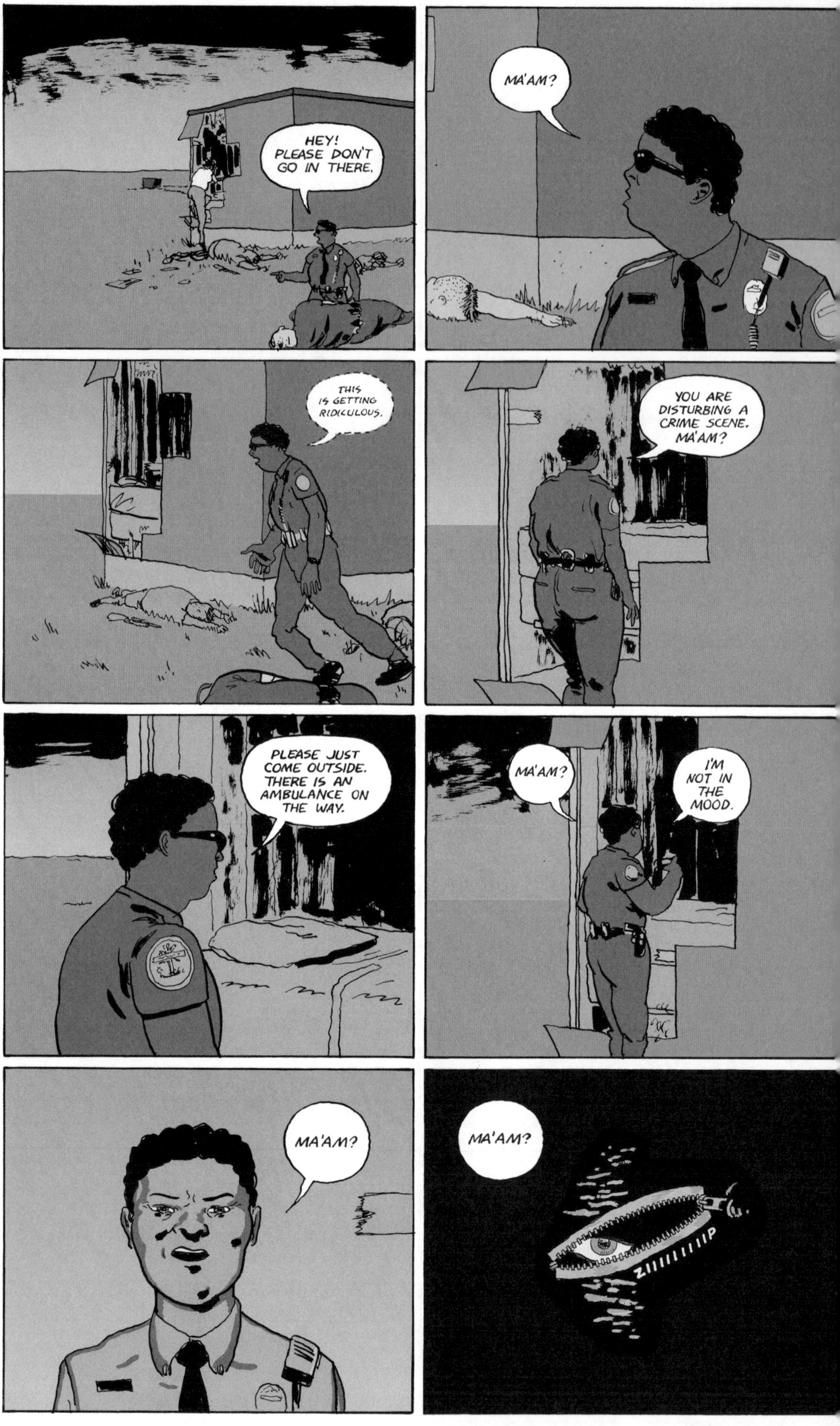
HEY! PLEASE DON'T GO IN THERE.
MA'AM?
THIS IS GETTING RIDICULOUS.
YOU ARE DISTURBING A CRIME SCENE. MA'AM?
PLEASE JUST COME OUTSIDE. THERE IS AN AMBULANCE ON THE WAY.
MA'AM?
I'M NOT IN THE MOOD.
MA'AM?
MA'AM?
ZIIIIIIIIP

5

MOMMY MOMMY

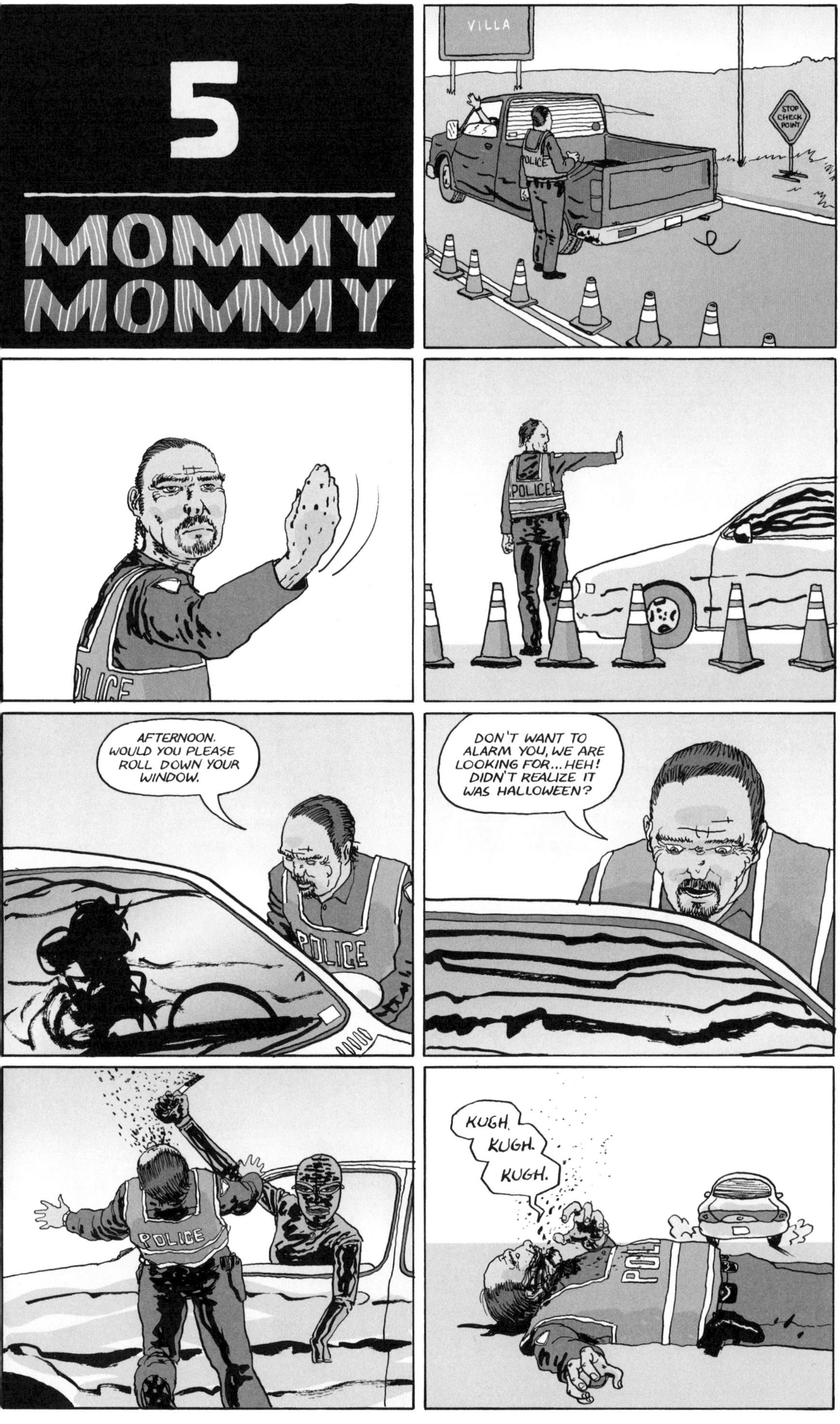
VILLA
STOP CHECK POINT
POLICE
POLICE
AFTERNOON. WOULD YOU PLEASE ROLL DOWN YOUR WINDOW.
POLICE
DON'T WANT TO ALARM YOU, WE ARE LOOKING FOR... HEH! DIDN'T REALIZE IT WAS HALLOWEEN?
POLICE
KUGH.
KUGH.
KUGH.

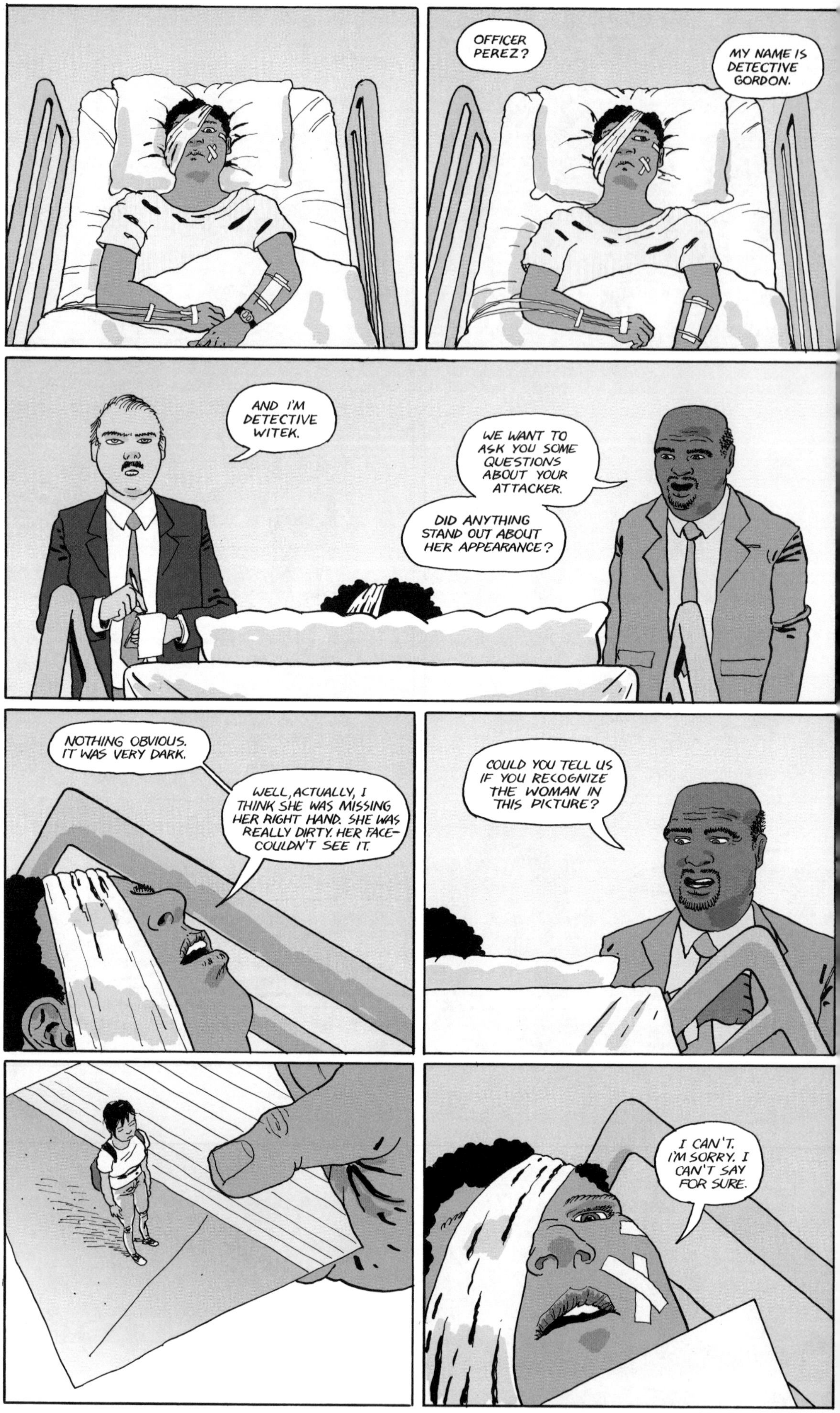
OFFICER PEREZ?
MY NAME IS DETECTIVE GORDON.
AND I'M DETECTIVE WITEK.
WE WANT TO ASK YOU SOME QUESTIONS ABOUT YOUR ATTACKER.
DID ANYTHING STAND OUT ABOUT HER APPEARANCE?
NOTHING OBVIOUS. IT WAS VERY DARK.
WELL, ACTUALLY, I THINK SHE WAS MISSING HER RIGHT HAND. SHE WAS REALLY DIRTY. HER FACE-COULDN'T SEE IT.
COULD YOU TELL US IF YOU RECOGNIZE THE WOMAN IN THIS PICTURE?
I CAN'T. I'M SORRY. I CAN'T SAY FOR SURE.

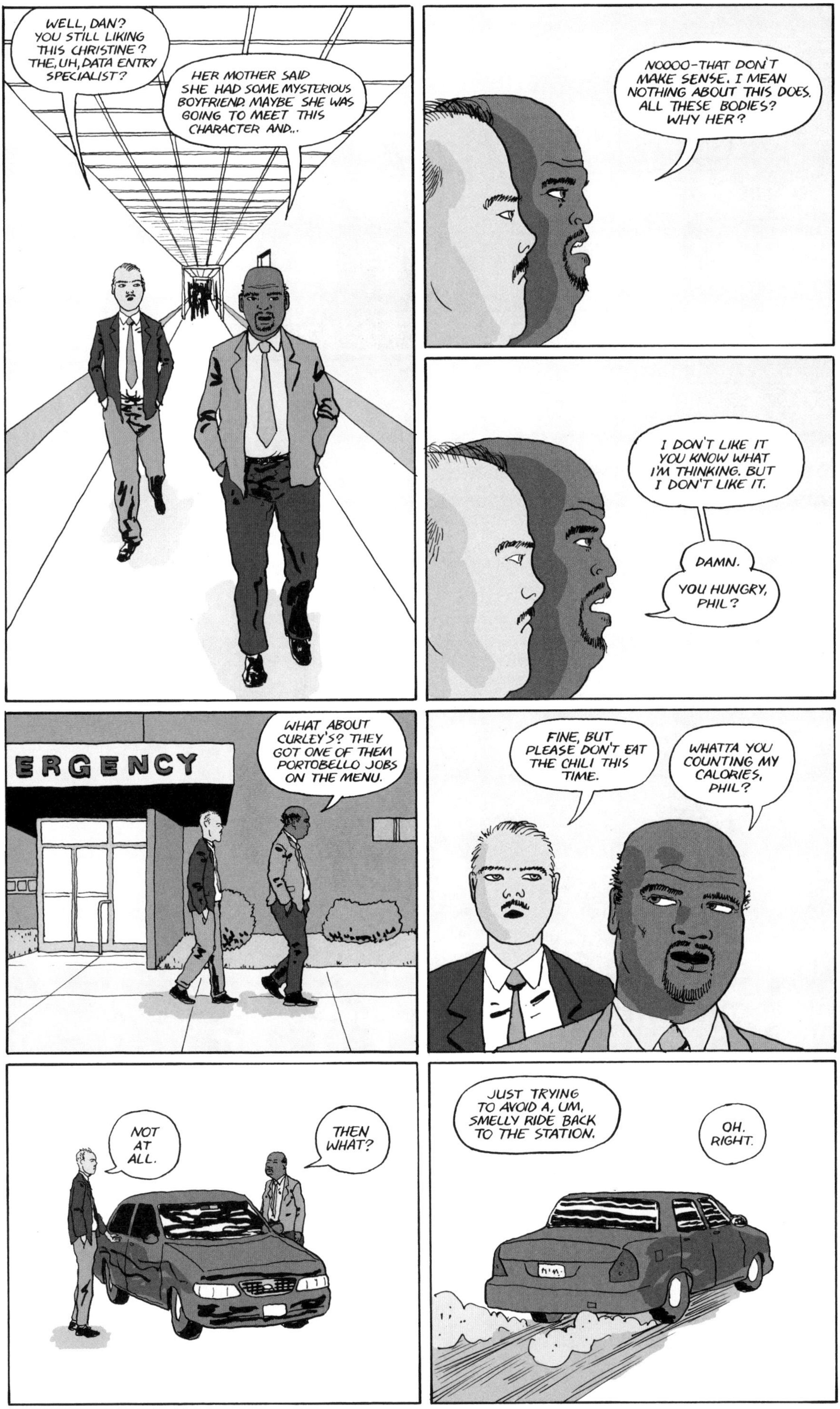
WELL, DAN? YOU STILL LIKING THIS CHRISTINE? THE, UH, DATA ENTRY SPECIALIST?
HER MOTHER SAID SHE HAD SOME MYSTERIOUS BOYFRIEND. MAYBE SHE WAS GOING TO MEET THIS CHARACTER AND...
NOOOO–THAT DON'T MAKE SENSE. I MEAN NOTHING ABOUT THIS DOES. ALL THESE BODIES? WHY HER?
I DON'T LIKE IT. YOU KNOW WHAT I'M THINKING. BUT I DON'T LIKE IT.
DAMN.
YOU HUNGRY, PHIL?
ERGENCY
WHAT ABOUT CURLEY'S? THEY GOT ONE OF THEM PORTOBELLO JOBS ON THE MENU.
FINE, BUT PLEASE DON'T EAT THE CHILI THIS TIME.
WHATTA YOU COUNTING MY CALORIES, PHIL?
NOT AT ALL.
THEN WHAT?
JUST TRYING TO AVOID A, UM, SMELLY RIDE BACK TO THE STATION.
OH. RIGHT.

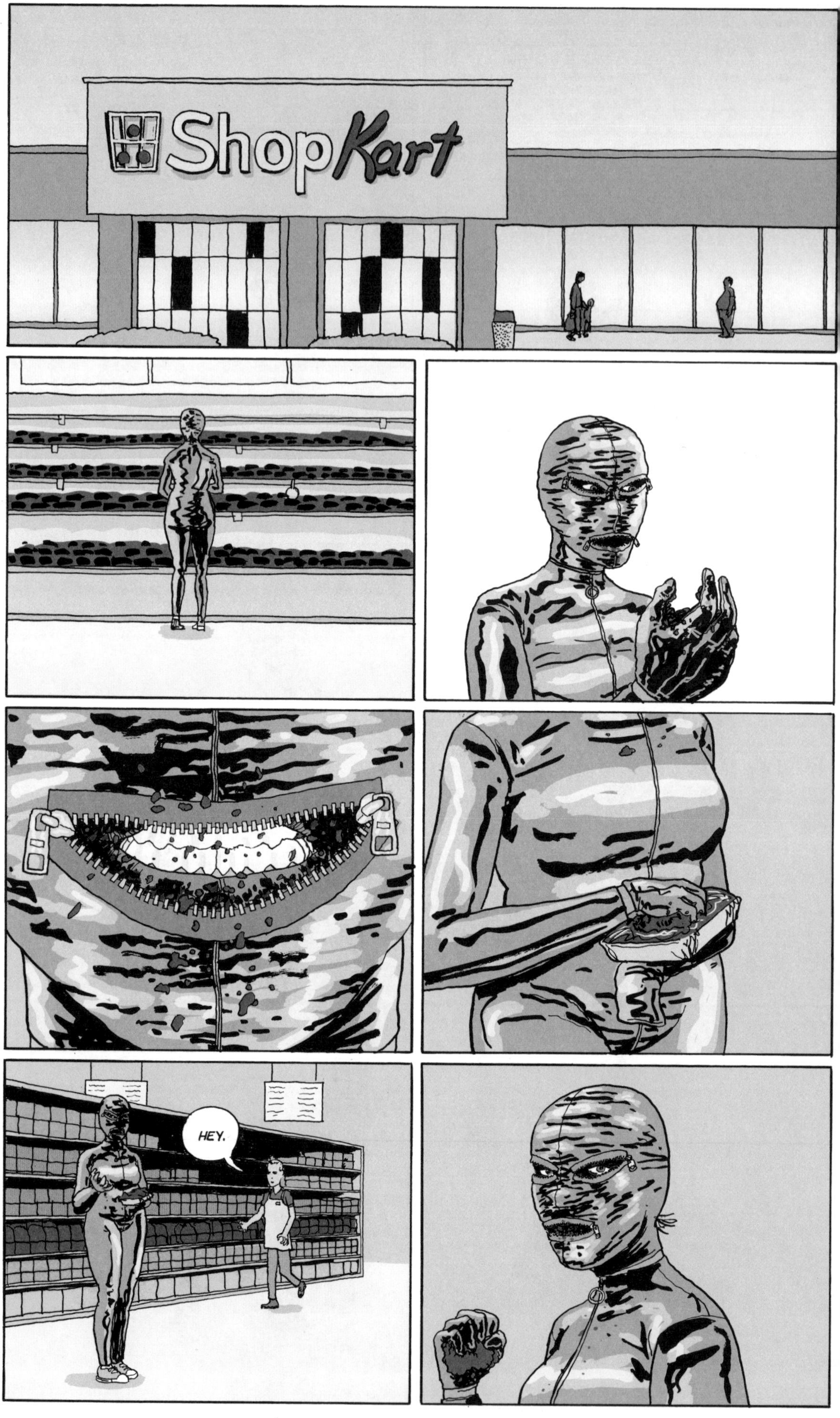
ShopKart
HEY.

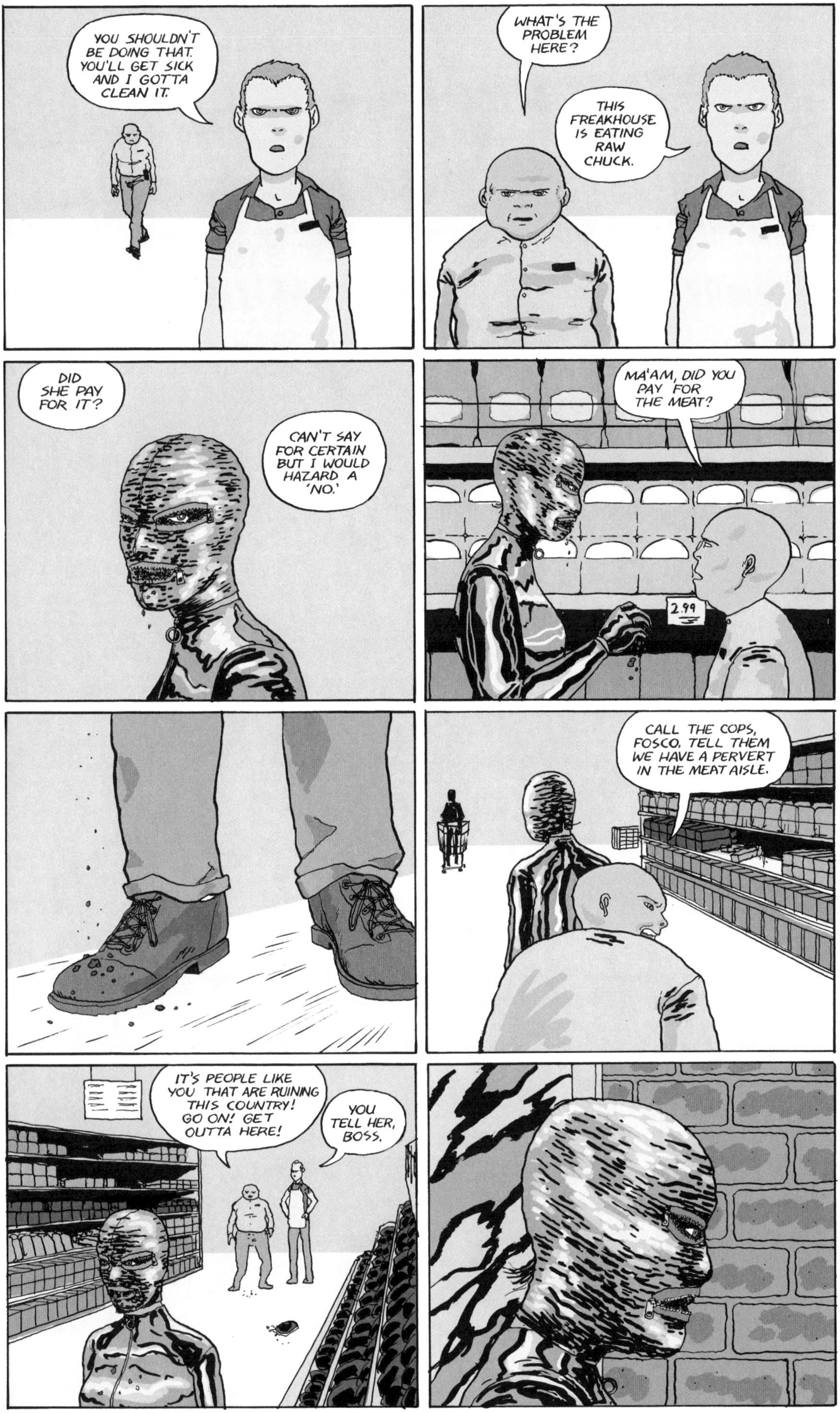
YOU SHOULDN'T BE DOING THAT. YOU'LL GET SICK AND I GOTTA CLEAN IT.
WHAT'S THE PROBLEM HERE?
THIS FREAKHOUSE IS EATING RAW CHUCK.
DID SHE PAY FOR IT?
CAN'T SAY FOR CERTAIN BUT I WOULD HAZARD A 'NO.'
MA'AM, DID YOU PAY FOR THE MEAT?
2.99
CALL THE COPS, FOSCO. TELL THEM WE HAVE A PERVERT IN THE MEAT AISLE.
IT'S PEOPLE LIKE YOU THAT ARE RUINING THIS COUNTRY! GO ON! GET OUTTA HERE!
YOU TELL HER, BOSS.

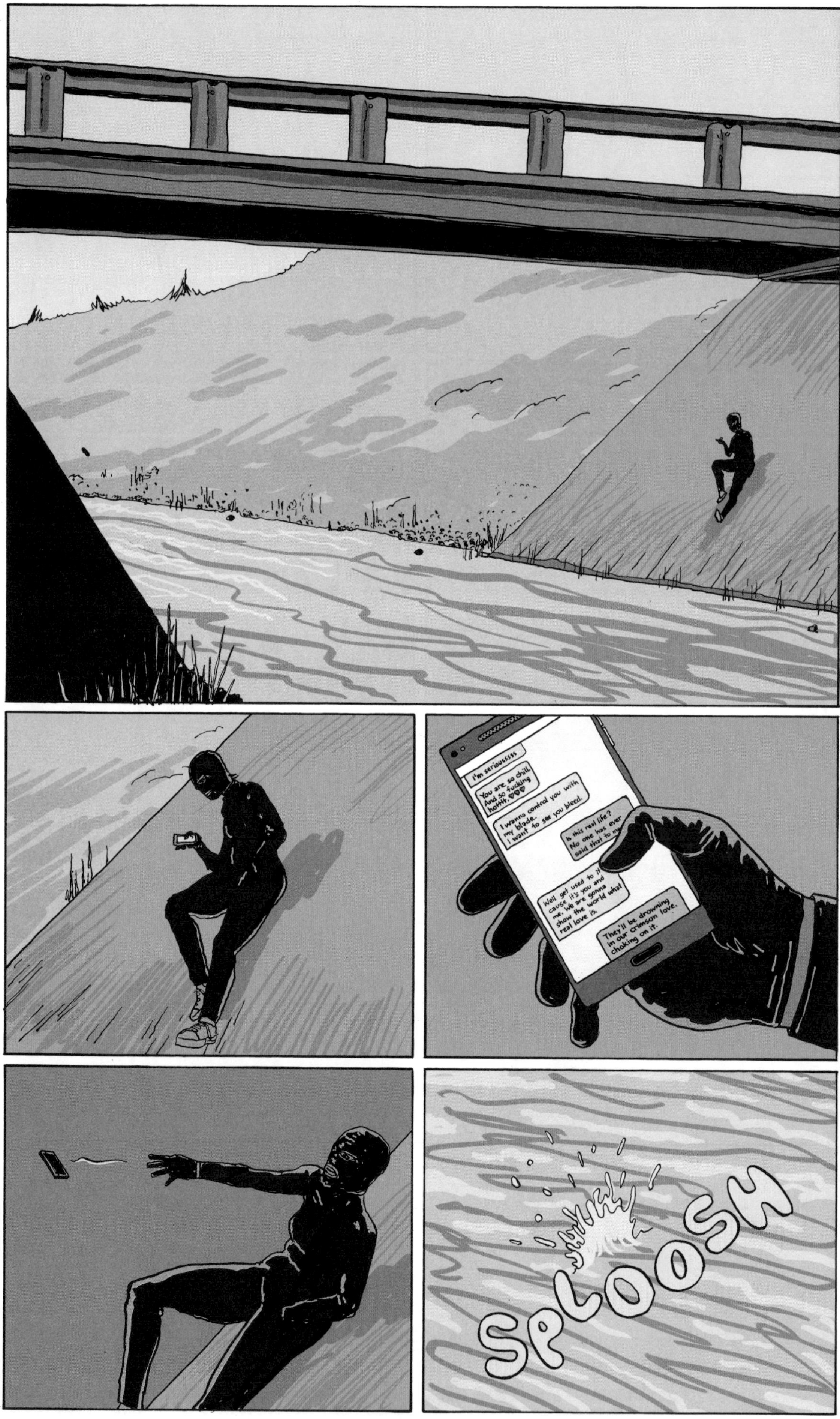
I'm serioussss
You are so chill. And so fucking hotttt.
I wanna control you with my blade. I want to see you bleed.
Is this real life? No one has ever said that to m
Well get used to it cause it's you and me. We are gonna show the world what real love is.
They'll be drowning in our crimson love, choking on it.
SPLOOSH

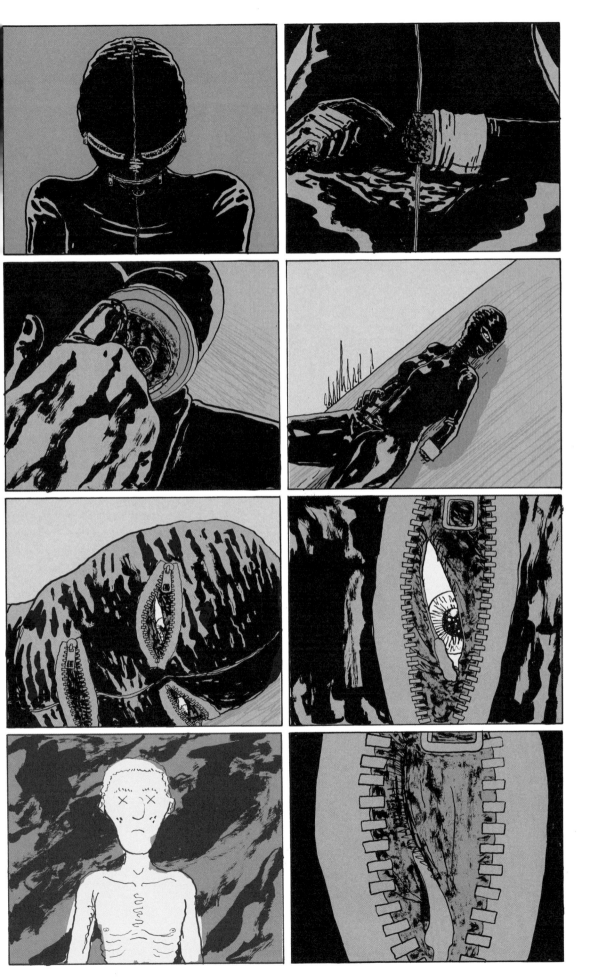

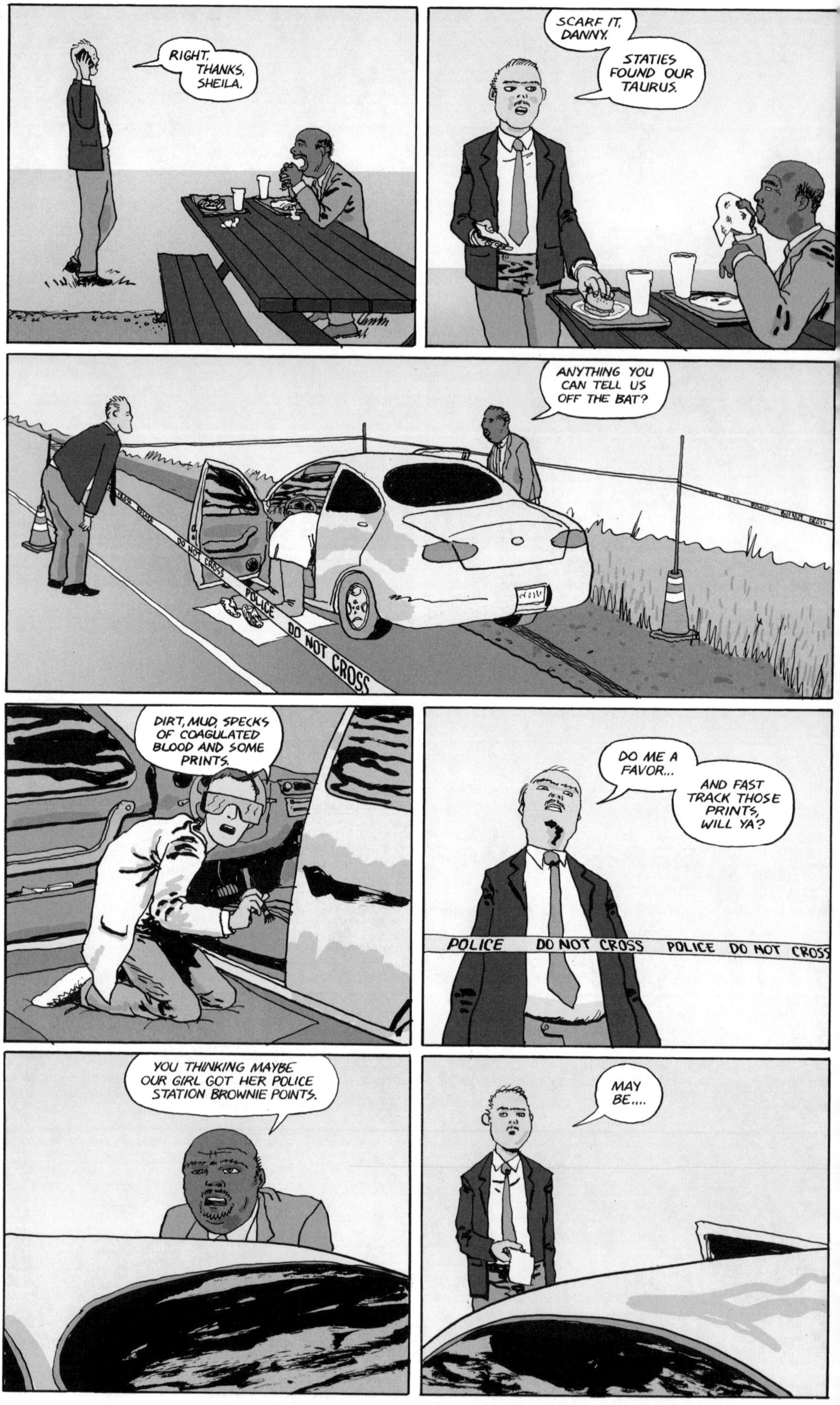
RIGHT, THANKS, SHEILA.
SCARF IT, DANNY.
STATIES FOUND OUR TAURUS.
ANYTHING YOU CAN TELL US OFF THE BAT?
POLICE
DO NOT CROSS
DIRT, MUD, SPECKS OF COAGULATED BLOOD AND SOME PRINTS.
DO ME A FAVOR...
AND FAST TRACK THOSE PRINTS, WILL YA?
POLICE DO NOT CROSS POLICE DO NOT CROSS
YOU THINKING MAYBE OUR GIRL GOT HER POLICE STATION BROWNIE POINTS.
MAY BE....

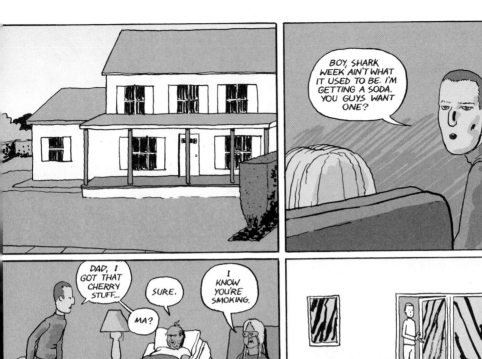

BOY, SHARK WEEK AIN'T WHAT IT USED TO BE. I'M GETTING A SODA. YOU GUYS WANT ONE?

DAD, I GOT THAT CHERRY STUFF...

SURE.

MA?

I KNOW YOU'RE SMOKING.

HI, JONATHAN.

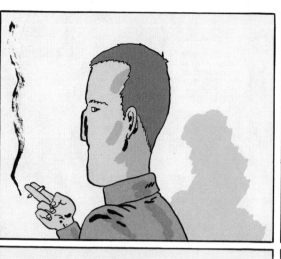

WOAH. UMMMM.

IT'S CHRISTINE.

I'M NOT GOING TO KILL YOU. I JUST NEED A FRIEND.

SINCE WHEN ARE WE FRIENDS, CHRISSY? AND THANKS FOR NOT SLITTING MY THROAT.

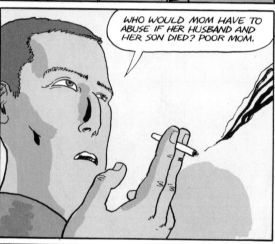

WHO WOULD MOM HAVE TO ABUSE IF HER HUSBAND AND HER SON DIED? POOR MOM.

YOUR DAD PASSED?

NOT YET.

OH.

SO DOES EVERY ONE THINK IT'S ME?

PRETTY MUCH.

CAN YOU TAKE THAT THING OFF? I FEEL LIKE I'M IN A LEATHER CLUB BUT IN MY PARENTS' BACK YARD.

YOU SHOULDN'T HAVE SLICED UP YOUR BOSS. KIND OF A DEAD GIVEAWAY.

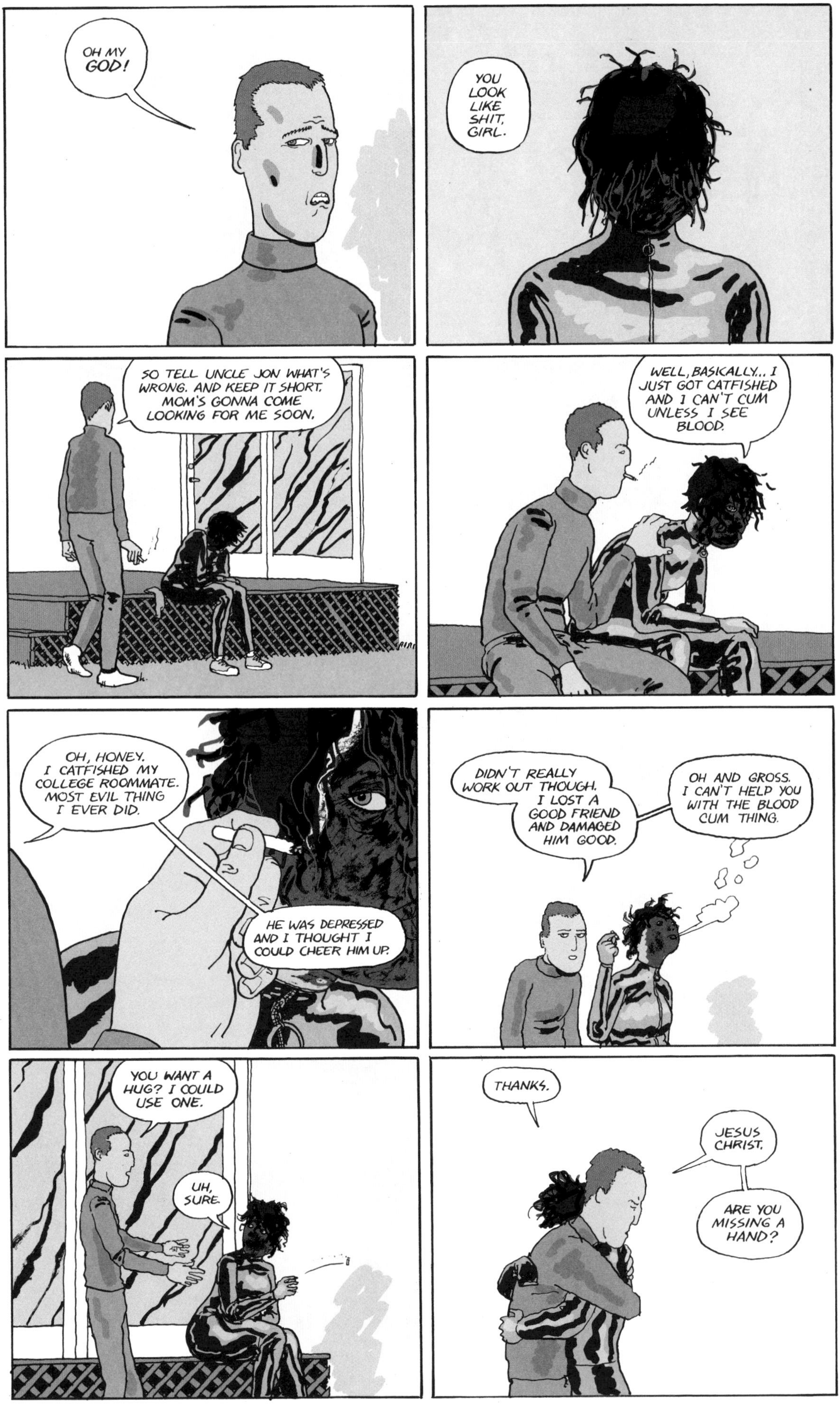
OH MY GOD!
YOU LOOK LIKE SHIT, GIRL.
SO TELL UNCLE JON WHAT'S WRONG. AND KEEP IT SHORT. MOM'S GONNA COME LOOKING FOR ME SOON.
WELL, BASICALLY... I JUST GOT CATFISHED AND I CAN'T CUM UNLESS I SEE BLOOD.
OH, HONEY. I CATFISHED MY COLLEGE ROOMMATE. MOST EVIL THING I EVER DID.
HE WAS DEPRESSED AND I THOUGHT I COULD CHEER HIM UP.
DIDN'T REALLY WORK OUT THOUGH. I LOST A GOOD FRIEND AND DAMAGED HIM GOOD.
OH AND GROSS. I CAN'T HELP YOU WITH THE BLOOD CUM THING.
YOU WANT A HUG? I COULD USE ONE.
UH, SURE.
THANKS.
JESUS CHRIST.
ARE YOU MISSING A HAND?

In an exclusive for C.N.X. News, We have learned from an unnamed source who the lead suspect is in the so-called Leather Slasher murders.

A string of murders have held the tri-state area in a fit of panic for the last ten days.

Peter Weathers

CNX NEWS

Now an anonymous tipster has revealed the lead suspect in the serial murders and their identity may shock you.

C.N.X.'s source claims to be a survivor of the Slasher's first attack.

Our source has been regularly attending church since the attack.

Saying, quote, "God was watching over me that night."

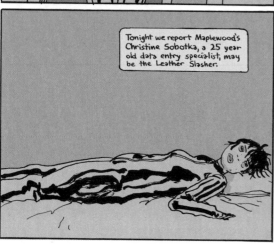

Tonight we report Maplewood's Christine Sobotka, a 25 year old data entry specialist, may be the Leather Slasher.

Miss Sobotka is still at large and is to be considered extremely dangerous.

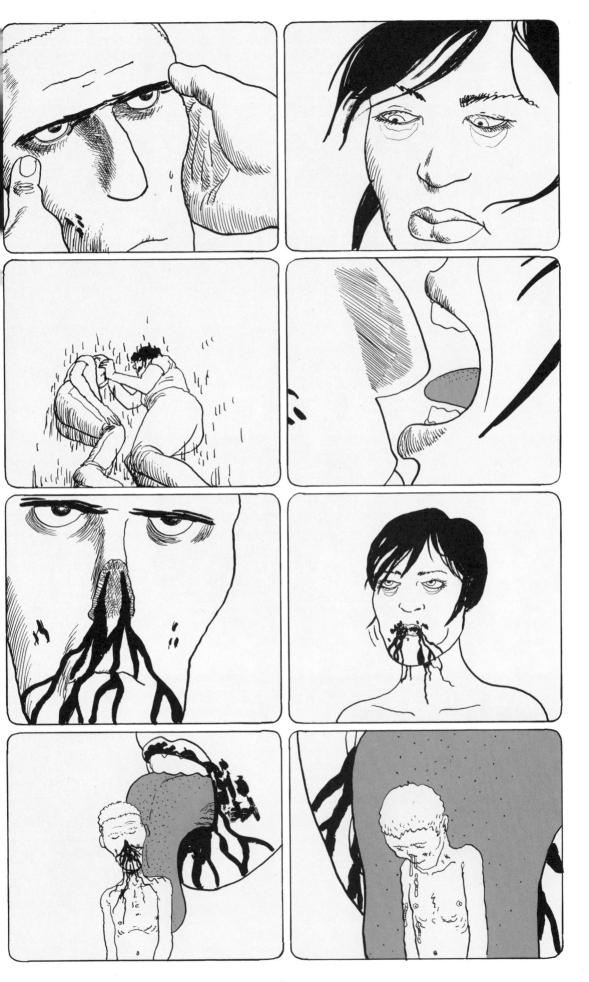

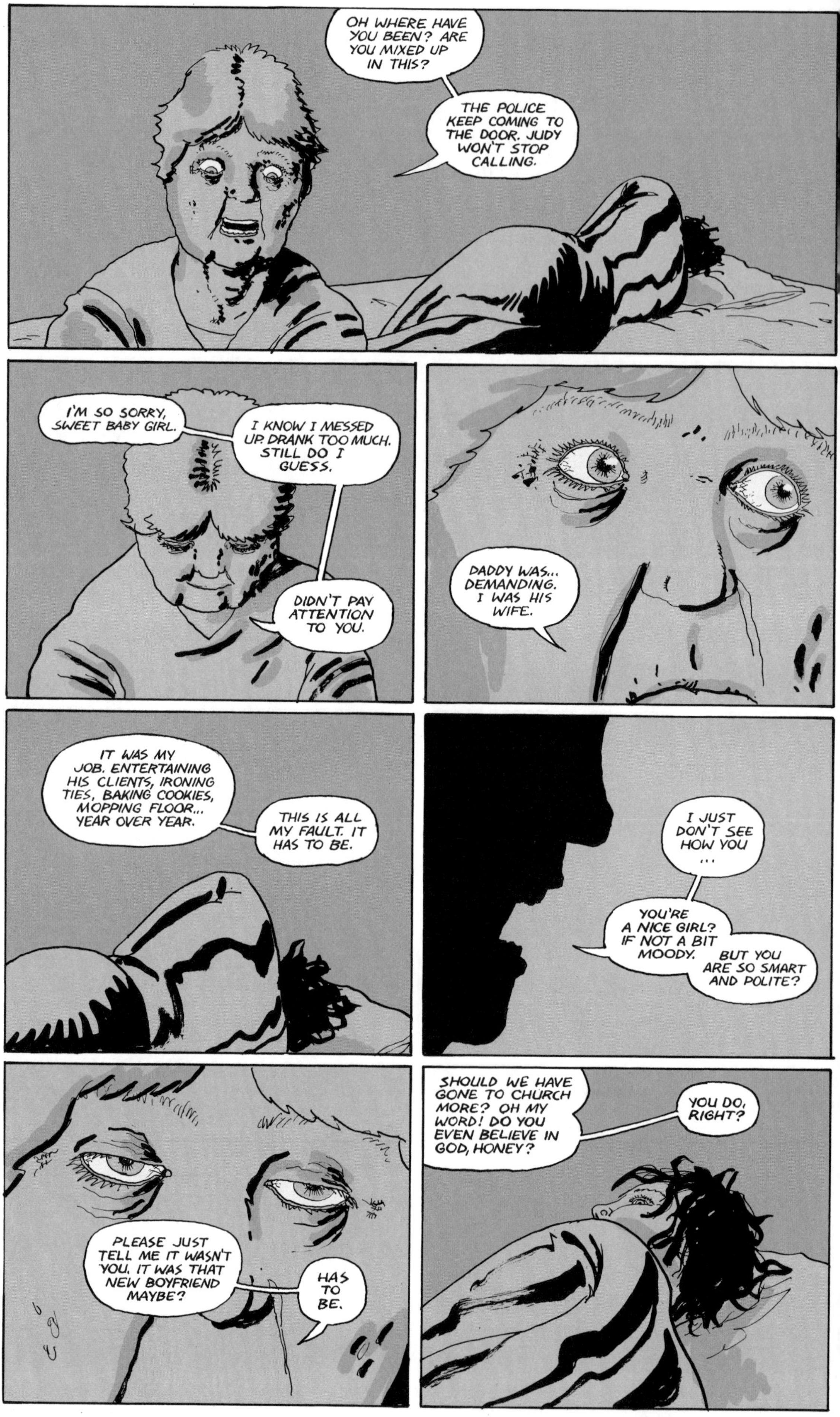
OH WHERE HAVE YOU BEEN? ARE YOU MIXED UP IN THIS?
THE POLICE KEEP COMING TO THE DOOR. JUDY WON'T STOP CALLING.
I'M SO SORRY, SWEET BABY GIRL.
I KNOW I MESSED UP. DRANK TOO MUCH. STILL DO I GUESS.
DIDN'T PAY ATTENTION TO YOU.
DADDY WAS... DEMANDING. I WAS HIS WIFE.
IT WAS MY JOB. ENTERTAINING HIS CLIENTS, IRONING TIES, BAKING COOKIES, MOPPING FLOOR... YEAR OVER YEAR.
THIS IS ALL MY FAULT. IT HAS TO BE.
I JUST DON'T SEE HOW YOU ...
YOU'RE A NICE GIRL? IF NOT A BIT MOODY.
BUT YOU ARE SO SMART AND POLITE?
PLEASE JUST TELL ME IT WASN'T YOU. IT WAS THAT NEW BOYFRIEND MAYBE?
HAS TO BE.
SHOULD WE HAVE GONE TO CHURCH MORE? OH MY WORD! DO YOU EVEN BELIEVE IN GOD, HONEY?
YOU DO, RIGHT?

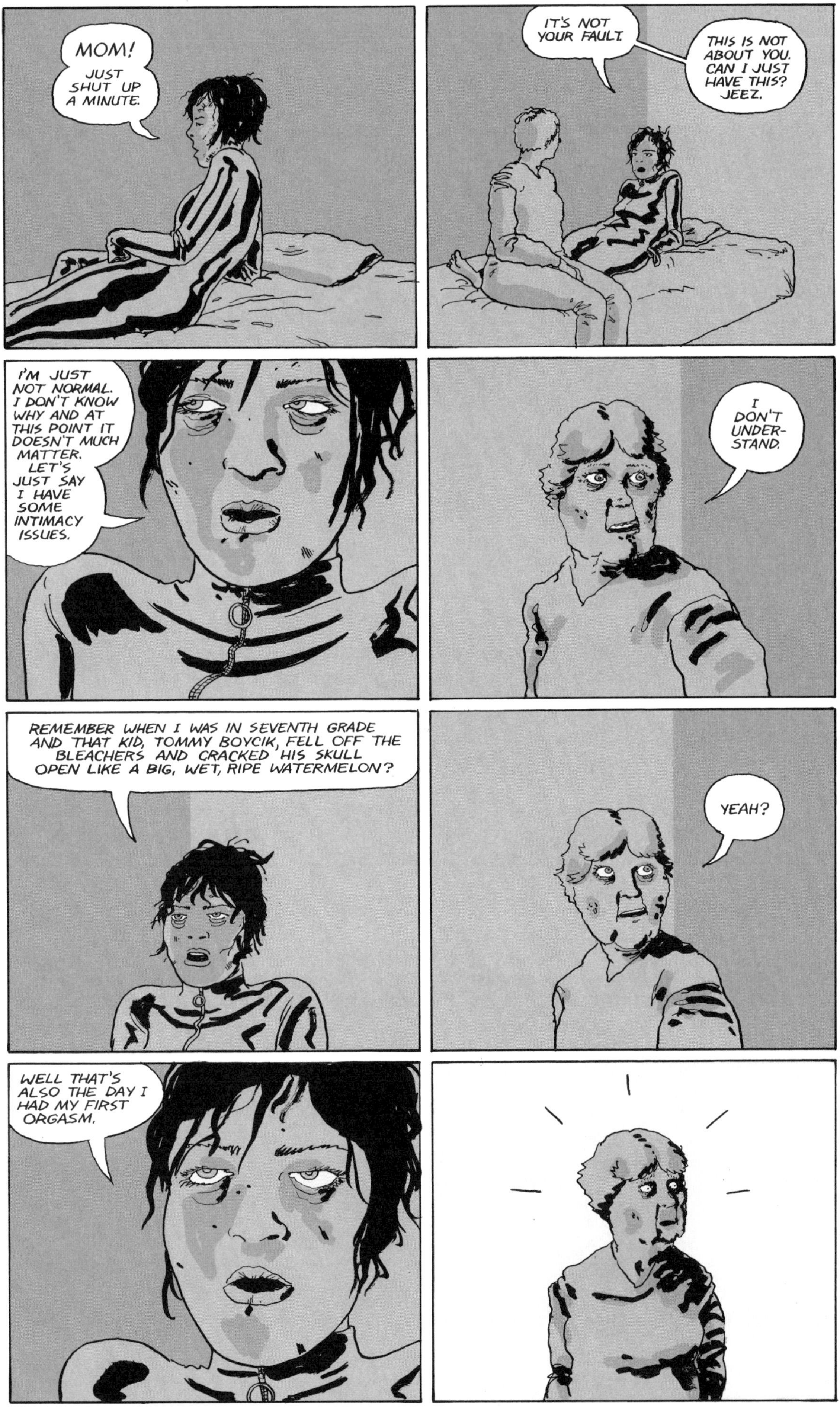
MOM! JUST SHUT UP A MINUTE.
IT'S NOT YOUR FAULT.
THIS IS NOT ABOUT YOU. CAN I JUST HAVE THIS? JEEZ.
I'M JUST NOT NORMAL. I DON'T KNOW WHY AND AT THIS POINT IT DOESN'T MUCH MATTER. LET'S JUST SAY I HAVE SOME INTIMACY ISSUES.
I DON'T UNDER-STAND.
REMEMBER WHEN I WAS IN SEVENTH GRADE AND THAT KID, TOMMY BOYCIK, FELL OFF THE BLEACHERS AND CRACKED HIS SKULL OPEN LIKE A BIG, WET, RIPE WATERMELON?
YEAH?
WELL THAT'S ALSO THE DAY I HAD MY FIRST ORGASM.

UM... OH! CHRISTINE! YOUR HAND, HONEY!
MOM...
MOMMY... HE BROKE MY HEART. HE BROKE MY HEART.
OH, BABY GIRL.
COME HERE.
SHH. SHH. THERE. THERE.
THERE WILL BE OTHER BOYS.

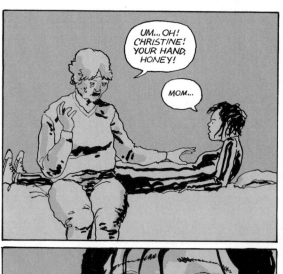

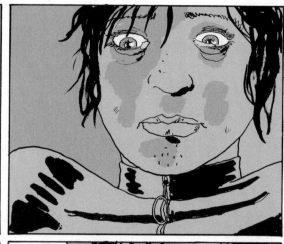

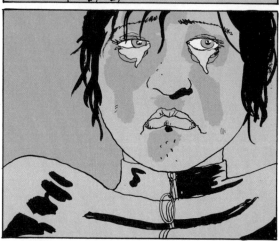

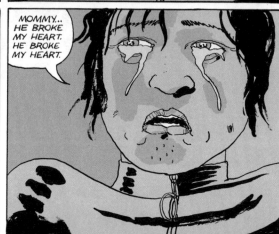

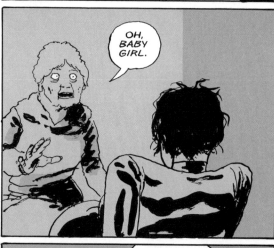

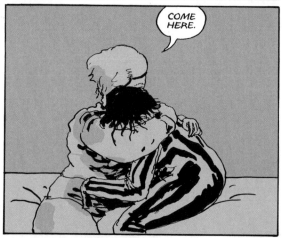

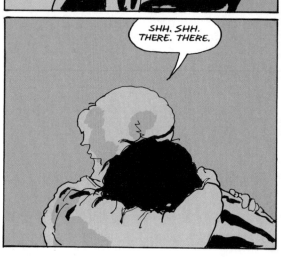

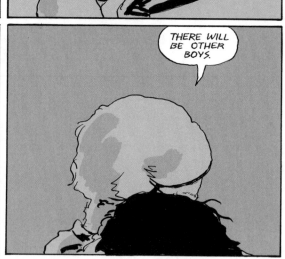

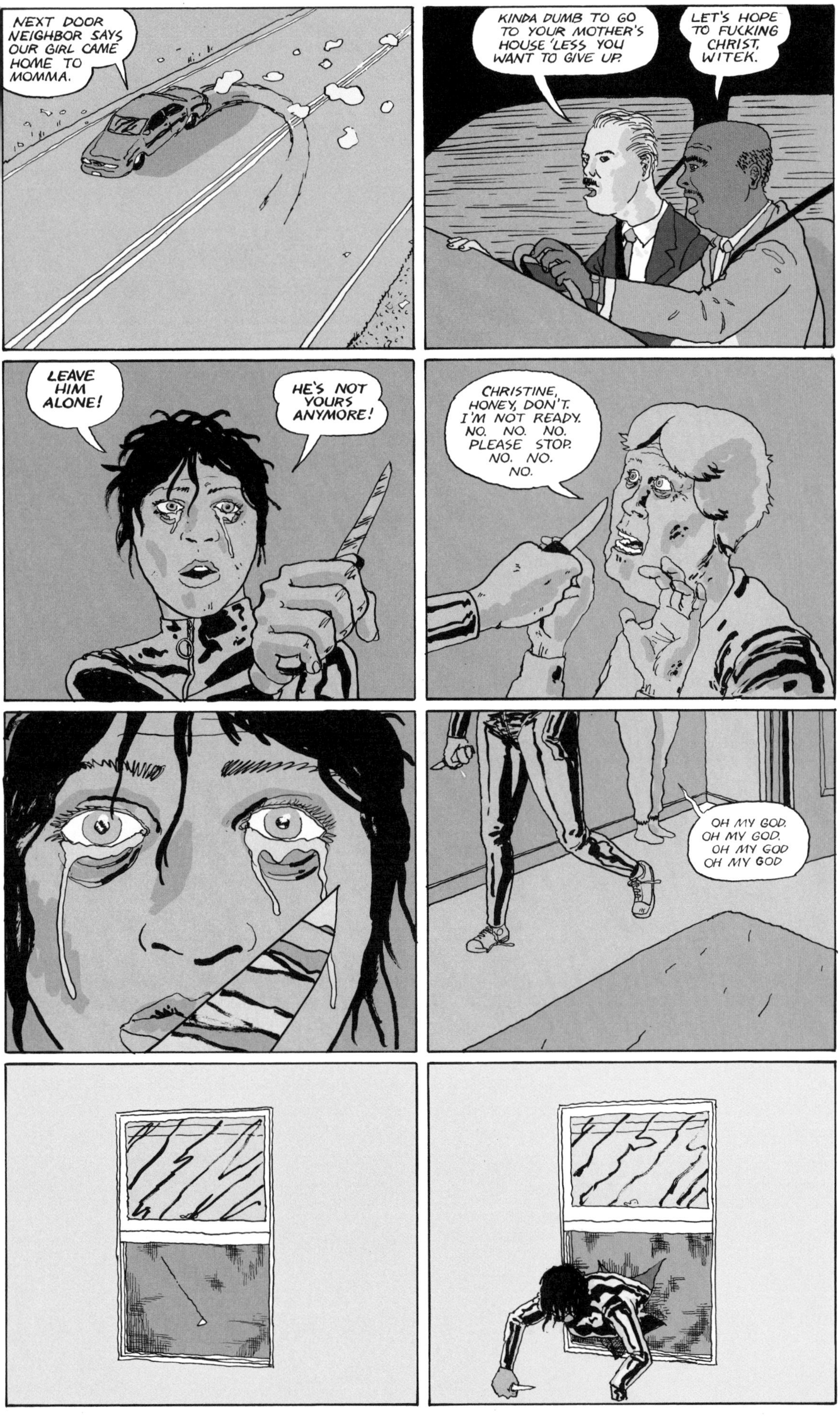
NEXT DOOR NEIGHBOR SAYS OUR GIRL CAME HOME TO MOMMA.
KINDA DUMB TO GO TO YOUR MOTHER'S HOUSE 'LESS YOU WANT TO GIVE UP.
LET'S HOPE TO FUCKING CHRIST, WITEK.
LEAVE HIM ALONE!
HE'S NOT YOURS ANYMORE!
CHRISTINE, HONEY, DON'T. I'M NOT READY. NO. NO. NO. PLEASE STOP. NO. NO. NO.
OH MY GOD. OH MY GOD. OH MY GOD OH MY GOD

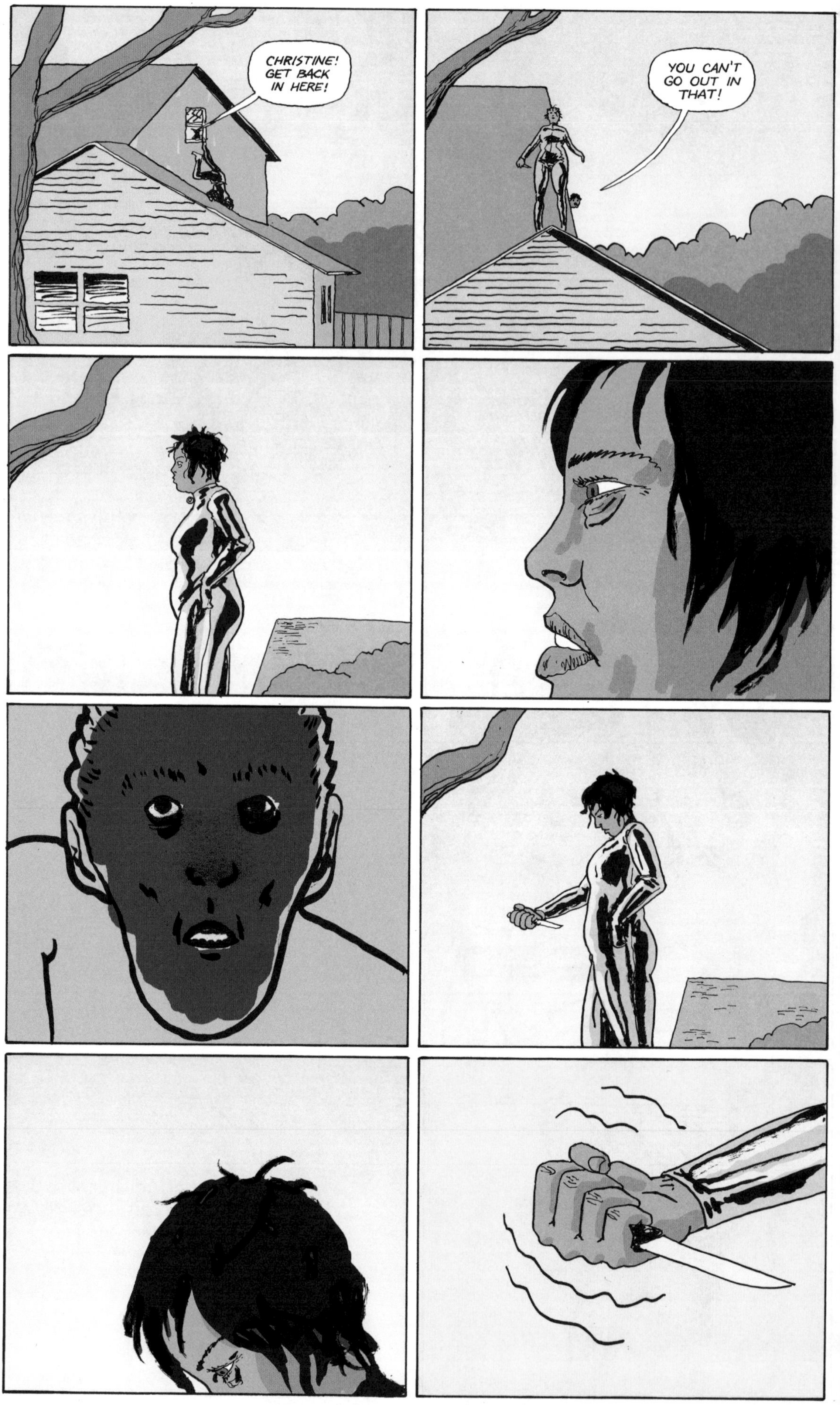
CHRISTINE! GET BACK IN HERE!
YOU CAN'T GO OUT IN THAT!

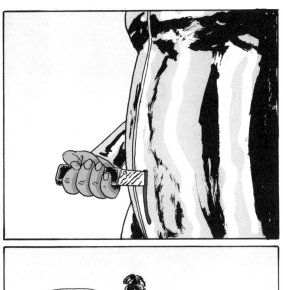
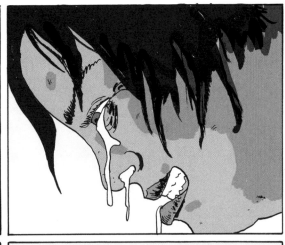

CHRISTINE? MY NAME IS DETECTIVE GORDON.

WHAT'S SHE DOING?

WE'VE BEEN LOOKING FOR YOU. WE WANT TO TALK TO YOU. YOU WANNA COME DOWN SO WE CAN DO THAT?

i love you Joshua.

WHAT THE EFF?

OH GOD.

CHRISTINE!

GET. IN. HERE.

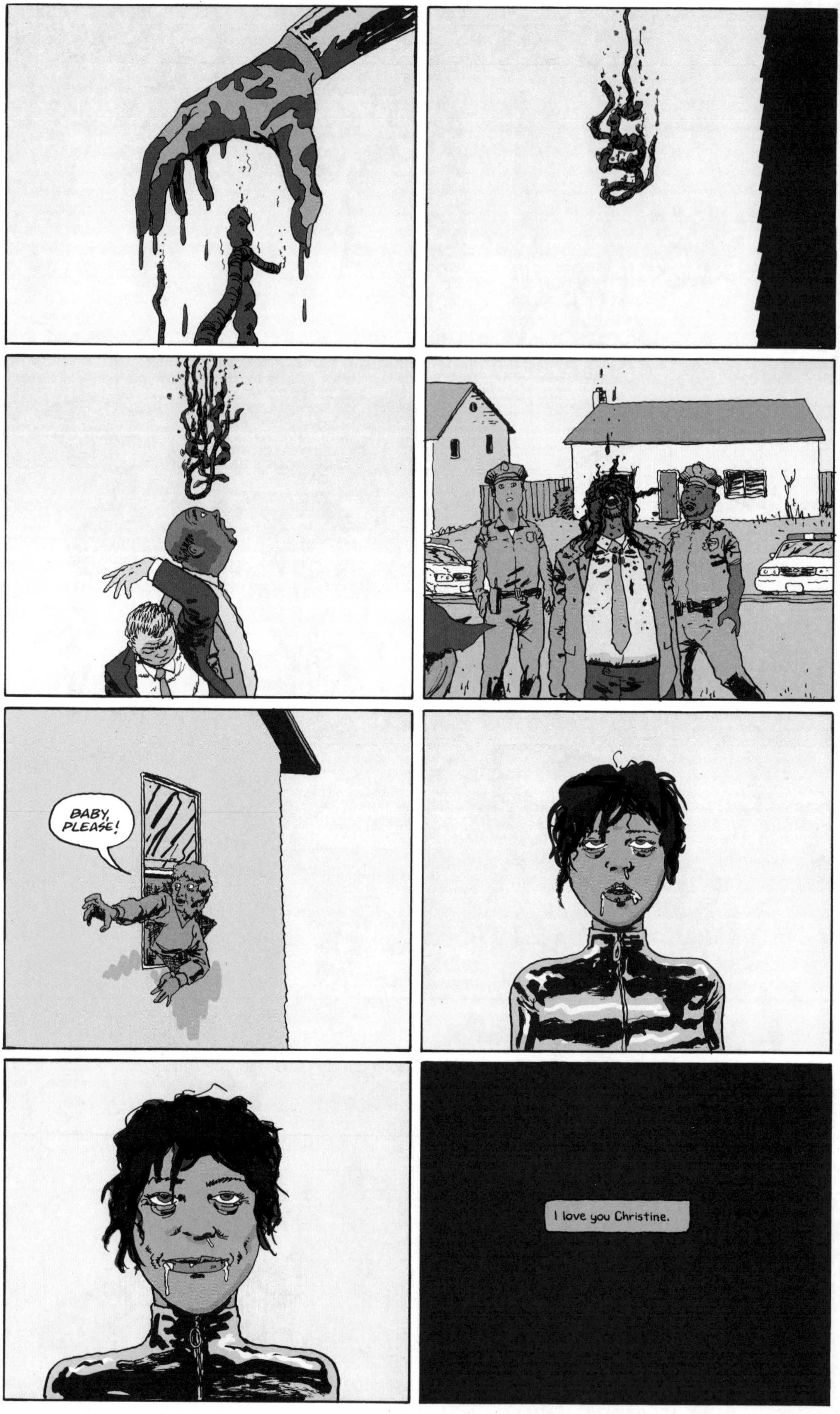
BABY, PLEASE!
I love you Christine.

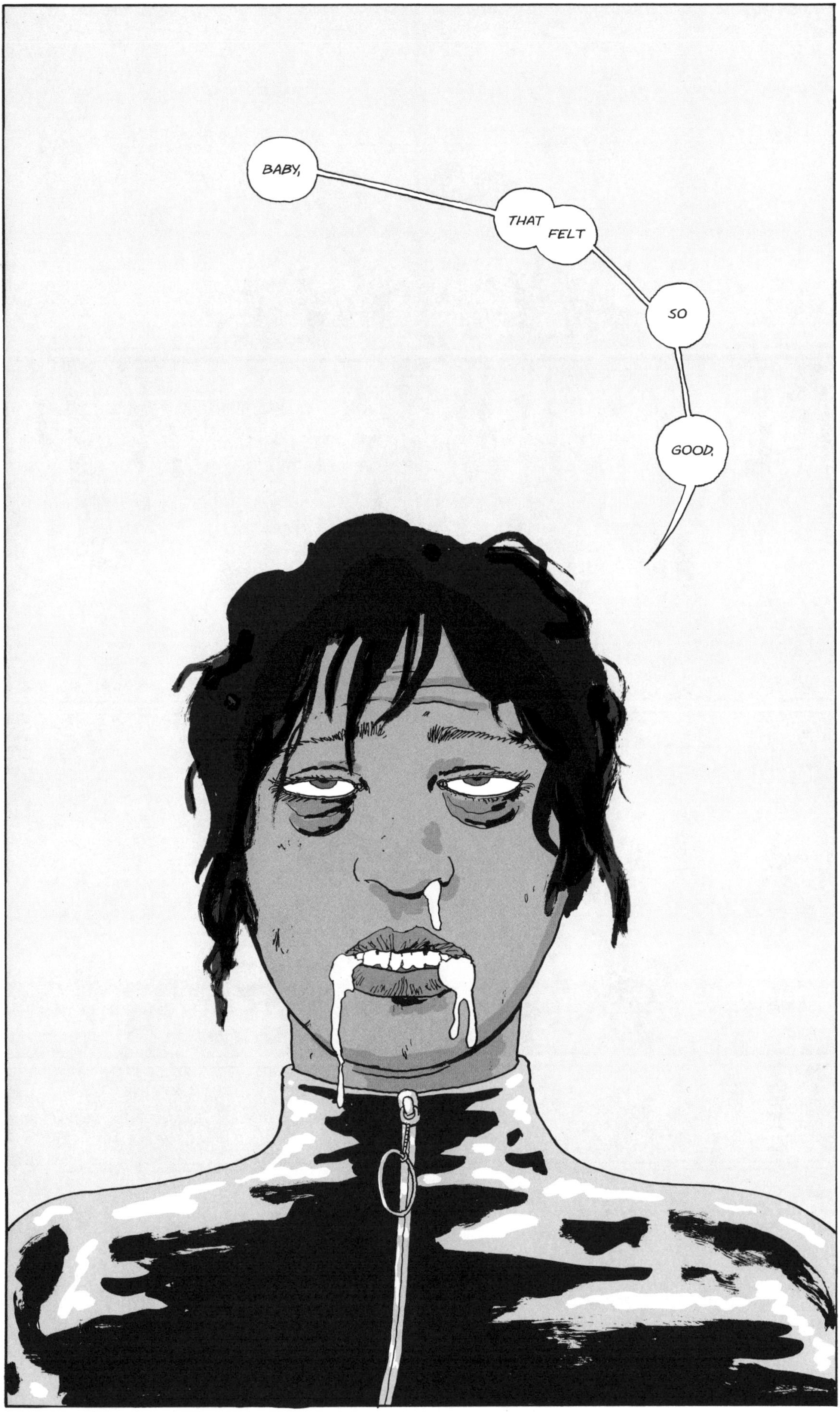
BABY,
THAT FELT
SO
GOOD.

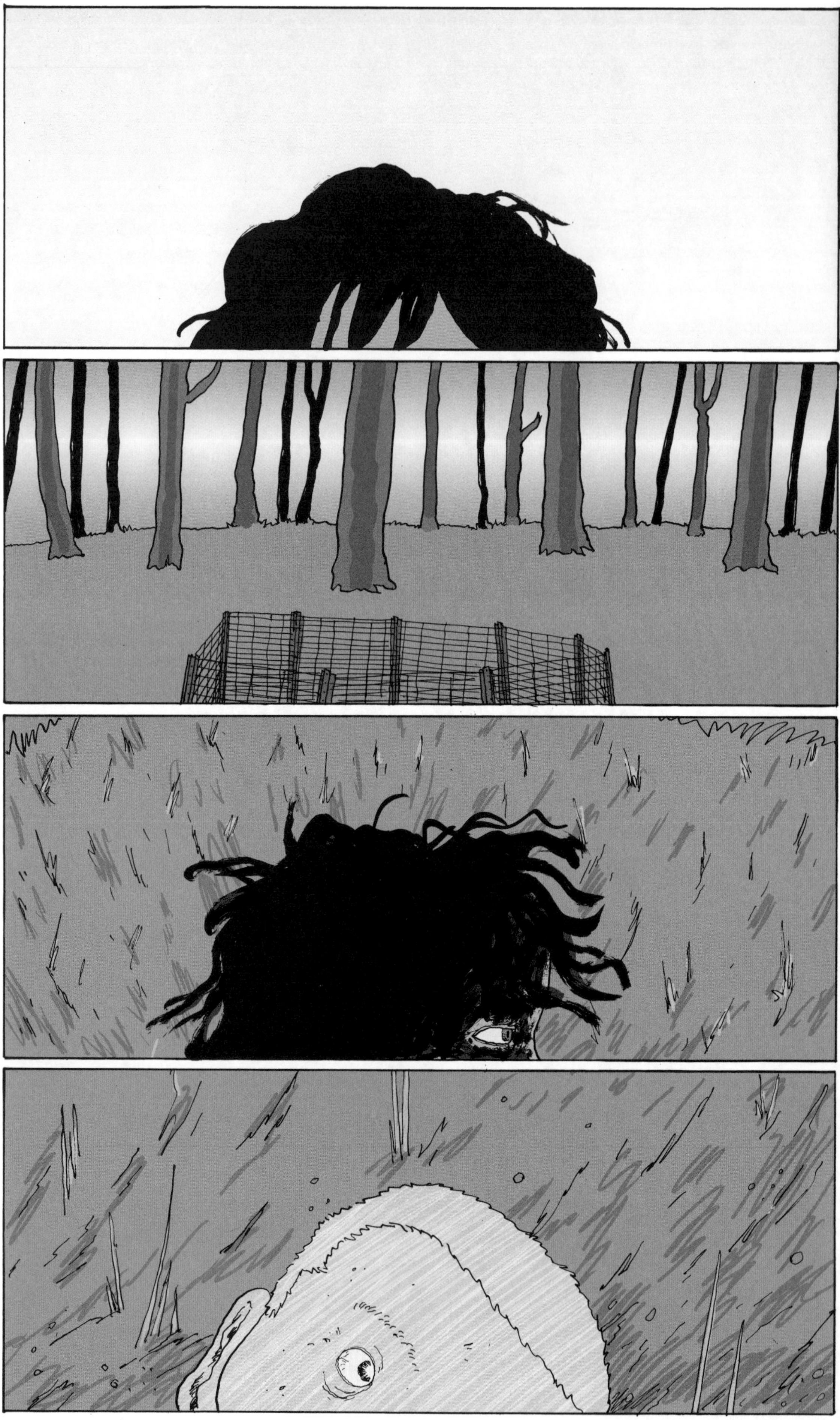

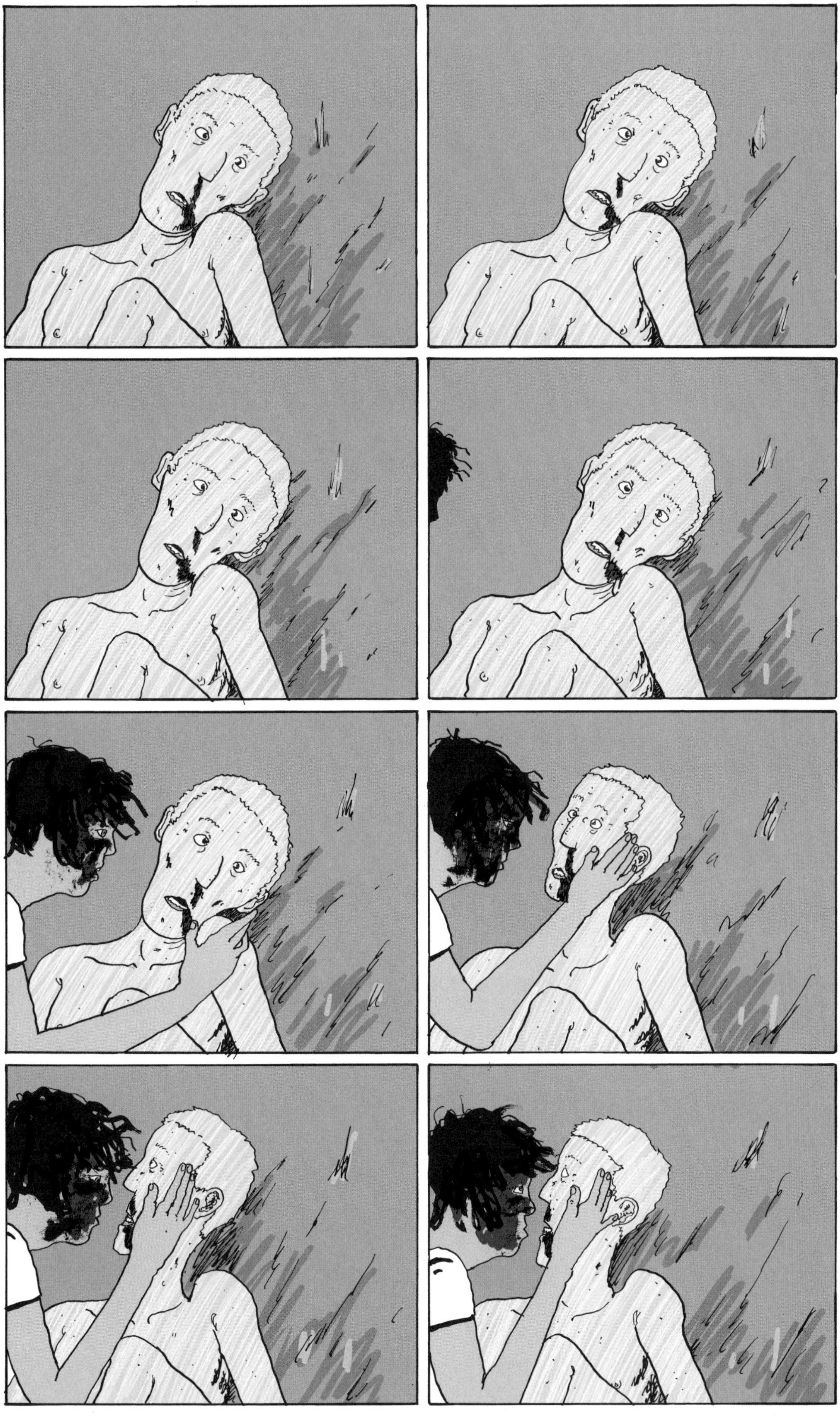

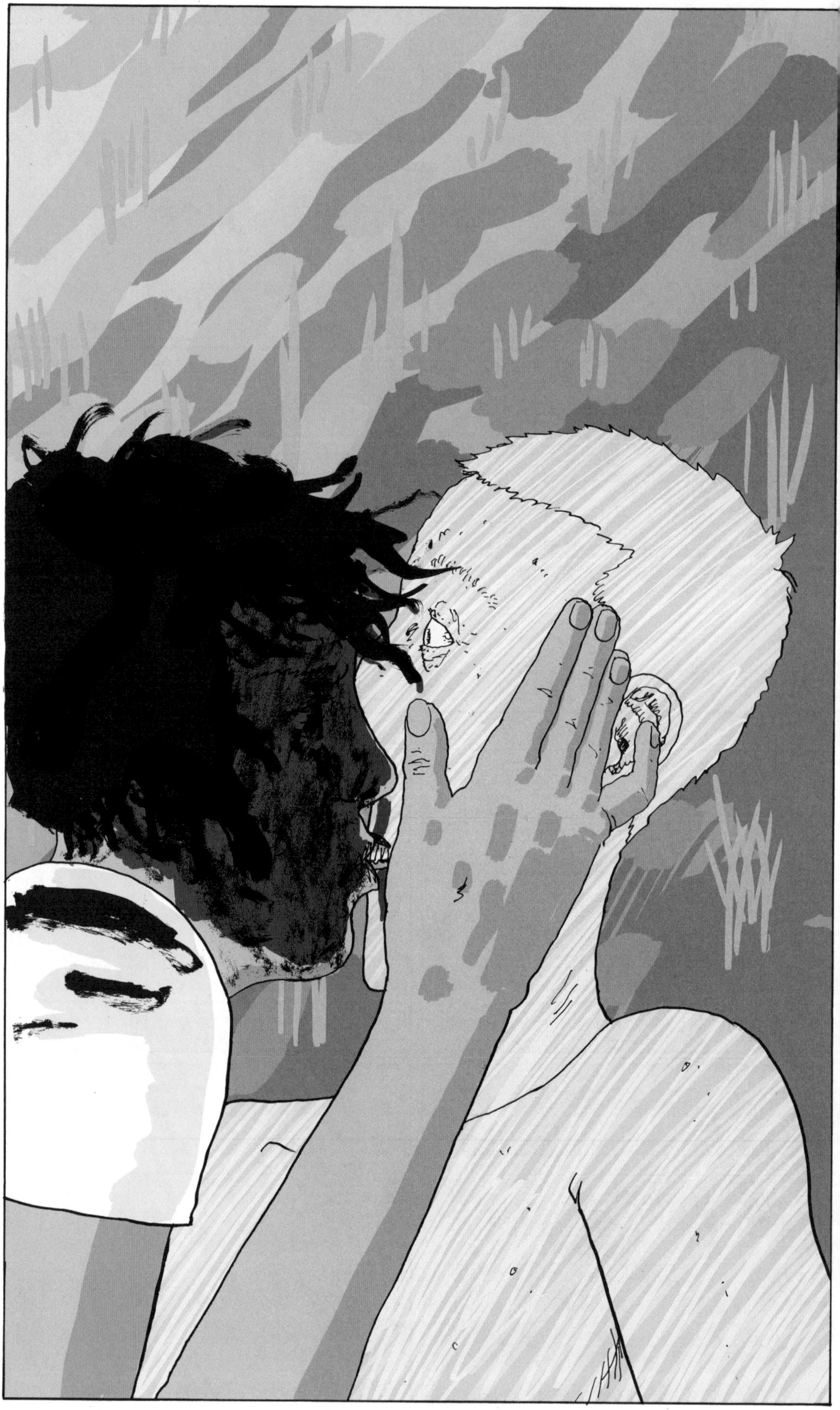

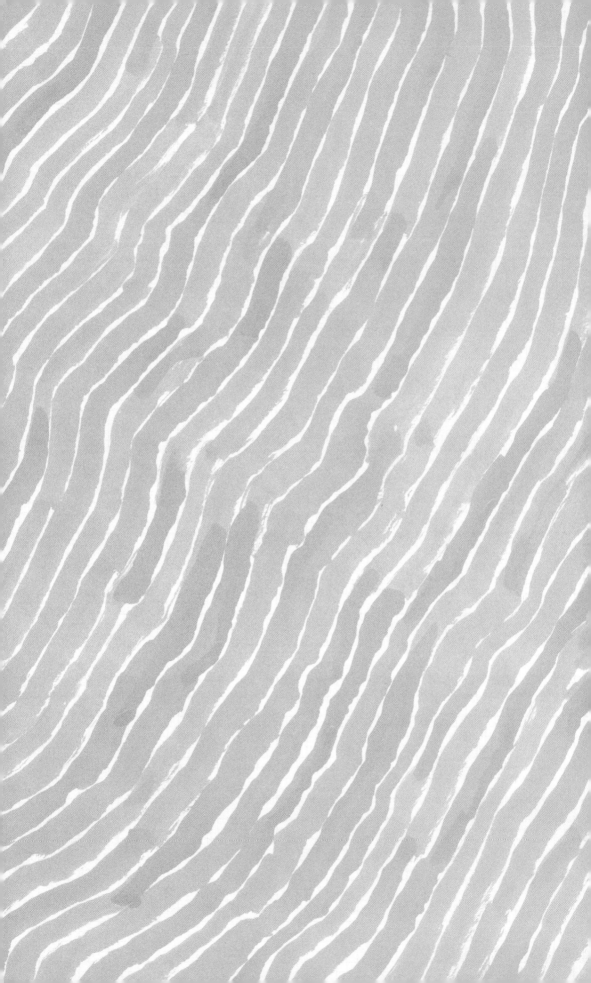

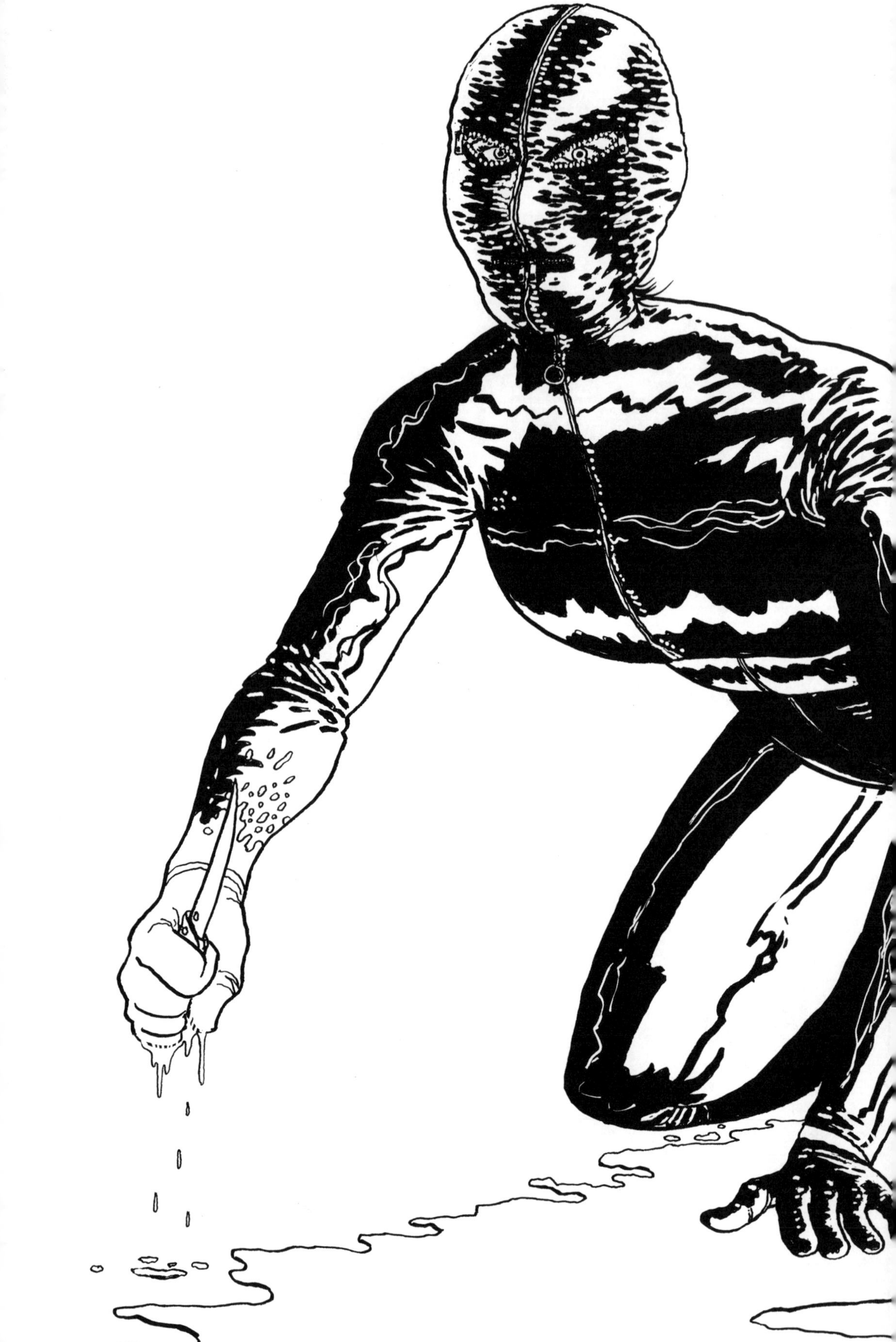

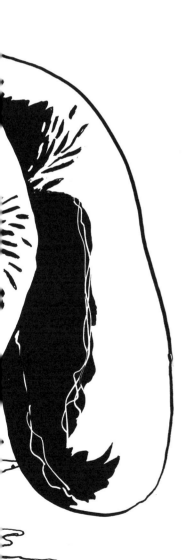

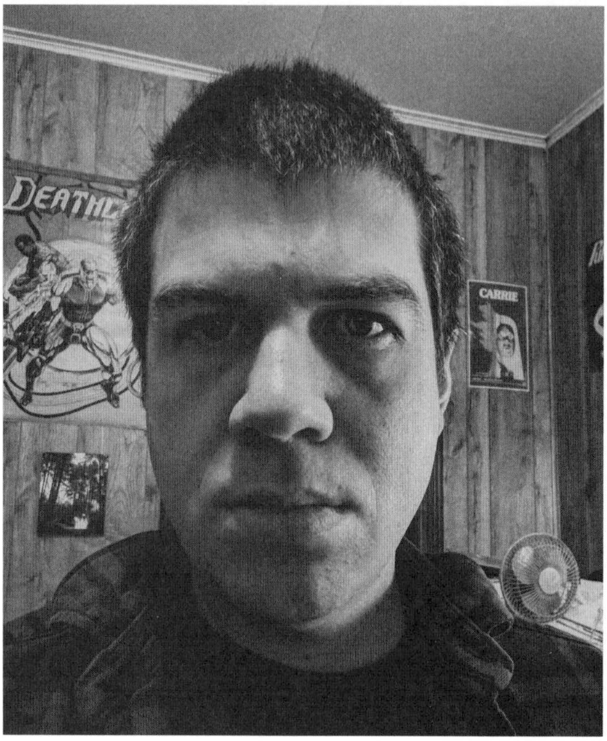
DEATH
CARRIE

photo by Chuck Forsman

Charles Forsman is a 2008 graduate of The Center for Cartoon Studies and a three-time Ignatz Award winner. His other comic books include *Revenger, Celebrated Summer, I am Not Okay With This* and *The End of the Fucking World* which has been adapted into a **Netflix Original Series**. He lives in Western Massachusetts.